INEQUALITY

Social Stratification
Reconsidered

LLOYD A. FALLERS

THE UNIVERSITY OF CHICAGO PRESS
CHICAGO AND LONDON

THE UNIVERSITY OF CHICAGO PRESS, CHICAGO 60637
THE UNIVERSITY OF CHICAGO PRESS, LTD., LONDON
© 1973 by The University of Chicago
All rights reserved. Published 1973
Printed in the United States of America
Internation Standard Book Number: 0–226–23684–6
Library of Congress Catalog Card Number: 73–78665

Lloyd A. Fallers is professor of anthropology and sociology and chairman of the Committee for the Comparative Study of New Nations at the University of Chicago. Among his many publications are *Bantu Bureaucracy*, *Law without Precedent*, and *The King's Men*.

1973

INEQUALITY

To L. A. F. and F. F. F.
son and daughter of
the prairie

Contents

Preface

THE PAST fifteen years have witnessed a revival of concern with equality and inequality in their various dimensions among critical thinkers about American society. Some have focused upon the distribution of income, stressing the persistence of a minority of poor within a generally affluent post–Second World War society,[1] and others have stressed the continuing resistance of racial and ethnic prejudice to equality of opportunity in a society proclaiming its attachment to the recognition of talent.[2] Still others have concerned themselves with the distribution of power, asserting or denying the existence of a monolithic "power elite."[3] Most recently there have been major controversies over the role of education in the achievement of, or the failure to achieve, greater equality and over the question of equality of opportunity versus equality of condition.[4] A major work has taken up the question of the place of equality in a theory of justice.[5]

These concerns are not, of course, new; debate concerning the desirable degrees and kinds of equality was prominent at the founding of the Republic and has continued to be so throughout its history, both within the society and among foreign observers. If Americans have rather generally agreed that "all men are created equal," there has seldom been anything like consensus concerning the actual or desirable meaning of the phrase. Nor, of course, has all this been limited to the United States. Egalitarian movements have appeared from time to time throughout modern European history, and in the twentieth century they have been projected onto the international scene with particular force in debates over relations among richer and poorer, more and less powerful nations. Indeed, the quest for greater equality—and of course the resistance to that quest—appears to be endemic to the modern world; the questioning of received inequalities seems an important aspect of the modern world's more general restlessness.

Unlike the literature I have cited above, the essays collected here are almost never directly concerned with what public policy toward inequality ought to be, in the United States or elsewhere. Most of them, reflecting my own research experience and competence, concern African and Asian societies (especially the former), and they are, most of them, designed either to yield greater understanding of particular situations of inequality or to contribute to the comparative study of such situations. Nevertheless, I suggest that the quality of policy debates on the subject, particularly in America, often suffers from a deficiency of such broader intellectual context. Comparative and analytic discussion at a stage removed from particular policy problems can suggest dimensions and possibilities which may be obscured by too narrow a focus upon the immediate in one's native milieu. At any rate, I myself (and I daresay most comparative social scientists) have learned some of my most valuable lessons about my own society while my attention has been most closely riveted upon some other society removed in time or space.

These self-revelatory moments occur because the social scientist is, after all, a mere mortal who cannot, however much he may try, fully escape from his own life-experience in his own society. The more deeply he penetrates the mysteries of another society, the more disturbingly the other society confronts his own within himself. If he recognizes these confrontations and follows them up with systematic thought and study, he may add something to his own and others' understanding of his own society and to policy debate within it. Certainly my own position as a skeptical egalitarian has been tempered and rendered more mature by my direct experience in East Africa and Turkey of equalities and inequalities quite different from those with which I had been brought up, and by my indirect experience, through reading, of equalities and inequalities in other times and places. Turks, Baganda, and Indians, as well as medieval and eighteenth-century Frenchmer and Englishmen, have all taught me much about the meaning, in America, of the assertion that "all men are created equal." The first of the following essays—the only one not previously published—recounts something of this experience.

I offer these essays in the hope that others, too, may find in these or similar confrontations with the unfamiliar some stimulation to further thought about inequality in American society.

PART 1
IDEAS AND COMPARISONS

1

Introduction

OVER the past twenty-five years, I have spent a good deal of time and energy, one way or another, on the subject which social science conventionally calls "social stratification." As a student at the University of Chicago I was taught by Edward Shils, whose lectures on the comparative political sociology of modern Western societies taught me much about stratification that I understood only a good deal later, and by Willam Lloyd Warner, at that time a veritable captain of industry in the study of "status class" in America. In East Africa, and more recently in Turkey, I have done research on the subject and have tried, at the same time, to keep in touch with the literature on stratification in Europe and America. Teaching in a department and a university in which South Asian studies are unusually well represented, I have perforce gained some exposure to the vast literature on caste. Although I do not believe my twenty-five years' interest in "social stratification" to have been wasted, I have nevertheless come to the conclusion that the phenomenon does not exist, or at any rate that "social stratification" is a poor name for it. If we need a general term to orient comparative discussion—and I believe we do —the term "inequality" seems to me both more straightforward and less loaded with cultural bias.[1]

I received my first practical lesson in relativity with respect to this subject in Africa, where I went in 1950 to do fieldwork in the Interlacustrine Bantu kingdoms of Uganda with the idea of "classes" and "strata" in my head and there found a world which seemed to be doubly "stratified." The African societies in which I worked were among the most hierarchical in Africa, and in the colonial order as a whole, Europeans, Indians, and Africans were clearly ranked, in that order. In both the colonial order and the African kingdoms, I saw the language and gesture of deference elaborated in what seemed to me then a quite fantastic way. Then I went to work, and one of the first things I discovered was that in the African kingdoms the hierarchy of chiefs, despite their great wealth and authority vis-à-vis their people, and despite the elaborate deference granted them, was very fluid. Except for the kings and a few princes, most persons in authority were "socially mobile": they were not in hereditary positions but instead were appointed by rulers on the basis of ability and personal loyalty. I had read Max Weber and I thought: Aha! I had found "patrimonial authority" in the flesh. But I still had "classes" or "strata" of society in my mind. Somewhat later I decided to systematize what I thought I had learned by drawing up a questionnaire which contained questions about "classes"; and then the bubble burst. The questionnaire was virtually untranslatable into the local language. It was possible to translate the word "class" only with the most elaborate and tortured circumlocutions, unintelligible to most people. There was, however, a rich vocabulary for speaking about dyadic interpersonal relations of superiority and inferiority—words of the "master" and "servant" type. Africans conceptualized their relations with Europeans, as well as the internal structure of European society as they knew it, in much the same way; although they perceived Europeans (*bazungu*) as a superordinate category (*bafuzi;* "rulers"), they continually probed that category in the effort to establish personal patron-client ties—with some success, thereby imposing, to a degree, their own definition of the situation. Their social world was pervaded by great "objective" differences in wealth and power, but my informants stoutly refused to conceptualize these in terms translatable as "classes" or "strata," and they behaved, for the most part, in accord with their own conceptualization of inequality in dyadic, patron-client, master-servant terms. Thus began a dissatisfaction with the stratificatory view of inequality which has grown over the years.

I shall not recapitulate the arguments of the essays which

follow. Each is concerned with some aspect or manifestation of inequality. In one of them ("Equality, Modernity, and Democracy in the New States") I attempt a systematic and comparative overview of the subject, and in part 2 I present an extended case study of inequality in the kingdom of Buganda. Instead of retracing any of these steps, I shall devote the remainder of this introductory essay to a question in which I have become increasingly interested since the last of the essays was written: the uses and abuses of the stratigraphic image of society. The argument is this: The term "social stratification" implies a hierarchy of pansocietal, horizontal layers, and I believe that a large number of social scientists think this a "natural" way of viewing societies. Some, however, have questioned its utility for analyzing particular societies, as I myself came to do in the case of the Interlacustrine Bantu kingdoms. Louis Dumont has expressed his dissent with respect to India at some length in his *Homo Hierarchicus,* and I and others have found difficulty in using the idea in the Middle East. This leads me to ask: What is the source of the stratigraphic image, and does it have any general utility? The answer I shall give is that it originated in rather specific historical circumstances and that it should be applied with caution to other times and places.

There are a few preliminary points to be made. First, it is central to my argument that what are often called "objective" inequalities—inequalities of wealth and power—can be understood only in their cultural contexts—only in the context of their *meaning* to those involved in them. Simply to chart the distribution of some "objective" attribute—say income or education—on a diagram with arbitrarily fixed intervals is harmless enough and even useful, if all one wants to know is the distribution of income or education—both important aspects of inequality. One might even safely call these intervals "income classes" or "educational classes," and use them to compare one society with another, so long as it is understood that they are purely conceptual creations of the investigator. No social scientific concept, of course, can be entirely culture-free, but then neither do sociocultural data vary entirely at random. If education and material income mean different things in different human communities, still one learns something, in a rough, first-approximation sort of way, by comparing them in these terms. Difficulties arise, however, when the classes are seen as sociocultural classes or strata—when, that is, it is whole persons or groups or roles that are portrayed in a vertical, layer-cake distribution, for this implies a great deal more about a society and its culture than can be safely assumed arbitrarily from an external observer's standpoint. The very use of a vertical dimension implies meanings—evaluative standards and cognitive images in terms of which a society's members, individually and in groups, perceive and evaluate (or grant deference to) one another—in short, it implies a *culture* of inequality. Furthermore, by portraying a whole society in a single image, it implies *a* culture of inequality—a particular set of cognitive images and evaluative standards—an implication which denies our common knowledge that in every society, even the "simplest," there is social differentiation—a division of labor —and that culture is to some extent differentiated into subcultures along whatever lines social differentiation takes. Thus persons and groups within a society may view themselves and each other differently and even competitively, and subculture may become counterculture. Here, too, enters the element of power—the power of a person or group to impose his or its culture of inequality upon others.

When these possibilities are recognized, the very motion of "a society" becomes problematical. Social scientists, like the literate public generally, often use the term as if its referent were obvious, and often this is indeed so. But very often ambiguities lurk behind the apparently patent. Where social and political boundaries are generally congruent the reference is often to a national state, but frequently they are not; "English society" and "British nationality" commonly refer to different units, whereas such terms as "mainstream" and "backwater," used in reference to "American society," direct attention to a somewhat different pattern of incongruences. Edward Shils's notion of a "moral center"[2] in which a society's "members" may participate differentially captures one dimension of variability here, the idea of "pluralism" another. With all these complexities and ambiguities, the effort to arrive at a universally useful, all-purpose conception of "a society" seems to me a misguided enterprise, which is not to say that one does not learn something from reflecting on the question.[3] This is also, perhaps, the best point at which to record my dislike of the term "socioeconomic status"—a hard-science-sounding term which achieves its quantifiability as a "variable" by fudging these complexities.

Max Weber, I believe, had it right when he said of structural-functional concepts in general—and general-purpose conceptions of society are usually of this sort:

> For purposes of sociological analysis two things can be said. First this functional frame of reference is convenient for purposes of practical illustration and provisional orientation. . . . But at the same time if its cognitive value is overestimated and its concepts illegitimately "reified,"[4] it can be highly dangerous. Second, in certain circumstances this is the only way of determining just what processes of social action it is important to understand in order to explain a given phenomenon. But this is only the beginning of sociological analysis as here understood. In the case of social collectivities, precisely as distinguished from organisms, we are in a position to go beyond merely demonstrating functional relationships and uniformities. We can accomplish something which is never attainable in the natural sciences, namely the subjective[5] understanding of the action of the component individuals.[6]

Thus the notion of "a society," with its implication of a moral center and relatively unambiguous boundaries, is useful to the degree that it enters into the complexes of meaning that inform persons' social action. But even its existence in this sense, which of course must be established by investigation, does not preclude dissensus in perception, differential evaluation, and the granting of deference, among many other matters. In contemporary Turkey, for example, the *Türkiye Cumhuriyeti* (Turkish Republic) created by Ataturk and his followers during the 1920s out of a part of the crumbling Ottoman Empire is today firmly established in culture and in personal identity as a "society," but there remains within it much dissensus concerning the location and nature of its moral center, resulting in *Kulturkampf,* and sometimes more physical sorts of *Kampf* as well.[7] The distribution of deference is very much at issue here. The recent fashion of classifying theories of society into "consensus theories" and "con-

flict theories" seems to me as unhelpful as a preoccupation
with what "societies" really and universally are. Empirically,
human groups vary widely in the degree and nature of their
internal consensus. When dissensus is marked, the result may
be relatively peaceful competition, secession, revolution, or
chronic incivility, depending upon other elements in the
situation—but the point is to *understand* these various situations, not to parcel them out among different theories and
theorists.

"Stratum" and "Class"

But to return, now, to the stratigraphic image: Louis Dumont has objected to its application to India on the ground
that it violates the Indian culture of inequality. His argument
(in part) is that it is a product of the modern Western culture
of individualism and egalitarianism—a culture he finds to
represent something like the polar opposite of Indian holism
and hierarchy.[8] In the Indian culture of inequality (my
phrase, not Dumont's) , which finds its most graphic representation in the scheme of the four *varnas* ("colors") found in
the Vedic literature—that is, *Brahman* priests, *Kshatriya* warriors, *vaishya* merchants and *shudra* servants—in this scheme
the separate elements are unified by a single principle of evaluation: purity and impurity. He takes pleasure in showing,
following Dumézil, that the *varnas* may be analyzed as a
series of contrasts and inclusions in the style adopted by
Claude Lévi-Strauss from structural linguistics. What this dem-
onstration adds to our understanding of what the *varna* hierarchy means to Indians escapes me, and in any case it is a way
of viewing things which is as clearly imposed by the outside
observer as are many of the social science terms Dumont criti-
cizes as alien to Indian culture. However, we may adopt his
suggestion that the idea of "social stratification" is a modern
Western one and look further into its origins. In the West,
words like "class" and "stratum," if not the idea behind them,
do appear to be relatively modern. The *Shorter Oxford English Dictionary* (third edition) gives 1772 as the date of first
occurrence for "class" in the social layer sense, 1902 for social
"stratum." Of course in medieval times there was much talk
of "orders" of men and of "estates" (*états, Stände*) , but in the

High Middle Ages this terminology was associated more with an organic conception of society as a "body politic" than with the notion of social layers. Thus John of Salisbury:

The servants of religion are the soul of the body and therefore have *principatum totius corporis,* the prince is the head, the senate the heart, the court the sides, officers and judges are the eyes, ears and tongue, the executive officials are the unarmed and the army is the armed hand, the financial department is the belly and intestines, landfolk, handicraftsmen and the likes are the feet, so that the state exceeds the centipede *numerositate pedum.*[9]

According to Gierke, the historian of these ideas, this image became the vehicle for ideological controversy, the partisans of church and state contending over whether the body should have two heads or one, and if one, whether this sole head should be prince or pope.[10] Parenthetically, Gierke's account should commend itself to Louis Dumont, who seems uncertain whether to contrast his Indian *homo hierarchicus* to a *modern* or to a *Western homo aequalis.*[11] Although Gierke (mercifully) lived and wrote before the tyranny of linguistics over cultural analysis, and hence is not as preoccupied as Dumont with dyadic contrast,[12] his (Gierke's) discussion of medieval Western thinkers shows that their conceptions of society were quite as "holistic" and free of "individualistic atomism" as were those of Vedic India—which is not, of course, to argue that the two sets of ideas are not different in other essential respects. Holistic or organic ideologies, of course, need not preclude competition and conflict, and one would be surprised if in Vedic times the theory of the four *varnas* did not also become the medium for ideological, and even physical, conflict, as indeed they have in historic times.[13]

However that may be, the stratigraphic conception of society, as contrasted with the organic one, seems to have appeared in Europe in the eighteenth century as a prelude to what R. R. Palmer has termed the "age of the democratic revolution."[14] In earlier times there had been the estates or "orders," which were categories of persons possessing a certain corporate character to the extent that they sat together in parliaments and enjoyed common rights and duties in relation to the king or prince. But these corporate solidarities and the conciliar institutions through which they operated were highly variable and local. The classical threefold division (nobility, clergy, burgess), Palmer makes clear, abstracts and summarizes almost as much on-the-ground complexity as does the four-*varna* scheme with respect to the local *jati* (castes) of India.[15] Further, the estates or orders were cut across by dyadic ties of interpersonal fealty. Palmer argues that the concept of "aristocracy" in the strict sense of a hereditary stratum was new in the eighteenth century and that it came into being, along with its contrasting concept "democracy," as the medieval "constituted (conciliar) bodies" became more hereditary, and as this development was challenged by those who felt left out. He writes:

> Aristocracy in the eighteenth century may even be thought of as a new and recent development, if it be distinguished from the older institution of nobility. A king could create nobles but, as the saying went, it took four generations to make a gentleman. . . . Aristocracy was nobility civilized, polished by that "refinement of manners" of which people talked, enjoying not only superiority of birth but a superior mode of life.[16]

"Aristocracy" and "democracy" are of course Greek words which have had a continuous scholarly currency since classical antiquity; but they became popular, partisan words in the context of the great revolutionary convulsion which, beginning in North America and France, swept across the Western world at the end of the eighteenth century. At this time, too, "democracy" seems to have begun its modern career as an essentially ambiguous term. Does it contrast more essentially with hereditary status or with the absence of self-government?[17] Although popular American usage has tended (optimistically) to blur the distinction, it can be argued—indeed, of course, often has been argued—that aristocracy, by acting as a check on monarchy, is friendly to the growth of democracy in the "self-government" sense precisely by being hostile to it in the (excessive) "equality-of-status" sense. This debate, in updated forms, lies at the heart of much contemporary political-ideological debate, at any rate in those societies in which such debate is allowed.[18] The point here, however, is simply that during the "age of the democratic revolution" "aristocracy" and "democracy" became, among other things, *stratificatory* words connoting a certain kind of equality and inequality—ascribed equality and inequality of power and status, or right to deference, embodied in society-wide, or even Western-world-wide strata. Some substantial part of the population of the Western world, under the influence of new ideologies, came to think of inequality in their societies as involving not merely dyadic, personal superiority and inferiority, but rather (or also) the ascribed inequality and opposition of layers of society.

Marx and Weber

But all this is intellectual history—or ethnosociology. What is the relationship of all these ideas to "social action"? Neither the four-*varna* scheme of classical Indian thought, nor the organic analogy-plus-estates theory of medieval Europe, nor the democracy versus aristocracy theme of the age of democratic revolution actually describes with any great fidelity the shape of inequality in the social order in which it was articulated. Are ideas, then, irrelevant? In pursuit of an answer it is useful to move from history to theory, as social science—in the course of the nineteenth century, reflecting upon the contemporary sociocultural situation in the light of its past —emerges by joining thought to empirical investigation. Much of what we should like to consider intellectual progress in thinking about inequality can be summed up in the work of Karl Marx and in Max Weber's response to that work. In "moving from history to theory" I do not, of course, mean to suggest that empirical social science was born at a moment in time—that ethnosociology suddenly became sociology—that there was not social science before Marx, or that Marx and Weber were not, like their predecessors, "men of their times." It is, on the contrary, my view that a social science completely free of historical context is impossible because we are men, not gods. We are "enculturated," at many levels. But in the modern Western world, beginning in the eighteenth century but especially in the nineteenth, there does emerge a kind of educated person, sufficiently "secularized" and disengaged from the daily life of society to engage in more concentrated reflection upon society and in empirical investigation of it. In Marx he is the "marginal man," the alienated scholar who depends for his livelihood upon his wealthy friend and patron, Engels. In Weber he becomes the fully institutionalized university professor. Both worked more with documents than with people, but Weber directed empirical investigations of contemporary social problems and if Marx's famous *enquête ouvrière* was a failure as survey research, it was at least a brave attempt.[19] The two of them, the one building upon the other, tell us much about the usefulness for social science of the layer-cake imagery inherent in the term "social stratification" and, more generally, about the relationship between cultural ideas and social action.

Marx and Weber shared an enduring central concern: the peculiarities of Western industrial capitalist societies and their characteristic inequalities. Marx had drawn attention to the crucial historical change: for the first time in human experience, most men would work not in family or neighborhood groups and not under, and for the benefit of, paternalistic masters who knew them as persons and took some responsibility for their fate, as had been the case in agrarian feudal societies, but rather in factories or other work places separated from kith and kin in an impersonal milieu, under the authority of masters with whom their only tie was the exchange of their labor for wages—a situation which encouraged a sense of common "class situation" and solidarity. By selling their labor they were alienated from its product as well as from the means of production. The market in which this exchange took place was formally free, but the bargaining position of the employer was far stronger and so the laborer was subject to exploitation. For Weber, this much was common ground, although with almost a half-century's additional historical experience at his disposal, he was able to see more clearly a further feature of modern Western societies: the growth of bureaucracy. By Weber's time, not only the governments of the nation-states, but also the great capitalist enterprises and even the trade unions and political parties— including the socialist ones—were coming to be bureaucratized as well. The managers and civil servants shared the condition of industrial workers with respect to the product of their work and the means of its production, though of course they were better paid and received greater deference.[20]

Where the two part company most decisively is in their views of history or, if one prefers, of sociocultural change. Marx's view of the matter is well known: society is "objectively" divided into broad strata, defined in relation to the means of production—that is, ownership or nonownership. Nonowners, who are thereby subject to exploitation, are a "class in themselves" until they become conscious of their common situation and thereby become a "class for themselves." History is made by nonowning classes' overthrowing owning classes, thereby establishing themselves, their characteristic means of production, and their ideology as dominant. Marx recognizes the existence of marginal groups not easily classified as owners or nonowners, but as time passes, he believes, these tend to disappear—to be assimilated into one or the other major party to the struggle for dominance. Thus the industrial bourgeoisie overthrew the feudal landowners and thus also the industrial workers will overthrow the factory-owners. But in this scheme of historical inevitability the industrial working class occupies a theoretically privileged place: All previous ruling classes imposed an ideology which supported their class interests, and to the degree to which other classes accepted this ideology it represented "false consciousness." But the interests and ideology of the industrial working class are "objectively" and "historically" correct for the society—and indeed for mankind as a whole—hence their triumph will mark the end of history as class struggle.

Now what is the nature of Weber's quarrel with Marx here? It is not that he saw no clash of interests in society, nor is it that he considers ideas, or ideology, or culture more important in shaping history than "material" interests. That one still occasionally encounters this misunderstanding can only be attributed to the vulgarization which seems to be the fate of most intellectual arguments possessing any degree of subtlety.[21] Weber was no Hegelian—rather less so, in some ways, than Marx. He was no "idealist," nor did he overstress "free will." He fully appreciated man's capacity to become entrapped by his environmental conditions, his technology, and his institutions. But he was concerned to *break open* the

Marxian scheme, to *relativize* it, to remove from it what he saw as the illusion of historical inevitability and thus to make of it a much more effective tool for empirical study.

Weber shared with Marx—perhaps learned from him and his successors—the notion that ideas—culture—have a social and material basis in the sense that persons, both ordinary persons and the creators of great ideas, are deeply influenced in the use they make of culture—the way they manipulate and shape it—by their social and economic milieu. Or, to put the matter somewhat more succinctly: Thinking is a social act. But Weber was concerned to round out the symmetry here; for him, it was equally important that social action and interaction were culturally framed; "social change" involved cultural creativity. For him there could be no such thing as "pure material interest" or social interaction in a cultural vacuum. This is why he so often speaks of social actors—individuals or collectivities—as "pursuing their *ideal and material* interests." This view fits, surely, with everything anthropology has learned about man. Man is, we say, *inherently* cultural; he has, in the course of his biocultural history, become irrevocably committed to guiding himself through cultural, much more than genetic, encoding.[22] Culture—particular cultures—must be recreated in every new generation of individuals, in old or new forms.[23] So, in Weber's view, the pursuit of material interests, even the most pressing material needs, presupposes "ideas"—cultural structurings of the world within which such pursuits become *meaningful* or make sense. Thus, what we perceive as the pursuit of "material" ends presupposes an element of "materialistic" culture which renders it meaningful to the pursuer.

To round off this all-too-skeletal account, it is perhaps useful to return to Marx's views on classes in history in juxtaposition with Weber's. Weber's discussion of differentiation and stratification is analytically more differentiated. He speaks of class (market situation), status (style of life, sense of honor), power (ability to influence the behavior of others), and ethnicity (perceived common origin) as analytic "ideal type" elements which may appear in varying degrees, forms, and combinations in the meaning-complexes of human groups. Perhaps most important, he takes from the medieval European estates the idea of a "status group": a collectivity bound by common "ideal and material" interests—by interests defined by culture—and sees in such groups an engine for social change, much as Marx saw his "classes." But there are crucial differences: Weber is less interested in broad societywide strata (although he uses the term "stratum") and more in occupational groups—entrepreneurs, lawyers, scientists, priests, politicians, and even musicians, and the industrial working class holds no theoretically privileged position. Insofar as it becomes a culture-bearing and culture-creating group, pursuing its ideal and material interests, it competes in the political and cultural arena with others and its "triumph" (in the sense of producing a classless society) is by no means assured, especially since trade unions and political parties have a tendency, shared by all modern institutions, toward internal oligarchy and bureaucratization, producing new inequalities. Nor is the "interest" of the industrial working class necessarily coincident with that of the society at large; thus, if socialism *were* to triumph, it would only reinforce the trend toward bureaucratization, which Weber sees as the most characteristically modern expression of inequality.

But this is a trend, not a "historical law." History is inevitably only in retrospect, and Weber foresaw the possibility of charismatic leaders who might break through the "iron cage" of bureaucracy and materialism, at least temporarily:

> No one knows who will live in this cage in the future, or whether . . . new prophets will arise, there will be a great rebirth of old ideas and ideals, or, if neither, mechanized petrification, embellished with a sort of convulsive self-importance.[24]

Weber's inclusion of the politicians among the modern occupations and professions is of particular significance, for it represents a recognition of the special role of the political professional in societies in which open politics are permitted. Politics in such societies constitute a calling and its practitioners live both "for politics" and "off politics";[25] that is, like members of other occupations and professions, they themselves have both ideal and material interests which they pursue in the social arena in competition with others. But politicians are peculiar in that it is one aspect of their calling to shape and to represent the competing ideal and material interests of others: their parties—both party organizations and their constituencies of voters. Again they are, as a group, the creators and custodians of the political subculture—the "rules of the game" of contest and compromise within which the competitive struggle is conducted. And this professional or occupational subculture, like others, contains an element of collusion against the public by virtue of the very fact of socio-cultural differentiation, since publicly expressed professional ideals must always be to some extent in tension with mundane professional-group interests. But politicians, charged with the triple responsibility of articulating policies for the public at large, representing their own and their constituents' interests, and at the same time maintaining the political subculture and the institutions within which it operates in good working order, face a most difficult set of demands—which is perhaps why "politician" and "political" are so often used as opprobrious terms and why, as Weber noted, the besetting sins of politicians are opposites: ideological absolutism and cynicism.[26]

The stratigraphic image of society, then, seems to have crystallized in the late eighteenth-century ideological clashes over hereditary power and status and to have been taken over by Marx as a means of conceptualizing the new inequalities of industrial capitalism. Weber's view was a more differentiated one which societies as arenas in which groups of various kinds—especially occupational ones—struggle for cultural and political dominance, in the process reducing old inequalities and producing new ones. This view, it seems to me, captures the modern situation more adequately than does Marx's stratigraphic scheme. Nevertheless, the idea of society-wide strata has remained prominent in Western social science, including that part of it which has been concerned with American society.

Inequality in America: Warner and Others

American society is fundamentally a European society, in its pattern of inequalities as in many other respects. Since the country is populated largely by immigrants from Europe, that thesis would hardly seem worth arguing were it not for the fact that so many Americans, both intellectuals and others, have been at such pains to deny it. Frequently Americans have even thought of theirs as a *counter*-European society. Many of the founders of the Republic, children of the Enlightenment that they were, thought of themselves as leaping right out of history and founding a new society on universal, rational principles. The fact that the revolution undertaken shortly thereafter by their French cousins was soon reined in and squeezed back into the European mold, whereas the new American republic with its open frontier could sail on into Jacksonian populism, seemed to confirm the idea that here was something quite different from "Old Europe." So it seemed, at the time, to Tocqueville.[27] And so it seemed, at the beginning of the twentieth century, to Frederick Jackson Turner, who perhaps contributed more than any other writer to the myth of the uniqueness of the American experience and whose "frontier thesis" so dominated American historiography during the early decades of the century as to (in the words of a biographer) convert the American Historical Association "into one big Turnerverein."[28] As Turner put it:

American social development has been continually beginning over again on the frontier. This perennial rebirth, this fluidity of American life, this expansion westward with its new opportunities, its continuous touch with the simplicity of primitive society, furnish the forces dominating American character. The true point of view in the history of this nation is not the Atlantic coast, it is the Great West.[29]

European observers, whether enthusiastic or horror-struck, have generally contributed to the idea of American novelty. More helpful are those (all too few) American historians who have given serious attention to American affairs in the context of European history. R. R. Palmer, for example, places the incipient American republic squarely within that history in *The Age of the Democratic Revolution*. There were "aristocrats" and "democrats" in America, too. "There were no lords in the British colonies. . . . But there was a good deal of hereditary standing, with an apparent tendency, as in Europe, toward its increase":

Each colony had a governor's council and an elected assembly . . . . A list of all who served on the councils before the Revolution, according to the estimate of Professor Larrabee, would include ninety percent of the "first families," that is, the socially prominent families, of the colonial period. By the 1760's in most colonies these families had repeatedly intermarried, until their genealogical trees had become veritable jungles of interwoven branches, the despair of the researcher but the pride of their descendants.[30]

Nor, of course, did this aristocratic element disappear with the Revolution. As Palmer summarizes it, the Revolution "remains ambivalent":

It was conservative because the colonies had never known oppression, excepting always for slavery—because, as human institutions go, America had always been free. It was revolutionary because the colonists took the risks of rebellion, because they could not avoid a conflict among themselves, and because they checkmated those Americans who, as the country developed, most admired the aristocratic society of England and Europe. Henceforth the United States, in Louis Hartz's phrase, would be the land of the frustrated aristocrat not of the frustrated democrat; for to be an aristocrat it is not enough to think of oneself as such, it is necessary to be thought so by others; and never again would deference for social rank be a characteristic American attitude. Elites, for better or worse, would henceforth be on the defensive against popular values.[31]

It is worth referring to Louis Hartz himself on these matters. In *The Founding of New Societies* he presents a theory of what happens when a "fragment of the larger whole of Europe is struck off in the course of the revolution which brought the west into the modern world."[32] I should say that Hartz is often too Hegelian for my taste:

What I am discussing here, of course, are not merely elements of cause and effect, but facets of the bottomless subjectivity which swallows up the fragment as even its memory of Europe fades. The latter is the instrument of the former, indeed its most powerful instrument. For it is because men are contained in the fragment that they cannot betray it, cannot give way to the alien thoughts of the future, cannot resist fostering the telos of the "present."[33]

For all his hypostatization of historical forces, however, Hartz has some interesting things to say about the dynamics of inequality in Western societies in general and in the United States in particular. Accepting the usual tripartite framework dividing European society into "feudal," "bourgeois," and "radical" elements, he says that the fragment societies overseas tend to be dominated by one or another element, depending upon the time and place from which they were "struck off." In the case of the United States, the fragment is a bourgeois one and this element comes to dominate society and culture in a way which is impossible in Europe, where all three elements remain powerful and in interaction. In the fragment, the dominant element comes to define the nation, so that to be American is to be middle class. The dominant element is "encapsulated," thus foreclosing further development of the "European dynamic."

Hartz's analysis of the bourgeois or middle-class ascendancy in America says something useful and convincing. This society has, indeed, demonstrated a large capacity to bourgeoisify its radicals and aristocrats.[34] But here it is again useful to turn from history to theory—or rather from theoretical history to social anthropology—and to consider the work of that most characteristically American student of inequality, William Lloyd Warner, and his five volumes on "Yankee City" (Newburyport, Massachusetts)—still the most complete ethnography we have of an American community.[35] Warner was not interested in continuities between European and American culture. Indeed, he was not interested in history at all, except as myth. He was a sometime pupil of A. R. Radcliffe-Brown and, perhaps through him, a Durkheimian—the very model of a Durkheimian, having, like Radcliffe-Brown, worked among Durkheim's favorite people, the aborigines of Australia. However, he was also very American (from California, actually) and therefore lacked that nostalgic hankering after the lost age of primitive simplicity that has marked the French Durkheimians down to our contemporary, Claude Lévi-Strauss. But if Warner's lack of interest in history was rooted in both his western American origins and his intellectual leanings, his work nevertheless says something interesting about European continuities in American society, particularly with respect to inequality.

American society, as represented by Yankee City in the early

1930s, was, Warner says, divided into six status-classes which
were ethnosociological; that is, they were elicited from native
informants. He assures us that this was not a view which he
and his collaborators brought to the research; rather, they
were in the first instance inclined to believe that "the fundamental structure of our society, that which ultimately controls
and dominates the thinking and actions of our people is
economic."[36] What he *did* bring to the study was this notion
of "fundamental structure," the idea that "all societies seem
to place emphasis on one structure which gives form to the
total society and integrates the other structures into a social
unity."[37] The Murngin of Australia, among whom Warner
had worked, "depend upon an elaborate kinship system for
their fundamental structure."[38] It was clearly for some equivalent of the Australian kinship groups, with their complex
rules of intermarriage, that Warner was looking in Yankee
City, and he found it in the system of status-classes. These were
the "something more," beyond the economic structure of the
town, which "integrated" and "gave form to" its social life.
One quickly discovers in the first volume of the study that
money is important, that the population of the town is ethnically very heterogeneous, that it has a complex associational
life, both formal and informal. But the "class order" is fundamental: Whereas Yankees (Wasps, in contemporary parlance),
who make up slightly more than half the total population,
monopolize the upper-upper class, they also make up 20 percent of the lower-lowers. The classes are characterized by style
of life, area of residence, a tendency toward membership in
common associations, and a marked propensity to marry en-
dogamously. There is a strong correlation between occupation and class, but Warner stresses that there are many important exceptions. The relationship between class and
political office is even weaker; the upper and middle classes
dominate the city government, but Warner gives great attention, in his volume on the symbolic life of the community, to
the career of "Biggy Muldoon," a lower-class Irish immigrant
who served several terms as mayor of Yankee City.

Warner and his colleagues subsequently carried out similar
studies of communities in the Middle West and the South and
developed more mechanical research methods ("evaluated

participation" and an "index of status characteristics") as shortcut substitutes for the laborious field techniques used in Yankee City.[39] For a time studies of status-class flourished, as did also, in reaction, criticism of these studies. It was said that Warner mistakenly viewed the small towns and cities he and his colleagues studied as microcosms of the country as a whole; that he neglected the so-called objective elements in inequality—wealth and power—in favor of the "subjective" sense of relative status; that his status-classes represented an unwarranted reification; that he was overly optimistic about the possibility of mobility in American society; that his perspective was ahistorical.[40] Many of these criticisms had merit, and in his later work Warner responded to some of them.[41] But it must be said that the view, rather widespread during his lifetime, that he was an apologist for the status quo in American life was quite unjust; for he and his colleagues were more forthright and searching concerning the defects of American society, in relation to professed American ideals, than were most other social scientists of his time. This was particularly true with respect to anti-Negro racism, a subject the Warner group probed with both subtlety and courage in their studies of southern communities.[42] Unlike many others, however, Warner did not consider it beneath his dignity to take American ideals—which is to say American culture—seriously.

However that may be, the storm over Warner has subsided —indeed his status-class terminology has, for better or worse, passed into the common language, as if he had only made explicit what lay just under the surface of the American consciousness—and it is possible now to assess more calmly his contribution to the study of inequality. In my judgment, that contribution consisted in a fuller appreciation of the *culture* of inequality, of the significance of styles of life and the symbols of status. His appreciation of the development from Marx to Weber appears to have been meager. He thought of himself, rather, as a Durkheimian, and he liked to assert that symbols of status were normative, that they were socially *real*, like the totemic symbols of the Australians. One may dismiss this as the sociology of snobbery, but it is only necessary to recall the mammoth exertions of millions of Americans to secure the marks of social acceptability and the countless rebuffs suffered by the "socially mobile" who have acquired the "objective qualifications" but do not yet know how to "behave properly" to recognize that the culture of inequality is a powerful force in American lives.

This force, as Warner saw it in Yankee City and other small American communities, is not a particularly American phenomenon—nor, in the broadest sense, is it a peculiarly Western one, though it is to its relevance to European continuities in American life that I wish to draw attention here. I suggest that the six-class system which Warner thought he had found in Yankee City does represent a reification—that is, that it is difficult, on the basis of his data, to sustain the notion either that there existed six clearly bounded, culturally distinguishable, stratified groups (upper-upper, lower-upper, upper-middle, lower-middle, upper-lower, lower-lower) or that the citizens of Yankee city (or some substantial proportion of them) viewed their inequalities in precisely this light. On the contrary the data can more plausibly be read as revealing, *in terms of persons,* an unbroken status continuum, from top to bottom, with persons classifying their fellow-townsmen into equals, superiors, and subordinates, so that a person's position might vary somewhat with the standpoint of the classifier— though it is easy to believe that there were unusually status-preoccupied persons from whom more general views and finer distinctions might be elicted. But the data also quite clearly reveal three (not six) rather distinct subcultures of inequality, and these are none other than our old friends from Europe: the aristocratic subculture, that of the bourgeoisie or "middle class," and what might be called the subculture of the unbourgeoisified poor. For those generally regarded as unambiguously "upper-upper," Warner describes a culture of birth and breeding, of genealogies and heirlooms, of self-confident standing and philanthropic "public service." For the great middling majority of the population, from "lower-uppers" to "upper-lowers" this aristocratic subculture appears to represent an ideal in the sense that participation in it stands as a goal to which their children or their children's children might aspire through here-and-now participation in the bourgeois virtues of "respectable" behavior and educational and occupational achievement—though Warner shows, through his account of the activities of "Biggy Muldoon," how ambivalent this commitment is: under the right circumstances, a gifted populist might make a career out of thumbing his nose at the "swells," in the process capturing the affections of much of this middling majority. Still lower in status is a much smaller group, the "lower-lowers," who work only as much as necessary and who, it is said, do not greatly value education and "respectability." It is difficult to evaluate the characterizations of lower-lower-class culture provided in the Yankee City volumes, partly because the attention given them is relatively slight and partly because their way of life is so often presented in the words of other, more "respectable," members of the community. To this day this issue simmers in American social science: whether the culture of the unbourgeoisified poor is a "genuine" subculture, with a cohesive integrity of its own, or simply a set of ad hoc behavioral and attitudinal adjustments to lack of opportunity.

This problem aside, however, one is impressed by the degree of continuity—cultural continuity, not continuity of persons (by descent) or of bounded groups—with the European culture of inequality. Of course participation in the culture of the bourgeois estate—the culture of achievement and respectability—has vastly broadened to include the greater part of the "working classes." To the despair of radicals, the American industrial worker has usually preferred the aspiration toward individual mobility to working-class solidarity, although American workers have on occasion been militant enough, and during the first two decades of this century, when industrial workers included large numbers of new and unassimilated European immigrants, socialist parties were able to draw substantial support at the polls through the rhetoric of social strata.[43] The bourgeois ascendancy has also inhibited the growth (or maintenance) of aristocratic culture, with its element of noblesse oblige, one consequence being that this society has been relatively ungenerous to those who, whether from lack of opportunity or from personal incapacity, have not been able to participate in the culture of achievement. Aristocracy was kinder, at any rate to its unquestioned inferiors, than the triumphant bourgeoisie, whose culture has always tended to view poverty as a symptom of moral inadequacy.

But this is far from being the whole story. If the American

bourgeois "fragment" has never quite succeeded in absorbing its lower orders, neither has it succeeded in eradicating its higher ones. Palmer speaks of an American aristocracy in the eighteenth century, and Warner finds one in twentieth-century Yankee City. Digby Baltzell has described their counterparts in Philadelphia.[44] If, as Palmer says, European aristocracy was "nobility civilized," American aristocrats have been successful merchants and industrialists civilized—grown to value birth and manners by the passage of generations. Relieved of the necessity to achieve occupationally in order to maintain what they have regarded as a suitable style of life, they have often become patrons of the arts and sciences, and even reformers or radicals.[45] Indeed, the sheer massiveness and vigor of the bourgeois element itself, and the distaste this arouses in "aristocrats," sometimes serves to "radicalize" the latter.

More important, perhaps (as Warner saw), in addition to the small number of "real" aristocrats, with many generations of ancestral wealth and status behind them, the aristocratic style remains a point of reference for many millions of middle-class American achievers. This is most clearly expressed in the American love of genealogy and armorial insignia. In many middle-class American minds, the rude farmstead of the European ancestor becomes a manor house, the blood line a claim to gentle birth. Such persons often take on a pretension to the symbols of aristocracy while neglecting its noblesse oblige sense of social responsibility. In another recombination of elements drawn from traditional European cultures of inequality, many American intellectuals combine aristocratic tastes with proletarian sympathies—both in a rather fragmentary and theoretical way.

Thus it is not quite correct to say, with Louis Hartz, that the "European dynamic" has been "foreclosed" in America by the "nationalization of the bourgeois fragment." The mix, of course, is different, but the cultural elements which frame inequality are all present. The dynamic proceeds in somewhat different terms—more in terms of a struggle to participate in more highly evaluated subcultures, less in terms of a struggle among "feudal," "bourgeois," and "radical" elements as such, embodied in cohesive social groups—thought at most times in the history of the new republic it has been possible to discern an element of the latter sort of struggle as well, in situations in which dissensus over criteria for inequality has produced a sense of "we against them." But is all this not also true in modern Europe? In Britain, for example, the class subcultures are more apparent—more palpable and clearly bounded—largely, perhaps, because they are more clearly marked by differences in speech, a status symbol difficult to acquire after childhood. But in Britain, too, a pervasive bourgeoisification of the working class is in progress, and a steady absorption of sturdy burgesses into the aristocracy has proceeded over many centuries. With appropriate variations to take account of varying national histories, much the same might be said of continental Europe. Thus, if America is not exactly European, there is much more of Europe in her inequalities than has commonly been acknowledged.

What is most novel, viewed from the vantage point of the third quarter of the twentieth century, is of course the role of race and ethnicity in American inequality. If it was possible in the thirties for Warner to argue that ethnicity was subordinate to status-class (he dealt with race in somewhat different terms) as the "fundamental structure"—and I should reject the very notion of "fundamental structure" as inviting a fatal oversimplification—it is much less easy today to make that argument. Neither racism nor ethnic antipathy has been absent from European cultures of inequality, but both have had a peculiar prominence in a society of immigrants and slaves. In this connection, one of the most important developments in American society is the progressive ethnicization of the Wasps—their increasing loss of a special relationship to the cultural "center" and their increasing assumption of a position of one kind of American among many. This process is not, of course, complete, but it was under way in Yankee City in the early thirties, as a close examination of Warner's data shows, and it has gone much further since, both through individual educational and occupational achievement and through organized political action.

It is fashionable today among writers on the "ethnic revival" to say that the "melting pot" has melted nothing, but here again it is essential to distinguish culture from its bearers, institutions from their personnel. Take, for example, language and law, the first the common medium of communication, the second the institution closest to the "cultural center" of the society,[46] and both together the elements most clearly associated with the Wasp heritage, in the strict sense of that which was brought over by English settlers. It has been said that in contemporary American literature Jews and southerners (the latter having been ethnicized by secession, defeat, and forcible readmission) excel because they each possess an "authentic idiom," but of course it is in both cases an idiom expressed in English. And the legal profession, long a favorite route into the "mainstream" for Irish, Jews, and, latterly, Italians, Slavs, and Negroes, truly, if partially, "melts" these bearers of diverse ethnic and racial traditions by training them in the skills of a historically English "common law" mode of legal thought. Of course in all these cases extraordinary effort and talent has often been necessary to overcome the resistance of Wasp persons, but it is not necessary to argue —it would clearly be false to argue—that American nativism and racism are dead in order to make the point that the time is past when Wasp persons could effectively dominate the culture and institutions established by English settlers; nor, of course, would it be right to ignore the creative vigor introduced into that culture and those institutions by persons of non-Wasp tradition, who perforce bring something of their ethnic experience with them. It is clearer today that the melting pot melts only insofar as not only persons, but also elements of their subcultures are admitted into the common culture.

Of course a price is paid by a society made up of the children of immigrants and slaves, not only in social conflict but also in the loss of that cultural coherence that Americans find so charming in the more "natural" communities of Europe. But either mourning or celebration would be pointless. Ethnic and racial heterogeneity are facts of the American pattern of inequality, and if these facts do not precisely determine its future, they do give definite shape to the problems it must face.

Inequality, especially in a human community of any substantial degree of sociocultural complexity, cannot easily be captured by grand dichotomies or typologies—*homo hierarchicus* versus *homo aequalis,* for example—or by images such as the stratigraphic one or by the idea of a "fundamental

structure" of status class. This is so because inequality—and
here lies the core of truth in Dumont's assertion that hierarchy is universal[47]—is inherent in sociocultural differentiation in all its dimensions: sex, age, descent, occupation, religion, race, ethnicity, and even—on a wider scale—nation.
This is not to say, of course, that subcultures of inequality
need be elaborated on all these bases (although I venture to
say that sex and age are never utterly neglected in this respect).
It is rather simply to say that wherever different sorts of persons *are* distinguished in thought and action, we may look for
cultures or subcultures that define the terms for differential
evaluation and the distribution of deference, both within and
among the sorts distinguished. And since a degree of commitment, a degree of investment of personal identity, personal
integrity, is involved in participation in culture and subculture, there follows power—the effort, however forceful or
muted, to cause other sorts to be like one's own or to conform
to one's own subcultural view of what being of another particular sort consists in. Given freer rein, these propensities
grow into such sociocultural complexes as the "generation
gap," the "war between the sexes," crusade and *jihad,* "class
conflict," racial and ethnic conflict, marketplace competition,
and the like. To view societies as *mere* arenas for playing out
power struggles, however, would be a distortion; for the extent to which societies exist in thought and action, they tend
to possess cultural centers, and common attachment to this
heritage of cultural traditions moderates the stresses among
creators and bearers of diverse subcultures. French workers
and employers are both French, American men and women
are equally American, so that personal ties may be formed on
the basis of common culture across lines of subcultural differentiation, within the contexts of home and workplace, neighborhood and place of worship, marketplace and political
arena. But both "society" and "cultural tradition" are all too
easily reified; neither is a mechanical thing; both exist only as
complexes of meaning in the minds of social actors and both
change with experience, an important aspect of which is
encounter with others who see things differently, and so act
differently.

The stratigraphic image, which looms so large in contemporary Western thinking about inequality, both ideological and

social scientific, appears to have developed out of a particular experience: a moment in Western history when increased ease of communication allowed the inequalities involved in local and diverse hierarchies of estates or orders and the routine tensions and conflicts indigenous to them to be generalized into a contest between "aristocracy" and "democracy"—between the claim to hereditary status and power and the egalitarian revolt against that claim. Interestingly, the "age of the democratic revolution" was also the age of the nationalist revolution. Persons increasingly saw their conflicts as part of larger struggles, but also increasingly developed a sense of common attachment to the nation. The French Revolution did not create the French nation, but it did consummate its sense of territorial unity. The slogan *"liberté, egalité, fraternité"* was accomplished by another: *"la France, une et indivisible."* As the sense of nationhood solidified in French minds, so also did the stratigraphic image—a view of the nation as divided among stratified layers, each "class" struggling to define the cultural center in its own subcultural terms. There seems to be, at any rate in societies of Western tradition, a certain affinity between the idea of the nation-state and that of the class/stratum sort of inequality. Perhaps the logic of this is as follows: The modern nation-state is more active than were the older sorts of polity, and it draws people into more active participation in its affairs, making them more conscious of the nation and its constituent elements and of their common citizenship, with its implication of a certain basic equality. Contained within the bounded national community of citizens, sociocultural differentiation more readily becomes sociocultural competition and conflict concerning the nation's character. The stratigraphic image, then, appears in the context of struggles between those whose power renders them more-than-equal citizens and those whose lack of it renders them less. Through the activities of ideologists who interpret social experience, it passes into cultural and subcultural tradition, where it appears as both sociology and ethnosociology and is reinforced in historical moments when conflicts become severe. Some few of these moments are revolutionary, but the stratigraphic image is seldom absent from the rhetoric of institutionalized electoral contest in Western societies.

The term "social stratification," then, has a certain historical appropriateness in contemporary Western societies. I suggest, nevertheless, that it is a poor term for which social scientists might well substitute "inequality." Not only is it quite
misleading when applied to the many non-Western societies
in which thought and action about inequality center much
more upon interpersonal relations of superiority and inferiority; it also oversimplifies by attempting to capture with a
single graphic image the multiple bases of differentiation
and inequality which exist within Western societies. Race,
ethnicity, occupation, and regionalism are not reducible to
"class" or "stratum," and all these terms, to the extent to
which they have meaning in non-Western societies, very often
have different meanings there. It may, perhaps, seem useless
to argue at such length about words, but there is, after all,
some relationship between the way we speak and the way we
think. There is some virtue in saying what we mean and
meaning what we say.

2
A Note on the "Trickle Effect"

MUCH has been written—and much more spoken in informal social scientific shoptalk—about the so-called trickle effect—the tendency in United States society (and perhaps to a lesser extent in Western societies generally) for new styles or fashions in consumption goods to be introduced via the socioeconomic elite and then to pass down through the status hierarchy, often in the form of inexpensive, mass-produced copies.

In a recent paper, Barber and Lobel have analyzed this phenomenon in the field of women's clothes.[1] They point out that women's dress fashions are not simply irrational shifts in taste but have definite functions in the United States status system. Most Americans, they say, are oriented toward status mobility. Goods and services consumed are symbolic of social status. In the family division of labor, the husband and father "achieves" in the occupational system and thus provides the family with monetary income. Women, as wives and daughters, have the task of allocating this income so as to maximize its status-symbolic value. Since women's clothing permits much subtlety of expression in selection and display, it becomes of great significance as a status-mobility symbol.[2] The ideology of the "open class" system, however, stresses broad "equality" as well as differential status. The tendency of women's dress fashions to "trickle down" fairly rapidly via inexpensive reproductions of originals created at fashion centers helps to resolve this seeming inconsistency by preventing the development of rigid status distinctions.[3]

Reprinted by permission from *Public Opinion Quarterly* 18 (1954): 314–21.

In the widest sense, of course, the "trickle effect" applies not only to women's dress but also to consumption goods of many other kinds. Most similar to women's dress fashions are styles in household furnishings. A colleague has pointed out to me that venetian blinds have had a similar status career— being introduced at relatively high levels in the status hierarchy and within a few years passing down to relatively low levels. Like women's dress styles, styles in household furnishings are to a substantial degree matters of taste, and their adoption is a matter of "learning" by lower-status persons that they are status-relevant. The trickling down of other types of consumption goods is to a greater degree influenced by long-term increases in purchasing power at lower socioeconomic levels. Such consumer durables as refrigerators and automobiles, being products of heavy industry and hence highly standardized over relatively long periods and throughout the industries which produce them, are much less subject to considerations of taste. They do, however, trickle down over the long term and their possession is clearly status-relevant.

The dominant tendency among social scientists has been to regard the trickle effect mainly as a "battle of wits" between upper-status persons who attempt to guard their symbolic treasure and lower-status persons (in league with mass-production industries) who attempt to devalue the status-symbolic currency. There is much truth in this view. Latterly we have observed a drama of this sort being played out in the automotive field. Sheer ownership of an automobile is no longer symbolic of high status and neither is frequent trading-in. Not even the "big car" manufacturers can keep their products out of the hands of middle- and lower-status persons "on the make." High-status persons have therefore turned to antique or foreign sports-cars.

It seems possible, however, that the trickle effect has other and perhaps more far-reaching functions for the society as a whole. Western (and particularly United States) society, with its stress upon the value of success through individual achievement, poses a major motivational problem: The occupational system is primarily organized about the norm of technical efficiency. Technical efficiency is promoted by recruiting and rewarding persons on the basis of their objective competence

and performance in occupational roles. The field of opportunity for advancement, however, is pyramidal; the number
of available positions decreases as differential rewards increase.
But for the few most competent to be chosen, the many must
be "called"—that is, motivated to strive for competence and
hence success. This, of course, involves relative failure by the
many, hence the problem: How is the widespread motivation
to strive maintained in the face of the patent likelihood of
failure for all but the few? In a widely quoted paper, Merton
has recognized that this situation is a serious focus of strain in
the social system and has pointed to some structured types of
deviant reaction to it.[4] I should like to suggest the hypothesis
that *the trickle effect is a mechanism for maintaining the
motivation to strive for success, and hence for maintaining
efficiency of performance in occupational roles, in a system in
which differential success is possible for only a few.* Status-
symbolic consumption goods trickle down, thus giving the
"illusion" of success to those who fail to achieve *differential*
success in the opportunity and status pyramid. From this point
of view, the trickle effect becomes a "treadmill."

There are, of course, other hypotheses to account for the
maintenance of motivation to strive against very unfavorable
odds. Perhaps the most common is the notion that the "myth
of success," perhaps maintained by the mass-communications
media under the control of the "vested interests," deceives
people into believing that their chances for success are greater
than is in fact the case. Merton seems to accept this explanation in part while denying that the ruse is entirely effective.[5]
Somewhat similar is another common explanation, put forward, for example, by Schumpeter, that though the chances
for success are not great, the rewards are so glittering as to
make the struggle attractive.[6] Undoubtedly both the "success
myth" theory and the "gambling" theory contain elements of
truth. Individual achievement certainly *is* a major value in
the society and dominates much of its ideology, while risk-
taking is clearly institutionalized, at any rate in the business
segment of the occupational system. Taken by themselves,
however, these explanations do not seem sufficient to account
for the situation. At any rate, if it is possible to show that the
system *does* "pay off" for the many in the form of "trickle-

down" status-symbolic goods, one need not lean so heavily upon such arguments.

It seems a sound principle of sociological analysis to assume "irrationality" as a motivation for human action only where exhaustive analysis fails to reveal a "realistic" payoff for the observed behavior. To be sure, the explanation put forward here also assumes "irrationality," but in a different sense. The individual who is rewarded for his striving by the trickling down of status-symbolic consumption goods has the *illusion,* and not the *fact,* of status mobility among his fellows. But in terms of his life history, he nevertheless *has* been rewarded with things which are valued and to this degree his striving is quite "realistic."[7] Though his status position vis-à-vis his fellows has not changed, he can look back upon his own life history and say to himself (perhaps not explicitly since the whole status-mobility motivational complex is probably quite often wholly or in part unconscious) : "I (or my family) have succeeded. I now have things which five (or ten or twenty) years ago I could not have had, things which were then possessed only by persons of higher status." To the degree that status is *defined* in terms of consumption of goods and services one should perhaps say not that such an individual has only the *illusion* of mobility, but rather that the entire population has been upwardly mobile. From this point of view, status-symbolic goods and services do not "trickle down" but rather remain in fixed positions; the population moves up through the hierarchy of status-symbolic consumption patterns.

The accompanying diagram illustrates the various possibilities in terms of the life histories of individuals. The two half-pyramids represent the status hierarchy at two points in time (X and Y). A, B, C, and D are individuals occupying different levels in the status hierarchy. Roman numerals I through V represent the hierarchy of status-symbolic consumption patterns. Between time periods X and Y, a new high-status consumption pattern has developed and has been taken over by the elite. All status levels have "moved up" to "higher" consumption patterns. During the elapsed time, individual C has "succeeded" in the sense of having become able to consume goods and services which were unavailable to him before, though he has remained in the same relative

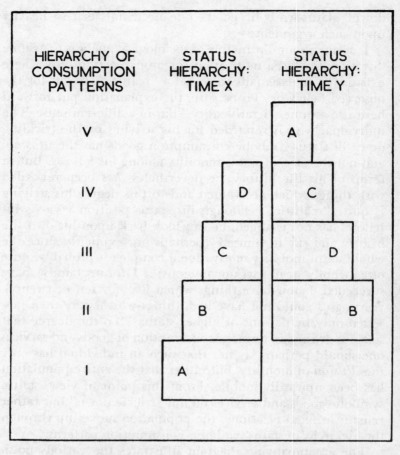

| HIERARCHY OF CONSUMPTION PATTERNS | STATUS HIERARCHY: TIME X | STATUS HIERARCHY: TIME Y |

status level. Individual B has been downwardly mobile in the status hierarchy, but this blow has been softened for him because the level into which he has dropped has in the meantime taken over consumption patterns previously available only to persons in the higher level in which B began. Individual D has been sufficiently downwardly mobile so that he has also lost ground in the hierarchy of consumption patterns. Finally, individual A, who has been a spectacular success, has risen to the very top of the status hierarchy where he is able to consume goods and services which were unavailable even to the elite at an earlier time period. Needless to say, this diagram is not meant to represent the actual status levels, the proportions of persons in each level, or the frequencies of upward and downward mobility in the United States social system. It is simply meant to illustrate diagrammatically the tendency of the system, in terms of status-symbolic consumption goods, to reward even those who are not status mobile and to provide a "cushion" for those who are slightly downwardly mobile.

Undoubtedly this view of the system misrepresents "the facts" in one way as much as the notion of status-symbolic goods and services "trickling down" through a stable status hierarchy does in another. Consumption patterns do not retain the same status-symbolic value as they become available to more people. Certainly to some degree the "currency becomes inflated." A more adequate diagram would show both consumption patterns trickling down and the status hierarchy moving up. Nonetheless, I would suggest that *to some degree* particular consumption goods have "absolute" value in terms of the individual's life history and his motivation to succeed. To the degree that this is so, the system pays off even for the person who is not status mobile.

This payoff, of course, is entirely dependent upon constant innovation and expansion in the industrial system. New goods and services must be developed and existing ones must become more widely available through mass production. Average "real income" must constantly rise. If status-symbolic consumption patterns remained stationary both in kind and in degree of availability, the system would pay off only for the status mobile, and the achievement motive would indeed be unrealistic for most individuals. Were the productive system to shrink, the payoff would become negative for most and the unrealism of the motivation to achieve would be compounded. Under such circumstances, the motivational complex of striving-achievement-occupational efficiency would be placed under great strain. Indeed, Merton seems to have had such circumstances in mind when he described "innovation," "ritualism," "rebellion," and "passive withdrawal" as common patterned deviations from the norm.[8]

This suggests a "vicious circle" relationship between achievement motivation and individual productivity. It seems reasonable to suppose that a high level of achievement motivation is both a cause and a result of efficiency in occupational role performance. Such an assumption underlies much of our thinking about the modern Western occupational system and indeed is perhaps little more than common sense. One British sociologist, commenting upon the reports of the British "productivity teams" which have recently been visiting American factories, is impressed by American workers' desire for status-symbolic consumption, partly the result of pressure upon husbands by their wives, as a factor in the greater "per man hour" productivity of American industry.[9] Greater productivity, of course, means more and cheaper consumption goods and hence a greater payoff for the workers. Conversely, low achievement motivation and inefficiency in occupational role performance seem to stimulate one another. The worker has less to work for, works less efficiently, and in turn receives still less reward. Presumably these relationships tend to hold, though in some cases less directly, throughout the occupational system and not only in the sphere of the industrial worker.

To the degree that the relationships suggested here between motivation to status-symbolic consumption, occupational role performance, and expanding productivity actually exist, they should be matters of some importance to the theory of business cycles. Although they say nothing about the genesis of upturns and downturns in business activity, they do suggest some social structural reasons why upward or downward movements, once started, might tend to continue. It is not suggested, of course, that these are the only, or even the most important, reasons. Most generally, they exemplify the striking degree to which the stability of modern industrial society often depends upon the maintenance of delicate equilibriums.

The hypotheses suggested here are, it seems to me, amenable to research by a number of techniques. It would be most useful to discover more precisely just which types of status-symbolic consumption goods follow the classical trickle-down pattern and which do not. Television sets, introduced in a period of relative prosperity, seem to have followed a different pattern, spreading laterally across the middle-income groups rather than trickling down from above. This example suggests another. Some upper-income groups appear to have shunned television on the grounds of its "vulgarity"—-a valuation shared by many academics. To what degree are preferences for other goods and services introduced not at the upper income levels, but by the "intelligentsia," who appear at times to have greater pattern-setting potential than their relatively low economic position might lead one to believe? Finally, which consumption items spread rapidly and which more slowly? Such questions might be answered by the standard techniques of polling and market analysis.

More difficult to research are hypotheses concerning the motivational significance of consumption goods. I have suggested that the significance for the individual of the trickling down of consumption patterns must be seen in terms of his life history and not merely in terms of short-term situations. It seems likely that two general patterns may be distinguished. On the one hand, individuals for whom success means primarily rising above their fellows may be more sensitive to those types of goods and services which must be chosen and consumed according to relatively subtle and rapidly changing standards of taste current at any one time at higher levels. Such persons must deal successfully with the more rapid devaluations of status-symbolic currency which go on among those actively battling for dominance. Such persons, it may be, are responsible for the more short-term fluctuations in consumption patterns. On the other hand, if my hypothesis is correct, the great mass of the labor force may be oriented more to long-term success in terms of their own life histories— success in the sense of achieving a "better standard of living" without particular regard to *differential* status. Interviews centered upon the role of consumption patterns in individuals' life aspirations should reveal such differences if they exist, while differences in perception of symbols of taste might be tested by psychological techniques.

Most difficult of all would be the testing of the circular relationship between motivation and productivity. Major fluctuations in the economy are relatively long term and could be studied only through research planned on an equally long-term basis. Relatively short-term and localized fluctuations, however, do occur at more frequent intervals and would provide possibilities for research. One would require an index of occupational performance which could be related to real income, and the relationship between these elements should ideally be traced through periods of both rising and falling real income.

3

The Predicament of the Modern African Chief: An Instance from Uganda

THE role of the modern African chief poses difficult problems of analysis because it is a role which is played out in a matrix of diverse and often conflicting institutions. Perhaps it would be better to say that the chief occupies many roles. On the one hand, he has a series of roles in the indigenous institutions of African society. On the other hand, he occupies roles in the imported institutions of colonial government. Of course, in various parts of Africa institutions of African and European origin have met under widely varying circumstances and have interpenetrated in varying degrees, but nearly everywhere the effect is confusing and bizarre. In Uganda, for example, if we were to visit a chief we might find him attending a committee meeting, helping to work out a budget for the coming fiscal year. If we ask for an appointment, we will be received in a modern office equipped with typewriters, telephones, filing cases, and the other apparatus of modern bureaucracy. If by chance we had called on another day, our chief would have been unavailable. He would have been meeting with his clan mates in the thatched hut of his paternal uncle, and the talk would have been of genealogical refinements and the wishes of the ancestors. If we are invited to have tea at the chief's house in the evening, we will be introduced to his several wives, and this may surprise us because

Reprinted by permission from *American Anthropologist* 57 (1955): 290–305. This is a slightly revised version of a paper read before a conference on "Stability and Change in African Societies," jointly sponsored by the Social Science Research Council and the National Research Council, at Princeton, New Jersey, 14–16 October 1953.

we have heard that he is a pillar of the local Anglican parish and a patron of the Boy Scout troop. I have chosen a rather extreme, though not unreal, example. Reading the literature on the various areas of modern Africa, one is impressed by the patchwork character of the chief's social milieu. It appears to be a collection of bits and pieces taken at random from widely different social systems. Modern African society as a whole frequently gives this impression, but in the case of the chief the effect is heightened because his role is so often the meeting point, the point of articulation, between the various elements of the patchwork.

It is perhaps because of this confusing diversity of elements in the chief's social world that relatively few attempts to analyze his role in systematic terms are to be found in the social science literature on Africa. There are, of course, important exceptions, notably the papers by Gluckman and his colleagues of the Rhodes-Livingston Institute on the village headman in British Central Africa[1] and Busia's recent book on the chief in present-day Ashanti.[2] Probably there are others. Generally, however, such published material as is available is of two sorts. First there is the large and growing body of official and semiofficial literature dealing mainly with what might be called the ideal structure of African politics as conceived by colonial governments. Notable here are Lord Hailey's five volumes[3] on the British dependencies and much of the content of the *Journal of African Administration*. This is the literature of what is called British territories "native administration," and it is concerned with those institutions which are the result of explicit planning on the part of the administering power. Sometimes these institutions embody many elements of indigenous institutions; sometimes they are wholly, or almost wholly, new. Everywhere they represent attempts by colonial governments to erect intervening institutions, manned by Africans, between themselves and African peoples. Familiarity with this literature on native administration is of course essential to the student of African politics, but by its very nature it seldom reaches deep levels of subtlety in the analysis of political process. It is concerned with formal arrangements, with the ways in which power *ought* to flow, and it treats such arrangements in quite general terms, emphasizing that which is common to native administration over wide areas often containing great diversities of indigenous social structure. It seldom concerns itself with the ways in which such indigenous diversities combine with the formal, official institutions to form the real pattern of politics within a tribal or ethnic area.

The second type of material generally available is that gathered by anthropologists in the course of investigations into the traditional structure of African societies. Such studies are most often concerned with the role of the chief in the *traditional* political structure and tend to treat those features of his role which are the result of modern conditions as peripheral to the main focus of study. If the official literature on native administration looks at the chief as he *ought* to be, or as the district officer hopes he will be tomorrow, the bulk of the anthropological literature looks at him as he was yesterday. There are reasons for this emphasis. Rightly or wrongly, anthropologists have frequently seen their primary task to be the documentation of the full range of variation in human society. They have therefore devoted themselves to the analysis of precisely those features of African society which existed before contact with Europeans. Modern developments are usually mentioned in monographs but most often only as representing the destruction of the integrated social systems which existed before. Judged by the task which they have set themselves—the analysis of indigenous institutions—the work of anthropologists in Africa has been of a high standard indeed, representing perhaps the richest body of monographic literature possessed by anthropology today. However, such studies do not often yield full analyses of the present-day role of the African chief.

The reason we have so few adequate studies of the modern chief's role may be found, I think, in certain characteristics of the conceptual schemes commonly applied by students of African societies. African studies have been the home par excellence of structural sociological or social anthropological analysis, a tradition founded by Durkheim, elaborated by Radcliffe-Brown, and more recently applied so brilliantly to empirical research by Fortes and Evans-Pritchard. The virtues of this frame of reference are obvious and familiar to anyone acquainted with the real classics of social science which have been its fruits. Its primary concern is to analyze the ways in which institutions dovetail to form an integrated whole—the ways in which, to put it another way, the institutional demands made upon individuals are harmonized so that the demands of institution X do not run counter to the demands of institution Y, but rather complement and support them. As a result of such studies we now have, for example, excellent detailed analyses of the relationships between political and religious institutions among the Nuer[4] and the Tallensi.[5]

The difficulty which arises when this point of view is applied to the present-day role of the African chief or, indeed, to many other features of modern African society, is that much of what we observe appears, as I have said before, to be a patchwork of diverse and conflicting elements. Institutions are constantly getting in each others' way, and individuals are constantly being institutionally required to do conflicting things. If our point of departure is a conception of the integrated social system, we can say of such situations only that "society has undergone disorganization" or that "cultures have clashed." We can say relatively little, I think, about why the particular kinds of disorder we observe occur. Increasingly, however, we want knowledge of precisely this kind.

One key to the escape from this dilemma lies, I think, in a recognition that the notion of "social order" or "social system" can have two referents, both of which are quite valid, but which must be distinguished. One consists in order or system in the sense of harmonious integration, the notion which I think structural social anthropology has stressed. Order in this sense exists to the degree that institutions making up a social system mutually reinforce and support one another. The other referent is order in the sense that the phenomena observed may be subject to systematic analysis leading to greater understanding by the analyst of the connections between events, whether these events relate to harmony or to discord. This meaning corresponds, I think, to the natural scientist's notion of "order in nature," leaving aside the philosophical question of whether the order really exists in nature or only in the scientist's head. In this latter sense, a society which contains major elements of disharmony or conflict may be studied just as fruitfully as one characterized by a high degree of internal integration. It would perhaps be better to say that the *dishar-monious elements* of a society may be studied just as fruitfully as the harmonious ones, since presumably no society is ever either completely integrated or completely at odds with itself.

If I am right in thinking that there are these two possible conceptions of order or system in social life, then it follows that the second conception, that of social life as subject to systematic analysis without regard to its harmonious or dis-harmonious character, is the more fundamental. It is in the nature of a first assumption which we must make if we are to study the disharmonious elements in societies. The first con-ception then, that of order in the sense of harmony, find its place in our frame of reference at the next stage and it defines a range of variation. The elements making up a social system will be harmonious or disharmonious in varying degrees and ways, and we will require concepts for talking about these various degrees and types of disharmony.

On the most general level, concepts of this kind are not hard to find. Delineating the elements involved in the *inte-grated* or *harmoniously functioning* social system has been one of the major preoccupations of social scientists, and lists of such elements may be found in almost any text or theo-retical volume. All that is required in order to utilize such a list in the study of relative harmony-disharmony is to treat each of the characteristics of the integrated social system as subject to variation. Perhaps the most generally agreed-upon characteristic of the integrated social system is the sharing of a common system of values by its members. If the actions of the individuals who are members of the system are to be mutually supporting, these actions must be founded upon common conceptions of what is right and proper. Actions which are in accord with the common norm will be rewarded, and those which run counter to it will be punished. Sometimes it is useful to distinguish "means" from "ends" within the general field of common values. Or one may find it useful to distinguish between situations in which value integration re-quires actual sharing of common values and those in which it requires merely that values held by groups within the system be compatible. Further distinctions under this general rubric might be drawn, but it is clear that integration among the values held by its members is one of the characteristics of the harmoniously functioning social system. It is also clear, however, that in actual social systems the degree to which value systems are integrated is subject to wide variation.

A second general characteristic of the integrated social system is a sharing of belief or a common system of cognition and communication. Persons must share not only a common system of means and ends but also a common system of symbols enabling them to interpret each others' behavior, as well as other events, in a common way. For traffic to flow smoothly on a crowded street, drivers must not only share the common value of obeying the law, but must also interpret red lights and green lights in the same way. Again, however, the sharing of symbols is by no means always complete, and we way expect to find social systems in which malcommunication is a common occurrence.

Again, the integrated social system is one in which the motivations of its component individuals are to a high degree complementary to the shared systems of value and belief. Actually, this is merely the other side of the social coin. To the degree that values and beliefs are actually shared, persons will "want" to do the "right thing" and will believe the "correct thing" and will be responsive to rewards and punishments which nudge them in this direction. The common values and beliefs of the social system will be built into the personalities of its members so that they will be adequately motivated to do the things others expect them to do. Where the system of value and belief is held in common and its parts harmoniously integrated, persons will not be expected to do incompatible things. All this, however, is also clearly subject to wide variability in concrete social systems. Individuals may be insufficiently motivated to socially valued behavior, or they may have placed upon them conflicting social demands.

I have been at some pains to spell out a point which may seem obvious to some and irrelevant to others because I believe it has a direct bearing upon the prospects for fruitful research into the role of the chief in modern Africa. In many areas the chief lives in a disordered and conflict-ridden social world, and it is important, if we are to reach some understanding of this chief's position, that we be able to talk about this

Peoples of Uganda Protectorate

conflict and disorder, if I may so put it, in an ordered way. In
many regions of Africa today, and indeed in many other
colonial and semicolonial areas, the situation is not simply one
of two radically different social systems colliding head on and,
as it were, holding each other at bay. Though in some areas
something approaching this situation may exist, it is not generally so. More commonly, African and European social systems have interpenetrated with the result that new social
systems embodying diverse and conflicting elements have come
into being. We must therefore be prepared to analyze systematically situations in which incompatible values and beliefs
are widely held by members of the same social system, where
individuals are regularly motivated to behavior which in the
eyes of others is deviant, and where other individuals have
conflicting motivations corresponding with discontinuities

among the values of the social system. We must be able to think analytically about these elements of relative disharmony and to determine their consequences for the functioning of such systems as wholes.

Something of what I have in mind may be illustrated by the situation of the chief today in the Busoga District of Uganda, where I have been engaged in field research under the auspices of the East African Institute of Social Research and of the Fulbright Program. Conditions in Busoga, and, indeed, in Uganda as a whole, have provided perhaps the optimum situation for the harmonious mutual adjustment of African and European social systems. The absence of extensive European settlement has meant that there has been little or no competition for land. The successful importation and cultivation on small peasant holdings of cotton, coffee, and groundnuts have provided a cash crop economy upon which a rising standard of living could be built without detriment to food crop cultivation. Administrative policy has stressed the recognition and gradual remolding of indigenous political institutions without sharp breaks with the past. In this situation, European and African institutions have, indeed, merged to a strikng degree, but the result remains a social system containing major elements of disharmony and conflict. In large measure, the role of the chief is the focus of this conflict.

Busoga was "discovered" by Europeans in 1862 and came under British administration in 1892; the temporal base line for the analysis of change in the Soga political system therefore lies in the latter part of the nineteenth century. At this time, Busoga was not a political entity. It did have sufficient linguistic and general cultural unity to mark it off from the other Bantu-speaking areas of southern Uganda so that in 1862 John Hanning Speke, the first European explorer of the area, was told that "Usoga" comprised the area bounded by Lake Victoria, Lake Kyoga, the Nile, and the Mpologoma River. These are the boundaries of the present-day Busoga District. (See map.) The inhabitants of the area, the Basoga, appear to have numbered some half-million. They were sedentary subsistence cultivators and livestock breeders, relying for staple foods mainly upon their permanent plantain gardens and plots of millet, sweet potatoes, and maize. The country is described by early travelers as being extremely fertile and closely settled, particularly in the south along the Lake Victoria shore.

Politically, Busoga was divided among some fifteen small kingdom-states, which varied widely in size but which shared a fundamental similarity in structure. The elements of this common political structure may be seen in three key institutions: *patrilineal kinship, rulership,* and *clientship.*

In its fundamentals, Soga kinship followed a pattern common in East Africa. Descent was traced in the patrilineal line, and kinsmen sharing common patrilineal descent formed corporate groups which were important units in the social structure. Kinship terminology was of the Omaha type. The most important unit formed on the basis of patrilineal kinship was the lineage, comprising all those persons within a local area who were able to trace the patrilineal genealogical relationships among themselves. This lineage group was important in landholding, through the rights which it exercised over inheritance and succession by its members. An individual was free to choose his heir from among his sons, but his testament was subject to confirmation or revision by the council of his lineage mates, which met at his funeral. The lineage also played a prominent role in marriage. Most young men were unable to meet from their own resources the marriage payment demanded by the bride's kinsmen and so had to depend for aid upon their lineage mates. Such dependency gave the lineage at least a potential influence over its members' choice of marriage partner and an interest in the stability of marriage. Finally, the importance of the lineage in temporal affairs was matched and complemented by its role in relation to the supernatural. The most prominent feature of Soga religion was the ancestor cult, founded upon the belief that patrilineal ancestors maintained an interest in and influence over the well-being and good behavior of their living descendants. Common descent thus involved a common sacred interest in the ancestors, and this in turn, through the ancestor's graces, which were the focus of the cult, reinforced the lineage members' corporate economic and legal interest in the land.

Units other than the lineage were also formed upon the basis of patrilineal kinship. The individual homestead was located in space by the practice of patrilocal residence, and where extended family homesteads were formed, these took the form of a small lineage group composed of a man and his sons together with their wives and children. Beyond the lineage, groups of lineages which were known to be related patrilineally but which were unable to trace the precise genealogical links among themselves formed clans which were unified by a common clan name, common totemic avoidances, and the rule of exogamy. Patrilineal kinship thus defined a large sector of the individual's life; it controlled inheritance and succession, structured marriage, gave form to religion, and strongly influenced the spatial distribution of homesteads.

Soga society was not, however, a segmentary society in which unilineal kinship constituted the only principle of organization. Through the institution of rulership, members of many patrilineal groups were bound together to form kingdom-states in which membership was defined, not in terms of kinship, but in terms of territorial boundaries and common allegiance to the ruler. In each of the kingdom-states there was a royal clan or lineage (in the case of the royal group, clan and lineage tended to be coterminous because royal genealogies were better remembered), which was set above commoner groups as having higher rank and an inborn fitness to rule. The ruler's position was hereditary within the royal clan. He was the active head of the kingdom and the overlord of all other holders of authority. He was also the chief priest, for as the ancestors of commoner lineages were thought to both assist and control the behavior of their descendants, so the royal ancestors were in a sense *national* ancestors who took a similar interest in the affairs of the nation as a whole. The ruler, being their descendant, was supported and controlled by them in his conduct of national affairs and was the intermediary through whom they might be approached on behalf of the nation. Inherited regalia and a courtly style of living centering around an impressively constructed capital symbolized and enhanced the ruler's political power.

To complete this outline of traditional Soga political structure requires the addition of the third of the institutions noted above—that of clientship. The administrative staff through which the ruler in each of the kingdoms governed was recruited neither through patrilineal kinship in commoner

lineages nor through membership in the royal group. The
ruler's leading lieutenants—the prime minister and the chiefs
of territorial divisions—were commoners bound to the ruler by
personal loyalty. Often they were chosen from the many servant boys, sons of ordinary peasants, who were sent to serve in
the palace and to seek social advancement. This mode of recruitment to positions of subordinate power was a partial solution
to a problem which apparently afflicted most Bantu kingdoms
in the Great Lakes region. All members of the royal group
shared in some measure the inborn fitness to rule, but within
the royal group there was no clear-cut rule of seniority.
Throughout the kingdom there were princes—junior members of the royal group—in control of villages or groups of
villages, and these persons were a potential threat to the paramount authority of the ruler. When the problem of succession
arose, any member of the royal group who could command
a measure of support might assert a claim to rulership, and
fighting not uncommonly broke out. The institution of clientship, through which commoners of administrative and military
ability were raised by the ruler to positions of authority and
thus were bound to him as personal followers, provided an
administrative staff which could be trusted with power. Not
sharing the inherited rank of the princes, they were not potential usurpers. At times of succession, the client under the
previous ruler participated along with members of the royal
clan in choosing a new ruler and thus exercised a disinterested
and stabilizing influence upon the ambitious princes. They
also acted as a check upon the ruler's power, since if he failed
to govern within the limits set by custom they might combine
in support of a rival prince and drive him from his position.

Traditional Soga society thus took the form of a hierarchy.
At the top was the hereditary ruler—the paramount holder
of authority and the central symbol of the kingdom's unity.
At intermediate levels were the princes administering villages
or clusters of villages and, counterbalancing them, the ruler's
administrative staff of client-chiefs administering other villages or village clusters in the name of the ruler. Forming the
broad base of the society were the communities of commoner
agriculturalists organized into corporate patrilineal groups.
Commoner and royal, kinsman and kinsman, patron and

client, were bound together by highly personal rights and obligations. Subordinates owed superiors economic support through the payment of tribute, military support in war, the recognition of judicial and administrative authority, and personal loyalty. Subordinates in turn received paternalistic protection and aid.

The sixty years which have passed since the establishment of the British Protectorate in Uganda have seen the radical reconstruction of this political system, to a great extent as a consequence of explicit planning by the administration. Innovations were introduced gradually, however, and under circumstances which contributed to the willingness of the Basoga to accept them. During the early years, little was changed in the formal structure of Soga political institutions, though their day-to-day functioning was substantially altered. Initially, the aims of the administration were limited to the establishment of "law and order," which meant an end to warfare and the creation of a system of revenue and trade. In the pursuit of these limited aims, the indigenous political structure was simply taken over intact, given new tasks, and allowed to continue functioning under the supervision of administrative officers. The rulers of the various kingdoms continued to hold hereditary office and to recruit their administrative staffs through personal clientship. The judicial and administrative powers of rulers and chiefs were recognized, and even enhanced, by Protectorate legislation which made them statutory judges and gave them the authority to issue administrative orders having the force of law. They continued to be supported by tribute paid by the commoner population. In recognition of the authority of the colonial government, they were required to collect taxes, to assist in public works, and to submit their judicial decisions to review by administrative officers. The one major structural innovation was the setting up of a district council composed of the rulers of the several kingdoms.

Even during this initial period of limited aims, however, important developments were taking place within Soga society. Though the additional functions which were imposed upon the indigenous political structure were minimal, they involved one important change. This was the introduction of literacy. Tax collection involved bookkeeping, and administrative supervision over the courts required the keeping of written records of litigation. Every chief or ruler now either had to be literate or required the services of a literate clerk. This development was made possible by, and in turn stimulated, the development of mission education. Soon the sons of important rulers and chiefs, and ultimately the rulers and chiefs themselves, were mission-educated and largely Christian.

The loss of political independence and the innovations which accompanied it were made much more palatable to the rulers and chiefs by the support which they received from the administration and by newly developed sources of wealth. As I have noted above, the position of the ruler or chief in traditional Soga society was not particularly secure. Warfare was more or less endemic and the threat of revolt served as a constant check upon the ruler's exercise of power. Now, not only were the traditional authorities backed by the superior power of the British administration, but they were also able to enhance their economic position. Cotton was introduced at about the time of the First World War and it soon spread rapidly as a peasant cash crop. Tribute could now be collected in cash or in labor upon the rulers' and chiefs' cotton plots. Within a few years there developed a new chiefly style of life, which included imported consumption items such as European-style clothing and houses, automobiles, and, incidentally, mission education, which required the payment of fees.

This early period thus saw the development of a new kind of elite position for the traditional political authorities in Soga society. With greater power and an enhanced wealth differential, they now stood above the common people in ways which had not been possible for them in preadministration times. This situation was very rewarding to them. It goes far to explain, I think, why they were so very ready to accept the supervision of administrative officers and why, later on, they were willing to accept much more profound innovations in the political structure. They had in large measure committed themselves to the new conditions.

The initial period, characterized by limited administrative aims and by the building up of the traditional authorities, came to an end in the 1920s and 1930s. The new policy of the administration came to be one of remolding the traditional political system in the direction of European-style civil service bureaucracy and electoral democracy. In a series of stages between 1926 and 1936, tribute was abolished and the chiefs and rulers began to be paid fixed salaries from a native administration treasury. The loss of tribute was painful to the chiefs and rulers, not only because it meant a reduction in monetary income, but also because tribute was in itself an important symbol of their power and prestige. Nevertheless, in part for the reasons I have mentioned, the change was accepted. A further fundamental change was introduced which concerned the basis of recruitment to office. Over a period of years, the administration came to insist more and more upon the recruitment of chiefs upon the basis of objective competence, and during the 1940s it became established that not only chiefs but also the rulers themselves, who had previously been hereditary, would be chosen upon this basis.

Since, at first, rulers' and chiefs' sons tended to monopolize the mission schools, "recruitment on the basis of competence" meant, essentially, recruitment of the most competent from this group. With more widespread education, the group from which chiefs were recruited became wider. Again, no serious opposition was encountered. What had previously been a hierarchy of hereditary rulers, princes, and client-chiefs thus became in a strict sense a hierarchy of civil service bureaucrats, recruited upon the basis of competence, increasingly as indicated by formal education; paid fixed salaries out of revenue from general taxation; subject to bureaucratic transfer and promotion; and pensioned upon retirement.

Within recent years, this bureaucracy has tended to proliferate, as the Uganda government has pushed forward its policy of devolving more and more responsibility upon the native administration, now known as the African Local Government. The hierarchy of civil servant chiefs which replaced the traditional hierarchy of rulers and client-chiefs has been supplemented by specialist officials concerned with taking over from Protectorate Government departments responsibility for matters such as finance, public works, agriculture and forestry, public health, and law enforcement. Concerned that this bureaucracy not become an irresponsible monolith, the government has also encouraged the growth of elected councils, leading up to a district council which is responsible for advising the bureaucracy, framing legislation, and preparing an annual budget. The strength of this trend toward devolution of responsibility upon the African Local Government may be seen in the fact that the share of direct taxation allocated to the African Local Government treasury is now four times that collected for the Protectorate Government. In 1952, the African Local Government budget called for the receipt and expenditure of more than a quarter of a million pounds.

During the period of British administration, Soga political structure has been radically altered by the introduction of new institutional forms, which have achieved widespread acceptance by the Basoga. The new civil servant chiefs are granted great respect and are popularly regarded as legitimate heirs to the former authority of the traditional rulers and client-chiefs. Appointment to the civil service is regarded as a highly desirable goal for the ambitious young man. The acceptance of new institutions does not mean, however, that a harmoniously integrated social system has resulted. In many cases traditional institutions which are in large measure incompatible with the new ones have survived. The result is a social system which shows deviations from harmonious integration in its value system, in its system of communication and belief, and in the social personalities of its members.

Traditional Soga political institutions emphasized the value of particular personal rights and obligations, a pattern which Parsons[6] has described by the terms *particularism* and *functional diffuseness*. Relations were particularistic in that they emphasized personal loyalty between individuals who stood in particular status relations with one another, for example, as kinsman to kinsman, patron to client, or royal to commoner. One owed particular loyalty to *one's own* kinsman, to *one's own* patron or client, or to one's ruler *as a person*. Relations were functionally diffuse in that they involved a wide segment of the lives of the persons involved. Kinsmen, for example, were expected to stand together as total persons and to take a legitimate interest in the most intimate aspects of each other's lives. A patron was similarly related to his client, as is indicated by the difficulty of distinguishing a political subordinate from a personal servant and by the common practice of linking client to patron through affinal ties. The basic virtue was personal loyalty between particular individuals.

The value system associated with bureaucratic organization is in most respects in opposition to this pattern. Here the guiding norm is, as Max Weber has expressed it, "straightforward duty without regard to personal considerations. . . . Everyone in the same empirical situation is subject to equality of treatment."[7] Relations in such a system are to be, in Parsons's terms, *universalistic* and *functionally specific*—universalistic in that universally applicable rules, and not particular statuses, are to be the determinants of conduct, and functionally specific in that they relate to specific contexts and not to the whole of individuals' lives. As a civil servant, one ought to treat everyone alike without regard to particular status considerations. One applies general rules and procedures. One's competence is severely limited to what are called "official matters" and one is enjoined not to become involved in, nor even to know about, the personal lives of those with whom one has relations *as a civil servant*. This norm of disinterested service is of course the constant goal of all Western political systems, and it was the aim which led the British administration to introduce the civil service system into Busoga.

In Busoga, these two value systems today exist side by side, and both are represented in major institutions. The patrilineal kinship system is very much a going concern, in large part because its stronghold, the traditional system of landholding, has remained intact. Corporate lineage groups continue to exercise jurisdiction over inheritance and succession and this keeps the ties of kinship alive and strong. The strength of kinship ties is, however, a constant threat to the civil service norm of disinterestedness. The wide extension of kinship bonds means that a chief is frequently put into the position of having to choose between his obligation to favor particular kinsmen and his official duty to act disinterestedly. He may, for example, be asked to favor a kinsman in a legal case or to exempt him from taxation. Again, the institution of clientship survives and leads a sub rosa existence within the civil service.

Although formally civil servants are chosen for their objective competence, in fact opportunities may arise for building up personal followings of clients. Senior members of the African Local Government, through their influence with the administration, are able to exercise substantial influence over the appointment and promotion of subordinates and are thus able to build up personal political machines. I want to emphasize that *both* these value systems are institutionalized in Soga society and that both are accepted by most Basoga as, in a sense, legitimate.

The system of belief and communication is also a focus of disharmony within the social system. Relatively widespread primary education and exposure to mass-communications media have produced a situation in which at least two sets of symbols and two views of the nature of the world are current in the society. Again, as in the system of values, it is not so much that different individuals interpret events differently as that the same individuals are trying to work with two sets of symbols at the same time. A chief may, for example, read a newspaper and have a good working knowledge of world politics, but he may still not be quite certain that Europeans are not cannibals or that witchcraft does not really work. Again, these disharmonies in the system of belief and communication center upon the chief because it is he who is most simultaneously involved in the two systems through his relations with European officers on the one side and with peasants on the other.

Discontinuities in the system of value and belief are reflected in inconsistencies in the social personalities of persons playing roles in the system. Since both the civil service norm of disinterestedness and the personal ties of kinship and clientship are institutionalized, both are also internalized in the personalities of individuals. It appears to be the case, though it is somewhat difficult to think about, that chiefs and most other Basoga hold both value systems and both systems of belief at the same time. This results in frequent conflict, both between persons and within persons. In social interaction, an individual is likely to uphold the value or belief which seems advantageous to him in a given situation. The kinsman of a chief is likely to expect preferential treatment in court and to bring the pressure of the lineage group to bear upon the chief if such preferential treatment is not granted. The same individual is outraged, however, if someone else does the same thing. Similarly, a chief is likely to exercise "pull" through a highly placed patron, if he can, in order to secure promotion, but complains bitterly about such a behavior on the part of others. A chief who is requested to exercise favoritism on behalf of a kinsman or a friend is put into a literally impossible position. Both his internalized values and the sanctions impinging upon him from society pull him in opposite directions. Whichever way he jumps, he will be punished, both by his own remorse at having contravened values which are part of his personality, and by sanctions applied by others.

One of the consequences of these conflicts and discontinuities is a high casualty rate among chiefs. Where conflicting demands pull him in opposite directions, it becomes very difficult for the chief to avoid falling afoul of sanctions. The adminstration, of course, strongly upholds the civil service norm. If a chief is caught engaging in nepotism or embezzlement, he is dismissed. But he may also be dismissed for upholding the civil service norm. If he offends a prominent superior by refusing to grant particularistic demands, he may find that charges of corruption have been "framed" against him, and he may be dismissed for the very thing which he has refused on principle to do. The poor communication prevailing between the Basoga and the administration and the consequent dependence of the latter upon senior chiefs for information make it unlikely that such fabrications will be exposed.

Thus, from the point of view of the chief acting in his role, the discontinuities in the Soga social system impose severe burdens. It is possible to view these discontinuities also from the standpoint of their consequences for the system as a whole. From this point of view, it would appear that some of the conflicts noted above act to stabilize the system in a period of radical institutional change. I have stressed the point that these conflicts do not consist primarily in discrete groups of persons holding opposed systems of value and belief; they consist rather in the *same persons,* to a great extent throughout the society, holding two incompatible systems of belief and value. They appear *in action* in the form of conflicts between

persons. A chief acts in terms of the civil service norm of dis-
interestedness and he is punished by others who wish him to
act in terms of particularistic obligations. The *persons* in such
situations, however, are interchangeable; on another occasion,
the same chief may act to fulfill particularistic obligations and
may have sanctions brought to bear upon him by the same
persons who now, however, wish him to act disinterestedly.
This *taking into* the social personalities of individuals of conflicts which might otherwise express themselves in conflicts
between discrete groups of persons acts, I suggest, to maintain
some unity and stability in the system. Very often—perhaps
most often—in societies undergoing rapid change, the latter
situation has developed. The society has divided into in-
transigently opposed factions or parties with the result that
consensus can be reestablished only through the defeat, often
by violence, of one group by the other. Of course, which of
these alternatives one considers "better" depends entirely
upon one's value position.

I have described the Soga political system only in outline
as an example of the sort of disharmonious situation which I
think we must be prepared to study if we are to reach greater
understanding of the present-day role of the African chief.
The situation is of course much more complex than I have
been able to indicate. If there were more time, I should like
to say something about what appear to be some of the consequences of the kind of institutional dilemma I have described for the personalities of chiefs. There are indications
that for chiefs who do contrive to avoid falling afoul of sanctions, and who remain in office, this success is achieved at
considerable psychic cost. The East African Institute of Social
Research is currently engaged in a program of research into
a number of contemporary East African political systems and
we hope, through a combination of institutional and personality analyses, to throw some light upon the reactions of personalities to such situations as well as upon other aspects of
political process in these systems.

I should like to add just a word about the situation I have
described in a comparative perspective. This situation, which
in its broad outlines is typical, I think, of Uganda as a whole,
is probably rather unusual in the broader African picture. In

Uganda, there have been few occasions for open conflict between European and African social systems as such. Economic conditions have been beneficent and administrative policy has emphasized gradual and orderly, though steady, change. The result has been a really astonishing degree of African acceptance of things European and a readiness to plunge into radical institutional change. New institutions have been quietly incorporated alongside old ones and conflicts between new and old institutions have been taken into the personalities of individuals who play roles in them. At considerable cost to its component individuals, the social system has come through radical transformation without splitting into opposed factions and without a serious showdown with European innovators.

Elsewhere in British Africa, two other types of situation appear to be more common. In the classical "indirect rule" territories, such as the Gold Coast and the South African High Commission territories, there was also, as in the early stages in Uganda, a recognition of indigenous political institutions, but it appears that there has been much less emphasis in those territories on remolding such institutions and on developing new responsibilities upon them. The traditional political systems have been preserved in more nearly their original form so that when new political institutions do develop the traditional ones tend to be bypassed and to remain as centers of conservative opposition. Such a process seems to have occurred in Ashanti where, one gathers, the Youngmen's movement arose as a "progressive" opposition to the "conservative," government-supported chiefs and ultimately contributed substantially to a self-government movement which was even more hostile to traditional political institutions. Another type of situation seems to exist in areas such as the Union of South Africa, parts of Central Africa, and in Kenya, where policy has stressed the rapid adaptation of Africans to the requirements of European settler communities. There again one sees African societies split into conflicting groups: traditional authorities who have had little recognition and who have gradually lost position and influence, government appointees who are often looked upon by others as stooges, and, occasionally, charismatic leaders of radical movements who oppose both the others. Comparisons with French and Belgian

Africa should prove illuminating, though I am too little familiar with those territories to attempt such comparisons. One has the impression, however, that the French policy of "assimilation" and the Belgian emphasis upon economic as against political development have produced situations substantially different from those found in British territories.[8]

I should like to end with a plea for more empirical studies of contemporary African politics. The great complexity and diversity of political phenomena there provide a fertile field for social scientists of many interests and disciplines.

4

Social Stratification and Economic Processes in Africa

SOCIAL stratification is a relatively complex phenomenon. Studying it involves more than simply plotting the distribution of power and wealth in a society, and more than securing ratings by a society's members of one another's prestige. Such simplifications may for some purposes be quite appropriate, but they are unsatisfactory if we aim to reach an understanding of the various ways in which economic processes may be involved in social inequality. For this purpose, a broader conception of social stratification and its place in human societies is required.

In its essential character, social stratification is not an economic phenomenon at all. This is not to say that economic phenomena are not involved or are unimportant in stratification, but simply that the economic aspect of stratification is secondary to another, and more basic, aspect: the moral or cultural one. The heart of stratification—what makes it universal in human societies—is man's tendency to evaluate his fellows, and himself, as "better" or "worse" in terms of some cultural notion of "the good."[1] To be sure, the content of such notions varies over a wide spectrum, but the universality of moral ideas forms one of the common roots of stratification. At this most basic level, economic phenomena may be involved in varying degrees and ways; goods and services of different kinds, and goods and services as such, may be differently evaluated in different cultures.

Reprinted by permission from *Economic Transition in Africa,* edited by Melville J. Herskovits and Mitchell Harwitz (Evanston, Ill.: Northwestern University Press, 1964).

Here we encounter the notion that "the economic" is founded upon a set of basic biological imperatives—a set of irreducible needs for food, clothing, and shelter. It is true, of course, that there are some kinds of goods and services which no culture is in a position to utterly disregard, but there are relatively few areas in Africa where considerations of this sort take us very far. The admirable reports and films on the Bushmen of the Kalahari produced by the Marshalls[2] impress upon us the precariousness of life in the desert and the marvelous ingenuity of the Bushmen in solving its problems through a single-minded adjustment of all aspects of life to the food quest, but for Africa as a whole this is an extremely unusual situation.

The vast majority of Africans have in recent centuries been reasonably prosperous agriculturalists or pastoralists, or often both, employing relatively efficient technologies. As Jones has put it: "Diets are those of poor people, but they are not necessarily poor diets. The total supply of calories appears to be adequate, and Africans rarely know hunger in the sense of persisting shortage of food energy."[3] As a matter of fact, in many areas, such as the highlands of eastern Africa, sheer subsistence requires of the ordinary man a good deal less attention than it did, let us say, of the medieval European peasant. Subsistence production can be left mainly in the hands of the female part of the labor force so that men may be largely available to work and fight for the king or chief. Consequently, "biological imperatives" do not take us very far in explaining the ways in which goods and services are evaluated in traditional Africa. Africans are relatively well off, and hence their cultures are free to give varying kinds and degrees of attention to goods and services.

On the other hand, traditional African cultures do not use the freedom which a relatively efficient technology gives them to actively *devalue* goods and services as, we are told, some traditional Asian cultures do. One must be cautious here; the stereotype of the "spiritual, nonmaterialistic East" can be very misleading if taken to mean a simple lack of avarice among Asian peoples. As Geertz has shown in his study of religion and economics in a Javanese town, the matter is more complex.[4] The people of Modjokuto see things—persons, modes of behavior, psychic states, and material objects—as ranging along a continuum of relative excellence bounded by the polar concepts *alus* and *kasar*—that is, roughly speaking, subtlety, control, inner serenity, as contrasted with crudity, awkwardness and uncontrolled animal passion. High rank, power, and wealth should be held by persons who are *alus*. This does not mean that persons in Modjokuto lack the desire for goods and services, but it does mean that concern for such things receives no sanction from the cultural definitions of excellence which are associated with the elite and hence remains unregulated by them. Economic activities of a sort which involve attention to the rationalization of production and exchange tend to be devalued or ignored, even while the products themselves may be greatly desired. Such activities are the concern of the *santri,* a more fully Islamized subgroup standing somewhat aside from the mainstream of Javanese life. No people —certainly not the people of overpopulated Java—are in a position to totally ignore the wants and needs of the biological man. But many Asian peoples do seem to have committed themselves to religious conceptions which regard the body as an unfortunate impediment to the perfection of the soul.

While recognizing that such generalizations, in the present very imperfect state of our understanding of such matters, inevitably oversimplify the cultural dynamics involved, it seems clear that this sort of cultural turning away from things economic has not been prominent in Africa. Whatever features of traditional African life may stand in the way of more rapid economic development, an absorbing interest in achieving states of inner spiritual perfection is not among them. On the contrary, Africans seem to have, on the whole a very utilitarian, matter-of-fact view of goods and services.

This is not to say that African cultures have made the organization of production and exchange a central concern. Except perhaps in those areas of Western Africa where trade has become a highly developed calling, this is clearly not the case. It will be argued below that, much more typically, production and exchange have been undertaken as an adjunct— a means—to the organization of power, the field in which, it appears, the African genius has really concentrated its efforts. But there is no evidence that in traditional Africa economic concerns were rejected as spiritually unworthy. Far from viewing the biological man and his wants as base and unworthy of concern, there is a certain tendency for traditional African religions to make the health, fertility, and prosperity of the living individual and the living community matters of central importance. A great deal of the ritual communication which takes place between living persons and the spirit world has as its object the maintenance or reestablishment of individual or group well-being in a quite material, biological sense.

With all the variation that may be found in traditional African religion, this seems to be one of the more persistent themes, appearing, for example, in the intricate cosmological religion of the Dogon of the western Sudan as well as in the ancestral cults of so many Bantu peoples.[5] In the context of this sort of culture orientation, the production and exchange of goods and services, while not the primary objects of human endeavor, are good and useful insofar as they contribute to individual and group comfort and well-being. In their recent economic contacts with the outside world Africans have on the whole responded in this essentially utilitarian way.

Thus far we have been discussing culture as one of the bases of social stratification. We have concluded that traditional African cultures, while not regarding economic processes as ends in themselves, have nevertheless given them definite positive value. We may now turn to the other universal root of stratificatory phenomena, the differentiation of roles in the social structure. No human community is a completely undifferentiated aggregation of like beings. The mutual expectations on the basis of which persons are enabled to interact with one another are always to some extent arranged into bundles or clusters on the basis of age, sex, and kinship—and usually, of course, upon other bases as well. Again economic phenomena may be involved—perhaps they always are, since the differentiation of roles always tends to involve some differential allocation of economic tasks and thus to be, in one of its aspects, a "division of labor." In general, the more complex the technological apparatus, the more complex the division of labor may become, though the relationship is by no means a simple and direct one. The division of labor between men and women, for example, seems to be largely independent of technological complexity.

The cultural and social structural roots of stratification are not, of course, discrete "things"; instead they come together in the tendency of the differentiated roles themselves, including their economic aspects, to be culturally evaluated. Since tasks are differentially allocated, the culture evaluates persons differentially; that is to say, not just pottery-making and praying are evaluated, but also potters and priests. Obviously, varying degrees of excellence in the performance of priests' and potters' tasks are also recognized.

In traditional African societies, the complexity of the differentiation of roles varies over a wide range, but it varies within definite limits. On the one hand, some degree of economic specialization beyond that represented by the sexual division of labor is present almost everywhere. Again the Bushmen, and perhaps some Pygmy groups, provide exceptions; but these, though they may be of great scientific interest for certain purposes, actually represent only an insignificant fragment of the population of Subsaharan Africa. In most African villages, an array of traditional crafts tends to be reflected in a corresponding array of semispecialized craft roles: potter, smith, woodworker, musician, bark-cloth-maker or weaver, and often others as well. In recent decades the bicycle mechanic and the tailor with his treadle "Singer" have often joined the ranks of "traditional" village specialists.

On the other hand, in village Africa, as in the rest of the nonindustrialized world, there is little differentiation of occupational from domestic organization. By far the greater part of the production of goods and services takes place in a domestic setting, that is, in some kind of local homestead unit. Workplace and homestead are the same and have the same inhabitants. Most homesteads in traditional Africa produce most of what they consume, and consume most of what they produce, and this probably remains true for a majority of African people today, despite the great changes of recent decades.

This relative lack of differentiation between homestead and work group has important consequences for social stratification. It means that what is stratified is not a series of autonomous occupational categories and organizations, but rather a series of domestic and other kinship units whose economic functions are but one among a number of characteristics on the basis of which their relative worth, in terms of cultural values, is judged. One of the great differentiating characteristics of industrial societies, from the point of view of social stratification, is their tendency to develop such autonomous organizations in which occupational roles may be played outside the domestic context. The modern business firm and the governmental bureaucracy, in their ecological aspect, are places spatially and socially segregated from domestic and other kinship units.

It was one of Karl Marx's great contributions to social science to point out some of the consequences of this separation. The point is not, of course, that occupational and domestic roles cease in such cases to influence each other, but rather that the autonomous occupational organizations tend to become the main foci of cultural evaluation and hence of stratification. The domestic unit of the job-holder comes to depend for its status, and even for its basic existence, upon the occupational system to which it is linked by a more or less "purely economic" tie. It is for this reason that students of stratification in industrial societies tend to focus their attention upon occupational ranking. Where occupational roles remain embedded in multifunctional domestic units, it is these latter which tend to be the units of stratification. Such units may remain economically more self-sufficient; a wider range of their characteristics and performances may remain relevant to evaluation and stratification.

Thus we have in traditional Subsaharan Africa the following range of variation: Almost anywhere there is craft specialization, but everywhere we also find that the production of goods and services is household production. Within this range, there is room for a good deal of variation in the degree to which households specialize economically. In most of Africa, craft specialization is predominantly part time. That is to say, almost every household engages in a basic subsistence activity —usually some combination of agriculture and animal husbandry, but in some cases fishing or transhumant pastoralism

—and in addition some households also engage in a part-time specialty like smithing or pottery-making.

In eastern, central, and southern Africa, crafts were almost always carried out in this part-time way. Even during late colonial times, in the villages of Buganda and Busoga, for example, one would be hard put to find a really full-time specialist of any kind. Potters, smiths, bark-cloth-makers and tailors, as well as modern schoolteachers, shopkeepers, and clergymen, maintained gardens, flocks, and herds to supply their staple diet. Even a large part of the employed population of the modern town of Kampala found it possible to grow much of their own food.

One gains the impression that this is common throughout the continent wherever urban dwellers are not crowded into "labor lines" or housing estates whose layout makes gardening impossible. In traditional eastern, central, and southern Africa really full-time craft specialists exist only at the courts of the more powerful and affluent kings, where they form part of the royal household. In Buganda, only the king's, and perhaps a few of the more eminent chiefs', bark cloths, pots, and music are produced by persons who work more or less full time; those consumed by villagers are made by fellow-agriculturalists for whom the craft is a sideline.

In traditional western Africa as Skinner points out in his discussion of the indigenous economies of this part of the continent,[6] full-time craft specialists are more common and the crafts themselves more highly developed. The old Yoruba towns contain many—perhaps a majority—of persons who maintain farms in the surrounding countryside, but they also contain weavers, smiths, carvers, and traders who are full-time professionals, dependent upon the sale of their products for basic subsistence.[7] Here, too, one finds the closest approach to the development of autonomous occupational organizations in the guilds of craftsmen and traders, which control entrance into these occupations and whose leaders represent their members' interests in the governments of the towns. It is not clear, however, how far these guilds as corporate bodies engage in production and exchange and how far they are structurally distinct from the lineage organization which is prominent in

Yoruba society.[8] The craft guilds of Bida, the capital of the Moslem Nupe, which tend to be hereditary and hence to be made up of a series of related kinship groups, are highly organized bodies exercising a substantial measure of control over their members.[9]

Throughout traditional Africa, however, full-time occupational specialization, in the sense of freedom from participation in subsistence production, is more commonly related to political than to economic tasks. Whereas full-time specialization in craft production or trade is relatively rare, the specialist in government is quite common. Indeed, there is in Africa a certain political efflorescence which is perhaps a corollary of the lack of the particular kind of other-worldly religious orientation found in parts of Asia. Authority is sought for and admired, both as a goal of individual ambition and as a means toward, and symbol of, group prosperity and well-being. This is reflected in the African passion for litigation, as well as in the tendency toward formalized political hierarchy. This characterization does not apply only to the great traditional kingdoms, which included much less than half the continent and were limited to relatively restricted areas of the Guinea coast, the western Sudan, the Great Lakes area, and parts of southern Africa and the Congo basin. Political specialists, such as kings and chiefs, are by definition found only in polities with a degree of political centralization, but the absorbing interest in things political of which these states are but a particularly explicit expression is common also, for example, to the decentralized, descent-organized polity of the Tiv, with its elaborate system of moots.[10] It is perhaps not going too far to assert that the *emphasis* in African systems of stratification is primarily political. The roles which are most highly regarded are usually authority roles, whether these involve the part-time political activity and adjudication of disputes which absorb the energies of the elders of a descent group, or the full-time exercise of authority engaged in by the rulers and chiefs of the great kingdoms.

One aspect of this peculiar prominence of the political in African systems of stratification, and perhaps the most important for the purposes of this discussion, is a tendency for economic structures and processes to be overshadowed by—

or, perhaps better, *contained within*—political structures and processes. It would not be unreasonable to hazard the guess that in Subsaharan Africa the greater part of the exchanges of goods and services which take place outside domestic units occur as incidents to the exercise or acknowledgment of authority. Wherever there are kings and chiefs, or even petty headman, goods and services pass upward in the form of taxes or tribute and back down again in the form of hospitality and gifts. In societies organized on the basis of descent, exchanges serve to mark the political alignment of corporate groups. Landholding, too, is commonly, in traditional society, a political matter. *"Omwami tafuga ttaka; afuga bantu"* runs a proverb of the Baganda: "A chief does not rule land; he rules people."

Again the matter is fundamentally the same in both centralized and decentralized societies; landholding tends to be merely the territorial aspect of political relations and groupings, not a distinct and predominantly economic relationship in itself. "Landlords" and "tenants" are exceedingly rare in traditional Africa, perhaps in part because on the whole land is not scarce. Of course we must be careful not to overstate the case. Throughout Subsaharan Africa there is also trade for its own sake, particularly, as we have noted, in western Africa. And a few peoples, perhaps most notably the Kikuyu of Kenya, seem always to have regarded land as a commodity.[11] But throughout the region, at any rate before the extension of the money economy in recent times, the predominant tendency has been for political structures to dominate and enclose economic ones and hence for authority to be the principal basis for stratification.

Thus far we have considered the two basic sources of stratificatory phenomena—the system of values and the pattern according to which roles are differentiated. There is clearly, however, much more to stratification than this. If the allocation and performance of differentially evaluated roles were a simple mechanical process, a catalog of values and roles would suffice. But societies are not machines, and the persons and groups who make up societies are not cogs and levers. Culture is not a set of engineer's drawings. Persons and groups interpret, feel, and strive, and in the process they react to, manipulate, and even create both the structure of social relations and the ideas which go to make up culture. All this results in certain additional complexities in stratification and in the economic processes related to it.

By differently evaluating roles, societies secure a commitment of energy and intelligence on the part of their members to tasks embodied in the roles which are more highly regarded, but in accomplishing this they assume the burden of assuring, explaining, and justifying the ways in which particular persons are selected to fill these roles. The range of possibilities here is of course very wide. Access to the more honorific roles is never entirely free and, to the degree to which it is not, culture may undertake to legitimatize inequality of access by means of an ideology of inborn differences in capacity or sanctity. Or it may attribute differential success to luck or the whim of the gods. Where a degree of openness is recognized, it may glorify competitive striving; and the qualities singled out for recognition may in varying degrees relate to actual superiority in the performance of the roles in question. The variations seem endless, but the problem is universal; as a result there develop what might be called "secondary cultures of stratification"—values and beliefs *about* stratification, in contrast with the basic values which give rise to stratification in the first instance.

These secondary cultures include both general public views of how stratification should or does work and also, commonly, a verdant growth of more or less "private," but typically standardized, ideas and beliefs through which persons and groups express their own aspirations, gratifications, and frustrations with respect to the results. Thus in Buganda, as in the contemporary United States, a public glorification of achievement is combined with an absorbing interest on the part of individuals and kinship groups in genealogy and the symbols of ascribed status, as well as in securing for their own children advantages in competition which are, from the point of view of the publicly expressed ideal, "unfair."[12]

The various elements which make up such a complex of ideas may in one sense be "contradictory," but they relate to each other in perfectly understandable ways in the context of the problem of linking and reconciling individual and group motivation with the overall system of stratification. The example just given pertains to systems in which achievement is publicly endorsed; but systems of hereditary status also have their public and private secondary cultures of stratification which, as materials from India demonstrate, allow lower-caste persons both to "accept" the fact of low hereditary status and, at the same time, to protest and work against it.[13] One would no doubt discover similar phenomena in the few real caste societies which are found in Africa, such as those of Rwanda and Burundi.[14]

Where different groups within a society become sufficiently separate from each other, the secondary culture of stratification may develop into distinct subcultures, based upon class, of the sort which interested Robert Redfield.[15] That is to say, relatively distinct "folk" and "elite" versions of the common culture may develop, expressing the respective interests, values, and beliefs of the elite and village levels of society. It has been argued elsewhere that such cultural differentiation, which is one of the marks of the true "peasant society," has not been prominent in Africa, in part because of the lack of a written religious literature of the kind which has formed the basis for elite subcultures in Europe and Asia.[16]

In this cultural sense, Africa tends to be rather strikingly egalitarian. This does not mean that Africans reject inequality of any kind; on the contrary, there is among them, as we have noted, a strong tendency toward political hierarchy. But, lacking the degree of cultural differentiation between strata which was common in medieval Europe, Africans do tend to be egalitarian about a man's class origins. The person who manages to acquire a position of authority and wealth is accepted as such; since the elite culture is not greatly differentiated from that of the villages, he can easily learn it and hence does not carry about with him linguistic and behavioral stigmata of the sort which have tended to mark the socially mobile European as a parvenu.

Along with this secondary culture of stratification there also develops what we may call a secondary structural aspect of stratification, an aspect commonly symbolized in the literature on the subject by the figure of a pyramid. Such figures are meant to illustrate, beyond the basic differentiation and differential evaluation of roles, the relative numbers of roles of various kinds that are actually available for allocation. The "shape" of the pyramid is clearly related in an important way to degrees of technological complexity. Thus the systems of stratification in those relatively complex, but nonindustrialized, societies which are commonly called "peasant" or "feudal" tend to be broad-based, with a small political and religious elite supported by a large mass of subsistence producers.

The traditional African kingdoms may be considered "peasant societies" in this structural sense, though they lacked the cultural differentiation characteristic of their Asian, Near Eastern, and European counterparts. Economic modernization of such societies tends to increase the number of "middle-class" roles, and thus to "push outward" the sides of the pyramid. Insofar as this image is an accurate one, it has important implications for the working of stratification. Peasant societies may to varying degrees emphasize achievement or hereditary status in their values, but if the elite is very small and the "common man" very numerous, the opportunity for mobility will be extremely slight, no matter how much the culture may glorify it, and no matter to what degree the small elite may actually be recruited from below.

There are other secondary structural aspects of stratification which are not so easily considered in terms of the pyramid image. Perhaps among the most important are family and descent systems, which greatly influence the allocation of roles and the nature of the units which are stratified. For example, systems of corporate unilineal descent groups, though of course by no means universal in Africa, are very common there. Given the sharply "peaked" shape of traditional stratification pyramids, that is, given the tendency for the powerful and rich to be relatively few and the weak and poor to be relatively numerous, with comparatively small numbers of persons in between, then it follows that extended kinship solidarities will tend to cut across stratification hierarchies in ways which are rather startling to Europeans and Americans. Solidary extended kinship groupings will tend to contain persons of widely varying degrees of power and wealth. This is particularly so where, as is common in Africa, persons of high status have higher rates of polygyny and fertility, with the result that in each generation there are many more elite children than can possibly inherit their parents' status.

In traditional European societies, although the phenomenon of the gradually declining "cadet" lines within a noble or gentry family is a familiar one, solidary kinship groups have tended to be narrower in range and more homogeneous as regards status. The kinship groups involved have been less ramified and marriage has tended to be endogamous with respect to class—or better, for the period of European history concerned, with respect to "estate." In Africa, however, solidary kinship groups tend to contain persons of widely varying power and wealth, both because they ramify widely and because marriage is seldom class-endogamous in any important sense. And this is particularly true of the kinship groups of elite persons, which status-differential polygyny and fertility tend to cause to expand more rapidly than others. Overall status distinctions, therefore, tend to be blurred and it is difficult to find clearly defined strata, even in the larger kingdoms.

African societies have worked out numerous ways of handling the apparent contradictions that result from the juxtaposition of sharp stratification of power and wealth and ramified kinship solidarity. Descent groups may be ranked, both internally and externally, by genealogical seniority, as in the southern Bantu states; or descent groups may be ranked vis-à-vis one another, while internal differentiation is determined by some form of election, as among the Akan peoples of the Guinea coast. Still another pattern is found in some of the interlacustrine Bantu states, where the political hierarchy, which here as elsewhere dominates stratification, is simply segregated structurally from the solidarities of descent groups. Except for the kinship, political office in these states is usually not hereditary. Chiefs are recruited by royal appointment, and thus a man's place in the state is one matter, his role in the internal domestic affairs of his lineage quite another.

Understandably, none of these ways of handling the problem entirely resolves the ultimate tension between stratification and the leveling influence of corporate descent groups, because every person remains influenced by both. This is another reason why relatively enduring, culturally defined, "horizontal" strata of the sort familiar in traditional Europe and Asia have not been prominent in Africa. Extended kinship solidarities work against their crystallization. Of course in the uncentralized societies organized on the basis of descent, where formal stratification and differentiation of authority are in any case relatively slight, these issues tend not to arise.

In the processes by means of which persons are distributed through the system of stratification of their society, economic phenomena may be involved in various ways and at different points. We have already, in discussing the cultural and structural roots of stratification, noted how the production of goods and services may be involved at the level of the primary evaluation of differentiated roles. Roles involving production and trade may to varying degrees be differentiated out and may in varying degrees be evaluated as elite roles. In traditional Africa, as we have seen, full-time specialization in nonagricultural production or trade is relatively uncommon, though it certainly exists, and in general authority roles tend to outrank those primarily associated with economic processes.

Apart from this primary evaluation of economic processes and roles, however, goods and services are also involved in other ways in the dynamics of stratification. For stratification, and indeed any element of social structure, always tends to have an economic aspect, even though this aspect may not predominate. Interaction between persons always involves the allocation of scarce goods and services—at a minimum those of space and time, and usually other things as well. Because they are scarce, their allocation is problematical, and this limits the ways in which interaction can proceed.[17] In the case of systems of stratification, it is useful to think of such goods and services as symbols and as facilities.[18] On the one hand, all systems of stratification tend to select some scarce goods and services as symbols of status. The differential allocation of such goods and services is in itself an expression of stratification and a reward to persons thereby favored. On the other hand, there are also goods and services, possession of which is not in itself particularly honorific, whose utilization is nevertheless essential to the achievement or maintenance of high position.

It is rarely possible to classify actual goods and services as falling wholly into one or the other of these categories, for the distinction is an analytic, not a concrete descriptive one. Thus the corvée labor which so many African kings and chiefs could demand from their people was simultaneously an expression of their superiority and a means of maintaining and strengthening it through the performance of useful work. But particular goods and services may vary considerably in the degree to which they function as symbols or as facilities and it is in the purer cases that the distinction becomes most clear.

Thus in eastern Africa cattle are particularly highly valued goods; indeed, they are valued to such a degree that Herskovits has given the name "East African cattle area" to the whole region.[19] But in many of these societies, cattle are very much in the nature of status symbols, whereas in others they are regarded as utilitarian goods. A good illustration of the contrast may be seen in the neighboring and closely related kingdoms of Rwanda and Buganda. In Rwanda, cattle are the elite symbols par excellence. Possession of large herds and consumption of a diet consisting as far as possible of dairy products are perhaps the most important expressions of Tutsi aristocracy.[20] Cattle are favorite subjects for poetry and exchanges of beasts validate the relationship of lord and vassal. The Baganda, also, value cattle—they are, for example, among the main objects in raids against neighboring peoples, just as they are in Rwanda.

But to Baganda, cattle are simply meat—the means by which king and chiefs may provide feasts for their followers. Mere possession of herds means nothing and cattle have no ritual significance in any context. Perhaps most striking of all, the tall, thin cattle people, whose Tutsi and Hima cousins in cattle kingdoms like Rwanda and Ankole form the ruling aristocracy, are in Buganda regarded simply as rustic and rather smelly herdsmen, who hire themselves out to look after the cattle of wealthy Baganda. However, the cattle of Baganda chiefs are not in any real sense more "economic" than are the more symbolic beasts of the Tutsi, though the uses to which they are put may be more mundane. Both facilities and symbols are "economic" in the sense that they are valuable and scarce and hence their allocation presents a problem in economizing for both persons and groups. The Tutsi chief in Rwanda, it is clear, allocates his cattle quite as carefully as he does his less symbolic possessions.

Here again we return to the point that in traditional Africa goods and services, both as symbols and as facilities, circulate primarily in terms of political relations, for it is the polity that dominates stratification. Persons and groups strive to control the symbols and facilities that are the expressions of authority and the means of strengthening and extending it. A good case could be made that, at least in eastern, central, and southern Africa, the most important facilities are people. This does not mean that people are regarded by their rulers as mere "things," though of course various forms of slavery have sometimes been involved, but rather simply that in the production of goods and services in this part of Africa, the most problematic factor is usually human labor.

As we have seen, land is on the whole not scarce and agriculture and military technology is relatively simple. The means of production are therefore controlled by groups of village cultivators. For the chief who wishes to strengthen and extend his rule, the main problem consists in securing an adequate supply of labor. The solution of this problem lies in attracting and holding the maximum number of subjects who, as cultivators and warriors, can then produce the maximum amount of tribute and booty in craft and agricultural products. These in turn can be redistributed as largess to the maximum number of loyal supporters. The principal danger to the authority of the chief lies in the ultimate ability of his disaffected subjects simply to pick up and move away, leaving him to be "chief of the pumpkins." Thinking, as we tend to do, of land and capital goods as the problematic factors, this tribute-largess-labor-starved economy may seem a tenuous base upon which to erect a highly centralized and stratified society, but the examples of the eighteenth- and nineteenth-century kingdoms of the Zulu and Baganda show that this can be done by rulers able to manipulate shrewdly the symbols and facilities of authority.[21]

Trade has also tended to be dominated by the polity, that is, to be directed to the political ends of rulers. In eastern Africa, where trade with the coast came late, rulers strove to monopolize the trade in such new facilities as firearms, which greatly reinforced the ruler's authority if he was in fact successful in controlling it, and through sumptuary laws such new symbols as tailored clothing. The Reverend Batulumayo Musoke Zimbe, who as a boy served as a page at the court of King Mutesa of Buganda, describes in his memoirs how Mutesa assigned different types of clothing to various ranks.[22] Even in western Africa, where trade is more extensive, more diversified, more professionalized, and of longer standing, it tends to be heavily influenced by political considerations. Rosemary Arnold's account of the domination of the port town of Whydah by the kingdom of Dahomey provides an excellent example of the tendency toward "administered trade."[23] The independent trading town of the sort described in the diary of Antera Duke of Calabar, where a kind of "lodge" or "guild" of trader-chiefs themselves ruled the town in the interest of trade, is a much rarer phenomenon in Africa.[24] Trade has most commonly been controlled in the interest of the polity.

Traditional African societies, then, have characteristically exhibited patterns of role differentiation in which political specialization has been more prominent than economic specialization. The ambitions of their members have been directed primarily toward attaining authority, and economic processes have commonly been dominated by the political needs of individuals and groups. While sharply "peaked" systems of stratification have been created in the great traditional kingdoms, even in these cases there has been relatively little cultural differentiation between elite and common folk and little concentration of the nonhuman means of production in elite hands. Extended kinship solidarities have worked against rigid status stratification. Keeping these indigenous patterns in mind, we may in conclusion draw attention to some of the consequences that contemporary processes of economic modernization seem to be having or, equally important in some respects, not having for these traditional patterns.

First of all, there has been taking place all over Africa, particularly during the past half-century, an ever-increasing commercialization of land and labor. This process was often initiated in the first instance by the demand for money created by the imposition of taxation by colonial governments, but it has also, and increasingly, been stimulated by the desire for the vast array of new goods and services, both imported and locally produced, which have become available. In some areas Africans numbering in the hundreds of thousands have gone to work for wages in mines and factories and on plantations; somewhat fewer have become white-collar workers— the ubiquitous "clerks" who tend the machinery of bureaucracy in both government and business firms. Others, in still larger numbers, have become cash-crop cultivators, producing cocoa, coffee, tobacco, cotton, and other crops for the export market.

Frequently cash-crop agriculture and wage work have competed for African labor, and in a great many areas vast numbers of men move back and forth between the two forms of money-making in cycles varying from daily commuting to periods of many years, combining agriculture and employment in ways that best suit their various situations and tastes.[25] Underlying all the variations in pattern, however, has been a pervasive and constantly deepening commitment to a money economy, in which both labor and land have increasingly become marketable commodities. If in very many areas traditional subsistence patterns have remained intact enough to make the money economy a rather superficial overlay, a source of "luxury" goods and services, the number for whom this is true has constantly diminished as the relationship of population to land has changed and as what were formerly merely "wants," have become "needs."

At the same time, ever-expanding educational systems have been busily producing practitioners of the learned professions —physicians, lawyers, clergymen, engineers, and teachers. Expanding literacy and the nationalist movements have encouraged the rise of politicians and publicists. Africanization of governmental and business bureaucracies has produced civil servants and junior executives. New opportunities for trade have stimulated a few real African entrepreneurs.

All this has meant a great proliferation of differentiated roles and, in particular, of occupational roles. In fact, over much of Africa, true occupational roles, in the sense of full-time roles played outside the domestic context in exchange for basic income, have essentially come into existence for the first time during this period. As a result we may confidently expect the emergence of new patterns of stratification. However, we may also expect that in these new patterns there will remain important elements of continuity with the past.

Almost without exception, direct continuity with traditional systems of stratification has been rendered nearly impossible by the lack of congruence between traditional and modern societal and cultural boundaries. Most African countries, having acquired their boundaries through the maneuvers of European diplomats, are extremely heterogeneous, and those lying south of the Moslem Sudan and Christian Ethiopia lack overarching literate elite cultures of the sort that, for example, give some unity to the otherwise quite diverse peoples of India. Thus, traditional elites, deriving their positions from societal and cultural units that have been absorbed and superseded by the new states or protostates, tend to have little legitimacy on a national level.

In Asia and the Near East, traditional elites can to a greater extent absorb and give birth to the new. Gandhi and Mohammed Abdu, for example, could in some measure reinterpret in modern terms traditional elite cultures that represented the common pasts of the peoples of their countries, thus contributing an essential element of continuity to the culture of new nations. In the African countries, however, there is inevitably a greater discontinuity between old and new cultures and between old and new elites. The only culture self-consciously shared by the new elites has tended to be that imported from France, Belgium, or Britain—or that formed in reaction to French, Belgian, or British domination. This is not to say that there are no underlying regional cultural unities in Subsaharan Africa, but these tend to be of a sort discovered by anthropological research. Not having been made explicit by being embodied in literary traditions, they are difficult for elites to utilize in the creation of new national cultures. Such concepts as "African personality" and "*négritude*" represent attempts by contemporary African leaders to solve the problem.

There are, however, other kinds of continuity between

traditional and modern systems of stratification which may
be even more important. Although direct cultural continuity
may be difficult to achieve, some characteristic features of the
traditional systems may perhaps persist and give a distinctly
African character to the new independent nations. For example, in the new African nations, as in the old, political
structures seem likely to continue to dominate economic ones,
and political elites to retain their preeminence. To be sure,
the place of economic processes in society has changed greatly.
Whereas in traditional societies an essentially static economy
was manipulated for political ends, the new independent
states make rapid economic development the principal aim of
public policy.

But this is precisely the point: Whereas in Europe and
America economic modernization was in great measure carried out by private entrepreneurs under regimes of laissez-
faire, Africa is attempting to modernize at a speed, and under conditions which require a more prominent role for state
entrepreneurship. This means a greater prominence, both in
numbers and in status, for civil servants, as compared with
private businessmen. As a result, the elite of a country like
Nigeria, recently studied by the Smythes, is perhaps as heavily
political as was, say, that of the old Yoruba state of Oyo.[26] The
traditional cultural emphasis upon authority coincides with,
and perhaps helps to produce, modern conceptions of planning for economic development.

It may be anticipated, also, that the new African states will
continue to be relatively "classless" in the same sense in which
the old ones were. To be sure, occupational differentiation has
greatly increased and the new educational systems hold the
potentiality for creating cultural stratifications of a kind unknown in traditional societies. In the colonial period, during
the early phases of educational development, many African
societies seemed to be producing new solidary elites of Euro-
pean-educated persons, and many writers have dwelt upon the
gap between such persons and the uneducated masses, often,
one suspects, reading into the African situation European attitudes toward status which were not really there. We certainly
should not expect egalitarianism in the sense of a lack of differentiation according to power, wealth, and prestige; such

differentiation was prominent in the past and is likely to remain so.

At least in the short run, however, extended kinship solidarities will tend to check the development of clearly defined strata. Welfare-state policies in education and other fields, policies which modern populist politics make almost inevitable, also will militate against the solidification of the new elites into hereditary estates or castes. Furthermore, the modernization of economies tends to increase the number of intermediate, or middle-class roles, thus increasing the structural opportunities for mobility. Thus, although the new African societies may be highly stratified economically and politically, they will probably remain relatively open to talent.

5

Are African Cultivators to Be Called "Peasants"?

THE TERM "peasant" has often been used of African rural folk, particularly when distinguishing them from political and religious elites in the larger and more complex societies. The word for the ordinary peasant cultivator in the kingdom of Buganda—*mukopi*—is commonly translated as "peasant," for example, and the literature of French Africa is full of references to "*paysans*." But most writers, one suspects, have used the word rather loosely; if pressed, most of us would be inclined to say: "Well, perhaps they are not *quite* peasants." Africanists tend to feel, perhaps, that the common folk of the complex African polities fall between the categories commonly utilized by those who have studied "peasant societies" in Latin America, Europe, and Asia, on the one hand, and, on the other those employed by students of aboriginal North American "tribes." They strike us as being not quite peasant but not quite tribal—something in between, a tertium quid. We may try to understand more clearly just what this tertium quid quality consists in by comparing some African societies with the notion of the "peasant society" developed during the past twenty years by students of Latin American, Asian, and European peoples. The point of this is not, of course, merely to play with definitions but rather to explore some of the implications of the fact—of which we are all aware—that the concept "peasant society" refers to a bundle of features which do not always go together. In doing this we may hope to indicate somewhat more precisely how these complex African societies resemble or differ from the classical peasant societies

Reprinted by permission from *Current Anthropology* 2 (1961): 108–10.

—thus satisfying our anthropologist's urge to fit all the peoples of the world into a grand classificatory scheme—and to suggest, indirectly, something about the significance of those peasantlike features which Africans do not share.

We may appropriately begin with Kroeber's definition (or description), since it has seemed to Robert Redfield, George Foster, Eric Wolf, and other peasant specialists to best describe their field of interest: "Peasants are definitely rural—yet live in relation to market towns; they form a class segment of a larger population which usually contains urban centers, sometimes metropolitan capitals. They constitute part-societies with part-cultures."[1] This last phrase—"part-societies with part-cultures"—we may take to be the heart of the matter. It can, however, be made somewhat more precise. On the other hand, the phrase *does* quite satisfactorily differentiate peasant societies from the societies we usually describe as "tribal"—societies whose constituent units, or segments, to use Durkheim's phrase, are all much alike and internally more or less homogeneous, in both structure and culture. Peasant societies, as Kroeber's definition suggests, are more differentiated, both socially and culturally. Peasant villages may all be much alike, but they are bound together into a larger whole by structures of a quite different kind, and the persons who man these other structures commonly have a different culture—a "sophisticated" or "urban" or "elite" or "high" culture. On the other hand, Kroeber's definition does not satisfactorily distinguish peasant societies from modern industrial ones, for the constituent units of these latter are also "part-societies with part-cultures"—even more partial than those of peasant societies, because modern societies are even more differentiated. We may suggest that the single most important difference between peasant and modern industrial societies lies in the nature of their constituent units. Whereas in peasant societies the household and the local community remain the primary units, in modern industrial societies occupational structures dissociated from households and cutting across local community units become important centers of cultural and structural differentiation. It is the vast increase in the differentiation and autonomy of occupational structures which industralization makes possible above all. Local communities thus lose their semi-self-sufficiency, the semidetached quality which they still retain in the peasant society and which led Redfield to emphasize—indeed .o overemphasize in his earlier work, as Foster has pointed out—the similarity between the peasant village and the tribal segment.[2] Unlike the latter, the peasant community is not completely isolable, completely capable of self-sufficiency; but neither is it so completely knitted into a larger fabric by crisscrossing occupational structures as is the modern community. The latter cannot possibly be imagined in isolation from the larger society. In contrast, the peasant community is relatively self-sufficient, leading many observers to comment upon its frequent indifference to changes in the political superstructure and hostility to members of the elite. Perhaps we may usefully alter Kroeber's characterization to read as follows: A peasant society is one whose primary constituent units are semiautonomous local communities with semiautonomous cultures. In this way we may differentiate the peasant society from both the tribal and the modern industrial varieties. It is perhaps necessary to add that we think of these as ideal, not concrete, types; actual societies will be in varying degrees "tribal," "peasant," and "modern industrial." The types are a means toward greater understanding, not a device for pigeonholing whole societies.

Now this semiautonomy of constituent local communities, which we may take to be the differentiating characteristic of the peasant society, may be decomposed into a number of aspects, of which we may here consider three: (1) the economic, (2) the political, and (3) what we may call, perhaps not very satisfactorily, the "cultural." We shall examine each of these briefly, attempting to see how far they find counterparts in the more complex African societies. It should perhaps be repeated that we consider here only trans-Saharan pagan Africa, excluding the Muslim areas and Ethiopia (see map).

1. In economic terms, a peasant is presumably a man who produces—usually through cultivation—mainly for his own household's consumption, but who also produces something to exchange in a market for other goods and services. This is the economic aspect of the peasant community's semiautonomy.[3] In this sense, peasants abound in Africa. The vast ma-

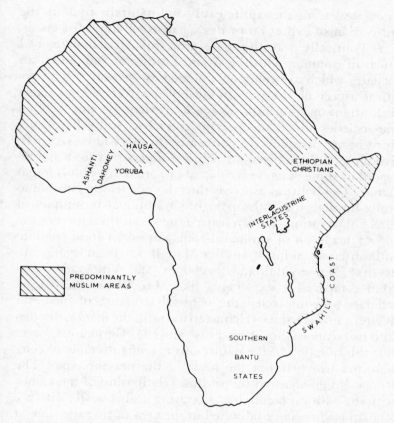

HAUSA

ASHANTI
DAHOMEY
YORUBA

ETHIOPIAN
CHRISTIANS

INTERLACUSTRINE
STATES

SWAHILI COAST

PREDOMINANTLY
MUSLIM AREAS

SOUTHERN

BANTU

STATES

Map showing Islamic areas of Africa and some of the major pagan states

jority of Africans were cultivators in precontact times—in
some cases intensive and devoted cultivators. They also traded;
the great markets of West Africa are famous, but also in most
other parts of the continent there was a good deal of craft
specialization and trade aboriginally. Cowrie shells, gold dust,
ivory, iron bars, and hoes in different areas provided semi-
generalized media of exchange. In the more centralized states
there was tribute, and sometimes even regular taxation to support and augment the authority of the nonagricultural superstructure. In short, in the economic aspect of the matter there
appears to be no problem. Economically, most Africans were
traditionally peasants and with the opening of the continent

to overseas trade they quite easily and naturally took up the cultivation of export crops in exchange for imported goods.

2. Politically, too, the more powerful African states had much in common with the Asian, European, and American societies which are commonly classed as "peasant." The political aspect of the peasant society has received relatively little attention from anthropologists, perhaps because so often the societies which the peasant specialists study have long since been "decapitated" politically (to use Kidder's expressive phrase), the indigenous political superstructure being replaced by those of modern colonial or nationalist post-colonial states.[4] The political aspect is thus the one least accessible to study through the anthropologist's traditional techniques of direct observation. We can learn more about this aspect of the society made up of seminautonomous peasant local communities from social historians like Marc Bloch, from legal scholars like Maine, Maitland, Seebohm, and Vinogradoff and from comparative sociologists like Max Weber. The legal scholars who unraveled the political structure of medieval Western Europe and its characteristic unit, the manor, divided into two schools, the "Romanists" and the "Germanists," over just this question of the nature of the semiautonomy of communities which lies at the heart of the peasant type.[5] The Romanists emphasized the vertical relationship of the manor with the political hierarchy, associating it historically with the Roman *latifundiae* established in the area during the time of the Empire. The Germanists, on the other hand, saw in the manor and its surrounding "vill" essentially a development out of the old solidary Germanic village community. If we understand this literature correctly—and it is easy for an anthropologist to go astray in the writings of legal historians —both were right, in the sense that both tendencies were present. They were debating, in a historical idiom, the relative importance of the two dimensions which always seem to be present in the peasant society and which constitute the political aspect of the semiautonomy of its constituent local communities: On the one hand there is the local community, hostile to the outside, sharing certain common rights in land and governed by local, often informal, mechanisms of social control; and on the other hand there is the hierarchy of patrimonial or feudal relations of personal superiority and re-

sponsibility (noblesse oblige) and subordinate dependence, which link the local community with the wider polity. Peasant political systems vary with the relative strength of the local community as against that of the vertical structure, as Eric Wolf has pointed out;[6] and also, as Max Weber[7] has shown, with the degree to which the latter is made up of appointed personal retainers as contrasted with hereditary feudal (using the term loosely) vassals.

These political peasantlike features, like the economic ones, are common enough in African states. The village community is a common feature everywhere (though it may be physically dispersed in scattered homesteads) and political hierarchies, where they exist, vary according to the degree to which they consist of appointed officials or hereditary chiefs. Africa is, of course, preeminently the continent of unilineal descent groups, and this gives to both village and communities and political superstructures a character which is less common in other regions. The village community often contains a core of lineage mates, and its corporate nature may be expressed in the idiom of unilineal descent.[8] There is an interesting range of variation according to whether strangers in such communities are relegated to a kind of second-class citizenship or are fictionally adopted into the core group. These phenomena are not, of course, universal in Africa. In the Interlacustrine area, the lineage is limited to such "domestic" functions as the control of inheritance and exogamy, and the village itself is defined purely territorially.[9] In the political superstructure of African states, unilineal descent groups often hold corporate rights to chieftainship; and thus the hierarchy, which in medieval Europe tended to consist of dynasties of individual hereditary lords and vassals, in an African state like Ashanti, or in one of the Southern Bantu states, consists essentially of representatives of corporate descent groups.[10] In some other states, like Dahomey and Buganda, the hierarchy is essentially one of patrimonial retainers, resembling in this respect the states of the Islamic world and Byzantium more than those of feudal Europe.[11] In general, allowing for peculiarities resulting from differences in patterns of descent, the politics of the traditional African states seem to fall well within the peasant range.

3. Thus, there would seem to be no reason why African

villagers should not be called "peasants" politically and economically. Doubts arise, however, when we turn to the culture that is characteristic of peasant life—that is, to the tendency, to which Redfield, Foster, and Marriott[12] have drawn attention, for the economic and political semiautonomy of the peasant community to be matched by a cultural semiautonomy. The culture of the peasant community of the classic conception is a "folk" version of a "high culture"; it is neither the same as the latter nor independent of it, but rather a reinterpretation and reintegration of many elements of the high culture with other elements peculiar to the peasant village. It is this cultural semiautonomy of the village, it would seem, which above all determines the relations which obtain between social strata in the peasant society. The elite possess, and live by, the high culture to a greater extent than do the peasants. The peasant, accepting the standards of the high culture to some degree, to that degree also accepts its judgment of him as ignorant and uncouth. At the same time, he possesses his own folk culture, containing high culture elements, and this provides him with an independent basis for a sense of self-esteem, together with an ideology within which he may express his partial hostility toward the elite and its version of the common culture. Excellent examples are provided by Homans's account[13] of how thirteenth-century English villagers caricatured the behavior of the elite.

Now it would seem to be just the relative absence of this differentiation into high and folk cultures which principally distinguishes the African kingdoms from the societies which have commonly been called "peasant." There is, of course, a substantial degree of cultural differentiation in many African societies. There are craft specialists with highly developed skills, and there are ritual specialists with great bodies of esoteric knowledge. There are courtly manners and there are recognized degrees of sophistication, ranging from the courtier who is "in the know" politically to the country bumpkin. Nevertheless, there remains an important difference between trans-Saharan pagan Africa in these respects and the differentiation which was possible in medieval Europe, China, India, and Islam. The word "peasant" denotes, among other things, a degree of rusticity in comparison with his betters which we do not feel justified in attributing to the African villager.

Lacking the more pronounced degrees of cultural differentiation, the African states characteristically exhibit a somewhat different pattern of stratification. African villagers do not seem to feel the same degree of ambivalence toward the political superstructure that European, Asian, and Latin American peasants do because, not standing to the same degree in contrast to the possessors of a differentiated high culture, they do not to the same extent feel judged from above by a set of standards which they cannot attain. Correspondingly, there is less development of a differentiated folk culture as a kind of "counterculture." Africans very commonly perceive themselves as being differentiated in terms of wealth and power but they do not often, except in the few real composite conquest states, view their societies as consisting of "layers" of persons with differential possession of a high culture. As is well known, they much more characteristically divide in terms of genealogical and territorial segments, even in instances where there are marked "objective class differences" in the Marxian sense. Not even those West African societies in which cities provide a basis for rural-urban cultural differentiation exhibit the degree of folk-high distinction commonly found in what we may now call the real peasant societies. Dahomean and Yoruba villagers were not separated from their urban cousins by a cultural gap of the same magnitude as that which divided medieval European and Asian countrymen from city folk.[14]

In large part this difference is due simply to the absence in traditional Africa of the literary religious traditions which formed the bases for the European and Asian high cultures. Written records make possible a vastly greater accumulation and elaboration of high culture. Furthermore, the mere presence of writing places between the literate and the illiterate member of the same society a barrier which cannot easily develop in its absence. The peasant's suspicious hostility toward the member of the urban elite is in large part a product of his realization that the latter, in his ability to read and write, holds a weapon against which the peasant cannot easily defend himself.

Thus the traditional African villager was, we might say, a peasant economically and politically, but was not a peasant culturally. Perhaps it would be better to call him a "proto-

peasant" or an "incipient peasant," for wherever literary culture has entered Africa, it has quickly made him more fully
a peasant. Thus the Muslim Swahili peoples of the east coast
and the Hausa of the Western Sudan were traditionally more
peasantlike than their nonliterate, pagan neighbors; and the
modern Baganda and Ashanti, with their imported Western
Christian high culture, are more fully peasants than were
their great-grandfathers. We may suggest that one of the
reasons why Christianity, Islam, and their accompanying high
cultures have been so readily accepted in many parts of Africa is that many African societies were structurally "ready" to
receive peasant cultures.

6
Equality, Modernity, and Democracy in the New States

SOCIAL stratification has fascinated students of modern Western societies and they have written about it with great perceptiveness and at great length. Equality and inequality and their place in modern society have been major themes in the work of such diverse figures as Burke and Marx, Tocqueville, and Weber. In recent decades, the study of stratification has become one of the most highly developed branches of professional sociology.

The reason for this great concern, quite clearly, is that the question of equality has played a peculiarly prominent role in the recent history of the West. It has dominated the ideologies of countless political movements and the personal aspirations of millions of individuals. Indeed, it would perhaps not be exaggerating to say that, from the point of view of most modern Westerners, including most social scientists, the progress of equality has been the central theme of recent history. For many, modernity and equality have seemed to be nearly synonymous; so also have equality and political democracy.

The very fascination with the subject, however, and the constant effort to refine our concepts and methods for study-

Reprinted by permission from *Old Societies and New States,* edited by C. Geertz (New York: Free Press, 1963).

I am deeply grateful to Marshall Hodgson, Milton Singer, Margaret Fallers, and the members of the Committee for the Comparative Study of New Nations for careful reading and criticism of successive drafts of this essay. They are, of course, in no way responsible for its remaining flaws.

ing it, may deceive us as we turn our attention to what seem to be analogous events and processes in the contemporary non-Western world. Concepts that have proved useful in the interpretation of the Western experience—concepts like "class," "feudal," "aristocracy," "democratic," "middle class," "proletarian," and "peasant"—may not have the same explanatory power when applied to processes that are different in important respects. That equality is also a central issue in the lives of contemporary non-Western peoples is apparent from the most cursory examination of the rhetoric of their leaders (though even here we must be wary; the Western experience has influenced non-Western politicians as well as Western social scientists, with the result that ideas and aspirations not entirely familiar to Western experience may be expressed in words that sound deceptively familiar). If we are to understand the *kind* of issue equality is in the new states, we must try to stand a bit outside the Western experience and ask ourselves just how far, and in what respect, equality, democracy, and modernity have been related at different times and places.

As a contribution toward a broadening of perspective in these matters, we shall try to outline some of the more general consequences of economic and political modernization for stratification systems. In doing this, it will be useful to include some explicit discussion of the Western case in order to achieve greater clarity concerning the relationship between the concepts we commonly use in thinking about stratification and the peculiarities of the Western historical experience out of a consideration of which these concepts have grown. This will inevitably involve oversimplification, for it is of course impossible within the scope of a short essay to do justice to the rich variety and complexity of the past few hundred years of Western history. Indeed, the very expression "the Western case" will no doubt be offensive to students of this historical complexity. There are, indeed, important differences among Western countries, particularly, for our present purposes, between those that modernized early and those that did so later. There are also differences between "old Europe" and its cultural outliers in America and Australasia (though these are hardly as great as many have assumed). Whatever the difficulties, the attempt at generalization seems justifiable and useful. Most historians would probably agree that there is sufficient unity among Western societies and cultures to give a measure of common pattern to their systems of social stratification, when contrasted with those of the other societies and cultures we shall consider. If, in a preliminary comparison of the modernization of the West with the contemporary situation of some non-Western societies, we misconstrue this common pattern, we shall at least have raised issues that may stimulate more adequate comparative discussion.

These caveats must apply also to our discussion of the non-Western areas whose systems of stratification, both traditional and modern, we shall compare with Western ones. We shall try to outline, briefly and schematically, the stratification systems of traditional India, the Ottoman Empire, and sub-Saharan Africa, and also those of the new states that in recent times have emerged in those areas. Three examples do not, of course, exhaust the wide range of forms stratification may take, but they do provide sufficient variation to make possible a preliminary exercise in comparative analysis.

The general theme we shall pursue is that the systems of stratification that emerge from the process of political and economic modernization are the products of the interaction between the forces of generic modernity (which of course we must define) and the traditional societies and cultures upon which, and within which, modernity works. This statement will seem obvious, and even trite, to all except those who see in modernization an all-consuming solvent of the past. That modern societies are different from others—that there will be features common to modern societies, East and West (and South), that set them off from their traditional predecessors —is of course assumed; or at any rate the discovery of some of the elements of the generically modern is one of the aims of this inquiry. But it will be argued that the outcome of the process of modernization will also be heavily conditioned by the nature of a society's traditional heritage—that, for example, modern Western society, including its stratification system, is what it is in part because of the special character of the late medieval European society and culture out of which it grew.

To anticipate the results of our comparative inquiry: The particular relationship between equality and political democracy that has been a feature of the modernization of stratification in the West appears to be the result of a pattern of interaction between tradition and modernity that is far from universal. While a kind of egalitarian politics seems to be one of the products of modernization everywhere, political democracy appears to be the result of more special circumstances. On the other hand, our inquiry will not suggest that these circumstances are so special that only the Western world is able to bring them together. Other societies and cultural traditions, undergoing modernization under different historical conditions, seem to exhibit features that suggest that they are capable of responding to political modernity in a broadly analogous way.

In pursuing this comparative investigation, we shall discuss in turn the various traditional societies and the forces of modernization that have impinged upon them. First, however, it will be useful to outline the conception of social stratification we shall use as a guide to more systematic analysis.

A Comparative View of Stratification

Much of the work on social stratification, as we have noted, has taken as it point of departure the data of a particular system or family of systems—usually Western. Consequently, it has been usual to begin with some prominent feature of one of these systems, say, with the differential relationship of persons to the means of production or with the differential prestige of occupational roles. Other students of the subject have stressed the cultural differences that distinguish the various strata of society, while still others have been interested in ideologies about equality and inequality. Each of these ways of looking at the field is, of course, "valid" enough in the sense that each leads us to a deeper understanding of some particular aspect of how the multifaceted phenomenon that is stratification works in the particular society in question. But if we wish to pursue comparative studies, it seems preferable to begin with a broader and more analytical view of the sort developed in Parsons's essays and implicit in much of the work of Weber.[1] Although we cannot, of course, hope to begin with a closed and final set of concepts that will be equally applicable to every situation and problem, we can start by considering some of the basic aspects and dimensions of stratification.

The Primary Roots of Stratification. Surely one of the fundamental bases for stratification phenomena everywhere is man's tendency to judge his fellow and himself as more or less worthy in the light of some moral standard. Thus a people's stratification system is rooted in its culture, and particularly in its culturally elaborated image of the "admirable man," the man whom everyone would like to be. Such images provide a spur to individual ambition—and to group ambition, too, since the unit of stratification is seldom in any simple sense a single person—thus providing a means by which individuals' and groups' energies and intelligence may be enlisted on behalf of society's goals. This is true in an important sense even when position in a stratification system is ascribed, for the qualities required of, say, a medieval European baron or an Indian Brahman are not, strictly speaking, inherited, either biologically or jurally. "Living up" to the demands of such a position always requires exertion on the part of the incumbent; and thus, even in such cases, there is an element of active pursuit of culturally defined standards.

Stratification, however, is equally rooted in social structure in the sense of the network of routinized relations, based upon mutual understandings and expectations about behavior, among persons and groups in society, for in this network of relations there is always some differentiation of roles, and thus the same image of excellence cannot be held before everyone. In addition to age, sex, and kinship roles there tends to be, certainly in societies with which we are concerned here, a division of labor with regard to economic, political, and religious tasks. As a counterpart to, and sustaining, these differentiated roles in society, culture must therefore present not just an undifferentiated image of the "admirable person," but also images of the "admirable woman," the "admirable son," the "admirable priest," and so on. This does not, of course, mean that by thus providing differentiated images of excellence to correspond with the differentiation of roles, the culture thereby relinquishes overall judgment among persons in general. Some dominant image of the "admirable person" tends to remain, and this image involves a selection and relative evaluation among differentiated roles themselves in terms of the degree to which they embody the features defined by the overall image of excellence.

Thus, the study of stratification may appropriately begin with a cataloging of the array of differentiated roles, with a delineation of cultural definitions of virtue and excellence in human behavior, and with a study of the interaction between these in terms of both cultural differentiation and overall differential evaluation of roles. This, however, is only the beginning, for the place of actual persons and groups in all this cannot be regarded as a passive one. If persons are assigned to different roles, and if culture evaluates these roles differentially, holding up some as more worthy than others, then the processes by which persons are allocated among roles may be expected to engage the interests and anxieties of persons and groups. Persons and groups may be expected to strive actively to achieve or defend their positions and, in the process, to manipulate, and even create, elements of the culture that evaluates them. A recognition of this "dynamic" element in stratification systems makes it useful to distinguish "secondary" structural and cultural aspects of such systems. By the "secondary structural aspect" of stratification we mean the structures and processes by which persons are allocated among roles, as distinguished from the "primary" differentiation of roles, or division of labor. By "secondary culture" we mean ideas and beliefs *about* stratification—about how and why persons are allocated among roles as they are and about the justice or injustice of this process—as contrasted with the "primary" definitions of excellence and the relative worth of roles.

Secondary Cultural Aspects. It is in relation to the secondary culture of stratification that we may most appropriately consider the famous concepts "ascription" and "achievement." These concepts certainly describe an important range of variation in cultural definitions of the proper allocation of roles, and one that has been particularly widely discussed in con-

nection with the process of modernization and the progress
of equality and democracy, it generally being assumed that
these involve a movement from ascription to achievement. It
has perhaps been recognized less commonly that neither occurs "pure" in the natural state and that consequently each
tends to be accompanied by additional cultural complexities
not encompassed by the concepts themselves. We have already
noted that persons who occupy high ascribed roles do not
really "inherit" the roles themselves; rather they inherit the
right to strive for such roles on favorable terms, often in
competition with others. The notion of noblesse oblige, for
example, expresses the obligation incumbent upon the legitimate occupant of an ascribed role to perform certain definite
kinds of behavior. From the point of view of the person assigned by ascription to a low position, the situation is still
more complex. For him there is probably always some difficulty in accepting as immutable a definition of himself as
unworthy by nature, no matter what he may do. This is not,
of course, to argue that he cannot, in some sense, come to
accept his position. It does mean that a culture that presents
to certain persons very much greater opportunity to occupy
the most admired roles must offer cogent reasons why this
should be so, and probably must also offer consolation in
some form to those thereby deprived of such highly valued
opportunity.

In addition to the dominant, public view of how the allocation of persons to highly valued roles should and does take
place, there also tends to develop a complex of more private,
yet quite standardized, subcultures that express the hopes and
fears of groups of persons variously placed in the stratification
system. A revealing example is provided by the tendency of
middle-class people in the West to combine great public devotion to the principle of achievement and equality of opportunity with an equally great, but less publicly expressed, concern with genealogy and the symbols of aristocracy. This
paradox is particularly marked in the highly achievement-
oriented society of the modern United States, where genealogy is nevertheless a major preoccupation. In a sense the very
emphasis upon the importance of achievement stimulates the
growth of a "counterculture" expressing persons' desire to be

"more equal than others." Everyone wants at least an equal
opportunity to achieve higher roles, but also wants to be pro-
tected from competition from below. In India, where, according to the theory of Hindu high culture, caste position is immutable, lowly placed castes find consolation in myths
explaining that they were once Brahmans, too, but that at
some time in the past were illegitimately demoted by caste
enemies.[2] Perhaps belonging to the same family of phenomena
are the more or less formalized dramatic and gamelike performances in which low-ranking persons sometimes express
ambivalently, in imitation that shades over into caricature,
both their acceptance and resentment of the culture that
places others above them in relative worth.[3]

Out of these complex crosscurrents of cultural attitudes
toward inequality there may crystallize, under certain circumstances, relatively compact bodies of belief and value
expressing the special position in the stratification system of
particularly cohesive groups of persons. Presumably the
growth of such subcultures is facilitated by the existence of
relatively closed social groups of the sort to which Max Weber
applied the term *Stand,* usually translated as "status group,"
thus giving analytical meaning to the German word for the
estates of medieval European society. Such subcultures may
pertain to broad horizontal strata within society or they may
be associated with occupational, or even territorial, groups.
Under some circumstances, as Weber noted, they may produce
very explicit and highly articulated ideologies that, borne by
aggressive social groups, may reshape substantially the cultural
orientation of whole societies. This is, of course, a matter of
central importance in the theory of modernization, involving
as it does the problems of innovation and class-consciousness,
and we shall therefore have to return to it later on in our
discussions of particular societies. Here it is sufficient to note
that the development of compact subcultures is one, but *only*
one, of the forms the secondary culture of stratification may
take.

Secondary Structural Aspects. These cultural phenomena do
not, of course, occur apart from the structure of social relations
in which the persons who are their bearers are involved. We

have spoken briefly of the primary structure of role differentiation and have suggested that beyond this, in order to understand the ways in which stratification actually works, we must examine the "secondary" processes and structures by which persons are allocated among the roles thus differentiated.

One aspect of all this is commonly conceptualized by writers on stratification by means of the image of the pyramid. The shape of the pyramid is meant to indicate the relative numbers of roles at the various levels that are available for allocation. (The height of the pyramid and the numbers and kinds of "levels" differentiated may indicate either the primary culture evaluation of various roles or the secondary cultural image of the system as a whole, depending upon the interests of the writer.) The important point for our present purposes is that the structural situation—the relative numbers of different roles that are available—may greatly influence persons' opportunities to occupy the more highly valued positions, quite apart from any cultural values concerning achievement and ascription. In traditional peasant societies, elites tend to be small and common folk to be numerous, with relatively few "middle-class" persons in between. In this situation, even though the elite may be very open to talent—as it is in traditional societies rather more often than has commonly been supposed—actual opportunities for mobility may be few. On the other hand, an increase in the number of middle-class roles available may greatly alter the structure of opportunity without any substantial change in the culture of stratification.

To an important degree, this may be an economic matter where the number of roles in question is determined essentially by the supply of goods and services of kinds that serve either as facilities for the performance of such roles or as symbols expressive of them. Thus changes in the supply and control of such goods and services may exert what is, in the short run at least, a relatively unilateral influence upon stratification. It is to such changes, and the changes in the degrees and kinds of role differentiation that frequently accompany them, that Marx draws our attention in support of his contention that the organization of the economy lies at the heart of social stratification, and indeed of society in general. Viewed in wider perspective and over the longer term, however, such processes take their place, along with processes of a more cultural nature, as only one among a number of "forces" making up the complex of social and cultural change.

Political systems, in terms of which legitimate authority to make binding decisions is distributed, influence and are influenced by stratification systems, much as economic systems are. Political roles are themselves the object of differential evaluation and the exercise of political power may influence the allocation of roles of other kinds. But politics is not synonymous with stratification any more than economics is, and hence democracy is not synonymous with equality.

There are still other structural features that influence the process of role allocation, among the most important being family and kinship structures. Stratification is probably never a purely individual matter, but rather always involves kinship groups of some kind, which is one reason why an element of status ascription is present in even the most achievement-oriented societies. Egalitarian ideologists have recognized this, hence their frequent attempts to eliminate the family. In traditional societies, kinship solidarities are commonly widely ramifying (although of course this phrase may cover a wide range of phenomena). With modernization, the kinship unit of stratification tends to shrink, principally because in modern societies occupational roles, played outside domestic contexts in functionally specialized economic, political, or religious organizations, tend to become the main focus of stratification. With this loss of direct articulation between kinship groups and the division of labor, the allocation of roles becomes a much more complex matter—comes to be mediated much more by special educational structures and a labor market external to the family and much less by training within the domestic or extended kinship group. Kinship solidarities, including quite widely ramifying ones, do not, however, automatically disappear under such circumstances; a tendency toward kinship ascription of status persists in all modern societies, influencing, sometimes quite profoundly, both the allocation of occupational roles and their cultural evaluation. We shall have to discuss later on some of the differences in traditional kinship structures and their consequences for the modernization of stratification.

These remarks should suffice to indicate in a preliminary way our view of the main dimensions of stratification systems. We may now turn to a closer examination of the patterns of stratification characterstic of the traditional societies and cultures that were the antecedents of the new states.

The Traditional Societies

Almost all the new states have grown out of peasant societies, and it is therefore part of our task to inquire into the forms stratification characteristically takes in such societies. The term "peasant society" is in some respects an unfortunate one because it refers directly to only one segment of the society's population; we use it principally in order to avoid such terms as "feudal society," whose historical connotations are too specific for our purposes. The term does have the merit, however, of drawing attention to certain important characteristics of the societies with which we wish to deal, including some important common features of their stratification systems. With all their real differences, the societies that in most cases preceded the new states shared a broad pattern of social and cultural differentiation whose main features are revealed by an examination of the peasant village in relation to the rest of society. This pattern may be contrasted, on the one hand, with that characteristic of what we may call "tribal societies" and, on the other, with that typically found in societies in which modernization has made substantial inroads.

The peasant village, as Kroeber has said, is what it is because of its relationship to the social and cultural superstructure above it; it is "a part-society with a part culture."[4] Standing alone, it would no longer be a *peasant* village. In contrast, the communities that make up a tribal society are functionally more autonomous. In Durkheim's famous image of the "segmental society"—an analogy he drew from the segmental worms—each local unit tends to be similar to the others and to be functionally complete in itself.[5] The analogy, of course, is not entirely satisfactory; analogies from biological to social systems seldom are. Tribal communities—those of most North American Indians and the pagan peoples of the Philippines, for example—are often bound together in a kind of interdependence by relations of trade and exchange of personnel through marriage, but there is something in the analogy, nevertheless: the communities that make up a tribal society do commonly have a kind of potential functional autonomy that makes it possible for them, for example, to multiply simply by fission.[6] The political order of the tribal society is often what Easton has called a "contingent" political order, a kind of miniature "international" order among essentially (or at least potentially) sovereign units.[7] Above all, the tribal community tends to be *culturally* more self-sufficient. There is little cultural differentiation, either within or among communities, and no overarching elite who might be the bearers of a differentiated elite culture. Each local community "contains" the whole culture.

The peasant community, however, has none of these kinds of self-sufficiency. Peasant villages may sometimes be little differentiated from one another, but they are bound together into a larger whole by a differentiated, superordinate elite, whom the villagers support through the payment of taxes or tribute and to whom they owe political allegiance. Most important, the elite are custodians of a distinct subculture, an elite or "high" culture, usually embodied in the scriptures and associated literature of one of the world religions. In relation to the culture of the elite, the peasant is a rustic whose culture is a "folk" version of the elite culture.[8] It is the association of the elite with the higher, "purer" version of the common culture that legitimates its economic and political supremacy in the eyes of the peasant. It is the relative crudity, in the eyes of the elite, of the villagers' folk version of the common culture that makes him truly a peasant.

Thus, the secondary structural and cultural aspects of stratification assume an importance in peasant societies that they do not possess in tribal ones. Cultural differentiation gives peasant systems a dimension of "depth," an added "distance" from "top" to "bottom"; and this, in turn, gives the secondary structural question of the placement of persons in the system an added prominence. It creates, or at any rate makes more important, the problem of social mobility. It also raises the problem of the legitimacy of the system and its placement of persons and thus stimulates the growth of ideologies, both public and private, about how the system does and should work. It is all this which makes the peasant society typically "more highly stratified" than the tribal society.

We may also briefly contrast peasant societies with modern ones, though we shall say more about this later on when we consider the process of modernization of stratification as such. If the peasant society is in important respects more differentiated, both structurally and culturally, than the tribal one, it remains less differentiated, in equally important respects, than the society to which we give the name "modern." In contrast with those characteristic of modern societies, the elites of peasant society tend to be relatively unspecialized, to consist generally only of rulers and those learned in religion. And although handicrafts may reach extremely high levels of skill and aesthetic expressiveness, and trade may become an important calling, they remain essentially domestic occupations, carried out in the context of the household of the practitioner or his elite patron, despite the important role that corporate bodies such as guilds have sometimes played in promoting the interests of craftsmen and traders and in controlling entry into these occupations. Even government is commonly carried out in a domestic idiom, the polity being treated rather like an extension of the ruler's household and public officials as his domestic servants.[9] Lacking are those functionally specialized political and economic organizations, so characteristic of modern societies, that are separated from the households of their members and in which the latter play purely occupational roles in exchange for basic income. Also lacking is the cultural commitment to constant innovation that lends a certain instability to both the cultural and structural aspects of stratification in modern societies.

We may now move on to an examination of some of the differences among the traditional societies, both non-Western and Western, out of which modern states have grown—the traditional settings that have influenced modern systems of stratification.

The Medieval West and the Empire of the Ottomans. One important range of variation in traditional stratification systems has been described by Machiavelli, with his usual matter-of-fact clarity, in the fourth chapter of *The Prince:*

the principalities of which there is any historical record are managed in two different ways: in the first, one man is prince and all others are slaves, who act as ministers and aid in governing the country through his grace and permission; in the second type, there are a prince and barons, and the latter hold their positions not through the grace of their lord but through the antiquity of their blood. Such barons have states and subjects of their own, who recognize them as lords and have a natural attachment to them. The ruler has most authority in governments administered by a prince and his slaves, because in all the province nobody is recognized as superior except himself, and if the people obey any other they think of him as a minister and appointee, and do not feel any special love for him.

The examples of these two kinds of government in our times are the Turk and the King of France.[10]

Max Weber has referred to this contrast to which Machiavelli draws out attention as that between patrimonialism and feudalism, adding his usual caveat to the effect that the concepts refer to ideal types and that actual cases are always mixed. This of course was true of the cases cited by Machiavelli. In medieval Europe there existed, along with the hierarchies of hereditary, aristocratic fief holders, appointed personal officials of kings and princes, like the English sheriffs and the continental *ministeriales*. And in the Ottoman Empire there were sometimes persons whose position approximated that of the feudal lord. The contrast, however, remains a real one and one that—since the empire of the sultans comprised the non-Western societies most familiar to Western thinkers—has played an important role in the development of thought concerning stratification, particularly in relation to the political order. It therefore provides an appropriate context in which to begin a discussion of some of the important differences to be found among traditional stratification systems. The Ottoman Empire does not, of course, represent the whole of the Islamic world, but as the last great premodern political focus of Islam it may appropriately serve as an example of Islamic society as a setting for modernization. Except where otherwise indicated, therefore, "Islamic society" will mean the realm of the Ottomans.

During the medieval period Islamic societies were at least as differentiated and sophisticated as were those of their Christian neighbors; during the earlier part of the period they were a good deal more so. Societies in both spheres rested upon peasant agriculture, skilled craftsmanship, and trade. Both were heirs to the culture of Greco-Roman antiquity, which the learned of each combined with their respective monotheistic faiths (and of course with other cultural elements) to create new "high cultural" syntheses. In their patterns of stratification, however, the two systems differed greatly, thus providing an excellent illustration of the inadequacy of the view of such matters that limits itself to primary structural features.

Medieval Western societies tended to be divided into broad, culturally defined, almost hereditary strata—the estates. Western political theorists of that age were fond of organic analogies that compared the estates to parts of a human body, each having its fixed and necessary function.[11] No doubt there was a good deal more mobility between strata than these images suggest; also, they obscure the asymmetrical, but nevertheless very real, vertical ties of personal loyalty that often bound together peasant and lord. But such notions did, clearly, represent an elite ideal, an aristocratic class consciousness that in turn was in some degree emulated by humbler folk in relation to their own inferiors.[12] Along with this ideology of aristocratic solidarity, and partly as an expression of it, there developed a marked cultural differentiation between the peasant, whose life and culture centered upon the annual cycle of agricultural tasks, and the noble knight, the bearer of a culture of chivalry that expressed his devotion to the protection of aristocratic honor and religion through military prowess.[13] Government was very largely in the hands of—indeed, essentially consisted of —the hierarchy of the noble lords and vassals.

Islamic societies of the time also exhibited great inequalities of wealth and power, but the secondary culture and structure of stratification were strikingly different. Never, apparently, did there develop anything really comparable to the European estates, and in particular nothing at all closely resembling the closed feudal aristocracy. Rather, Islamic societies remained comparatively fluid and open to talent. As von Grunebaum's description of the social order of the Abbasids makes clear, this tendency toward social fluidity already existed in early medieval times:

Money, though deprecated by the moralist, played its customary part. Education opened the doors of the great to the ambitious poor, and it was a prerequisite for public office, though princely whim did not always stop to scrutinize a favorite's qualifications. Political influence, military power, administrative rank, wealth, birth and schooling, in every possible combination, strengthened or counteracted one another in assigning a given individual his place in society.[14]

Under the later bureaucratic regime of the Ottomans, more relevant to our purposes, aristocracy of birth came to count for even less. The whole of what Gibb calls the "ruling institution"—the imperial administrative service—came to be staffed by men conscripted as young boys from among the non-Moslem subjects of the sultan, whose personal slaves they were considered to be.[15] It was this independence of recruitment to political office from considerations of ascribed status, and the resulting great personal power of the sultan and grand vizier over the appointment and control of officials, that so attracted the attention of Machiavelli and other European thinkers familiar with the more decentralized and aristocratic polities of Europe. It was this that gave rise, in Western minds, to the image of "Oriental depotism." Nothing, indeed, is more indicative of the gulf that separates medieval European and Islamic secondary cultures of stratification than their different attitudes toward the legal status of slavery. In Europe, degrees of freedom correlated directly with social worth, and over the centuries the achievement of full personal freedom became a common goal of personal ambition and of social movements. In the Domain of Islam, however, legally unfree persons could so thoroughly monopolize the highest positions in the state that it became advantageous to freeborn Moslems to assume slave status fictionally.

To be sure, this was not the whole story. In the countryside there were peasants who, while not formally unfree, labored

under restrictions that sometimes led them to escape to the
greater liberty of the city, much as their Christian contemporaries did. And there were "feudal" landholders, often members of the imperial cavalry, who held semihereditary "fiefs"
and stood in something like the relationship of "lord" to
those peasants. "Noble" blood was cherished by descendants of
the Prophet. But a striking difference remained, nevertheless:
the main lines of cleavage in society ran not between hereditary, culturally differentiated estates, but rather between
rulers and ruled, however these positions might in particular
circumstances have been acquired.

How may we account historically for these differences between societies that otherwise were so closely related? This is
of course too large a question to embark upon here. In any
case, we are interested here more in the subsequent fate of the
two systems under the impact of modernization than in their
origins. We may, however, ask a more modest question and
one more pertinent to our present concern: What part did
Islam and Christianity, respectively, play in developing these
differences?

A common answer has been given in the phrase "Islamic
egalitarianism"; but so simply put, this seems inadequate, for
Christianity also, in its primitive Gospel form, proclaims the
religious equality of believers. In any case, religious doctrine
seldom acts so directly upon social structure. Perhaps the difference lies, in part at least, in the greater concern of Islam
to derive from its scriptures and traditions a concrete and detailed code of behavior covering every aspect of life. While, of
course, law and government in medieval Christian Europe
were also infused with religious influence, Islam, in a very
real sense, simply *is* the *shari'a*, at least in relation to the external life. The Islamic ruler is thus not merely the defender
of the faith; he is its direct administrator, and this in itself
must have given added force to a universalistic code for behavior. It also meant that the holder of authority, whether
religious or civil (to the limited extent to which such a distinction is possible in the Islamic polity) had to be educated
in the law in a manner that was not required of the European
lay feudal lord, although of course the clergy required education. Islamic "high culture" was thus embodied, to a

greater extent than was the chivalric culture of the European nobility, in formal courses of study pursued in schools and universities, which thereby became channels for relatively universalistic recruitment into the political elite. The ultimate decay of the Ottoman state consisted in a retreat from this universalistic pattern into de facto hereditary recruitment and the purchase of office.[16] The decay of the Western feudal state, in contrast, involved greater political centralization and a strengthening of patrimonial universalism.

Traditional India and Sub-Saharan Africa. If the traditional Islamic social order was more fluid and open than that of the medieval West, that of traditional India, with its multiplicity of closed groups, was a good deal less so. Despite, therefore, the bewildering variety and seeming uniqueness of Indian patterns of stratification that, as Marriott has said, have tended to make them resistant to analytic treatment,[17] some discussion of these patterns seems to be useful to our purpose. The obvious importance of India in any consideration of processes of modernization in the non-Western world makes this doubly desirable.

Our discussion of stratification in feudal Europe and in the Ottoman Empire has been centered upon the state in a way that is less appropriate in the case of India, for two reasons: First, Hindu religion, which presumably has been the dominant influence in molding the culture of Indian stratification, appears to have been less directly concerned with the political order. There have, of course, been Hindu monarchies and, in connection with these, a tradition of thought concerning right government,[18] but Hinduism has on the whole directed its attention more to the perfection of the inner spiritual life and to the regulation of symbolic interpersonal behavior between persons presumed to be in different states of spiritual excellence than to the religious guidance of the polity as such. This tendency has been reinforced by a second factor: the Indian society upon which modernizing forces worked had been to a large extent politically "decapitated" by several centuries of Mogul and European domination. During the latest premodern period, therefore, indigenous patterns of stratification were reflected in village life and in a degree of

Indiawide Brahman cultural leadership but not, to the same degree, in the organization of a wider political order.

There are two principal aspects of traditional Indian society and culture that require some discussion because of the peculiar importance they may have had in creating a setting for the process of modernization of stratification: the "other-worldly" character of Indian religion as it enters into the "primary culture" of Indian stratification—the value system in terms of which roles are differentially evaluated; and, of course, the caste system. Both are exceedingly complex phenomena, and we can here do no more than outline some of their principal dimensions in relation to our present concerns.

Indian traditional religion was "otherworldly" in the sense that the application to everyday economic and political problems of a religiously informed body of thought was not for it a matter of major concern. The primary object of religiosity was rather the achievement, through contemplation, learning, and physical and emotional self-discipline, of a state of inner spiritual perfection leading to a union with the divine or to a favorable reincarnation. This concern was reflected both in the classical scheme of the fourfold division of society (*varna*) and, in large measure, in the reality of traditional social life in the high position accorded the Brahman as the most complete embodiment of this ideal. It was also conversely, reflected in the less worthy role assigned to the warrior-ruler and the trader, in that order.

Here oversimplification is fatally easy. It is certainly not the case that Brahmans and other Indians have lacked economic and political interests, as many village studies have shown and as Max Weber has emphasized in his discussion of the general character of Asian religions.[19] Indeed, Weber speaks of an "unrestricted lust for gain in Asians large and small," which, he argues, is precisely the result of a lack of religious guidance in the economic and political fields— guidance of a sort that, we may add, was provided by St. Augustine and the Moslem jurists.[20] For the problem of the distribution of wealth and power is present in any society; and in addition in any peasant society, as we have noted, the political and economic "pyramid" tends to be sharply "peaked," whatever view the high culture may adopt with regard to it. Thus, it is impossible to exclude political and economic problems from social life, but it is perfectly possible for religion to neglect or denigrate them, and this is what traditional Indian religion seems to have done. The principal creators and bearers of Hindu high culture, and the persons allocated highest status in its view of society, were not primarily exponents of religious law or moral virtue or wise statecraft but rather persons who expressed most fully the ideal of detachment from the world and the body in order to achieve the fullest possible association with a transcendent divinity.

Furthermore, this role of principal bearer of the high culture was allocated in a strictly ascribed way, and this brings us to the second essential feature of traditional Indian stratification—the castes. In traditional thought, the idea of caste was represented by the scheme of the four *varnas*. In traditional social life it appeared in the form of the thousands of closed groups, ranging in scale from local clusters of a few families in a single village to very large bodies of persons stretching over wide regions of the subcontinent. The complexity of the caste hierarchy also varied widely, both in the numbers of distinguishable groups and in the numbers of ranks into which groups were classified.[21] Beneath all this variation, however, certain characteristic features stand out: Castes were hereditary and endogamous (or hypergamous), both features tending to maximize differentiation and exclusiveness; they were internally highly homogeneous with regard to rank, at any rate in terms of the wider stratification system; and they were ranked with respect to one another in terms of relative closeness to Brahman patterns of ritual behavior, commensality, and occupation. Within a local community, members of different castes tended to be bound to one another by obligations to supply mutual though often rather asymmetrical services, assigned in terms of a division of labor by caste.

The system (or systems!) was of course not so static or so universally accepted as has sometimes been made out; if intercaste mobility was virtually excluded, there was certainly much competition for position among castes, both at regional and local levels, for the relationship of actual groups to the theoretical *varna* scheme could always be challenged. In the short run, however, and from the point of view of the life career of any individual, stratificatory position was probably more nearly fixed by ascription, and this ascription was probably more thoroughly legitimated by religion, than in any society of which we have knowledge.

This combination of thoroughgoing mysticism with rigidly ascribed status would seem to provide a singularly unpromising setting for modernization, for, whatever else the latter may consist in, it is generally agreed to involve a fundamental commitment to technological innovation and a degree of universalism in the allocation of occupational roles. That India nevertheless has thus far been in many respects one of the most successful modernizers among the new states indicates that the process of modernization is more complex than would at first appear. We shall have to return to this interesting problem subsequently.

There have, of course, been many other traditional societies and cultures upon the basis of which new states have arisen, and we cannot discuss them all. Before leaving the subject, however, it may be useful to draw attention to some of the peculiar features of Africa as a setting for the development of a number of the very newest among the new states. That part of Africa that stretches south from the Mediterranean to the southern borders of the Sudan belt and the Ethiopian highlands, and down the eastern coast as far as Sofala, was traditionally included within the world of Islam and Christianity. The remainder of the continent, however, differed from the other regions we have discussed in lacking the unifying influence of overarching literary high cultures. This is not, of course, to say that the many autonomous kingdoms and tribes lacked any sort of wider cultural community. Indeed, recent research on the linguistic and cultural history of Africa suggests that a very large part of the traditionally non-Islamic and non-Christian area was populated by peoples who were historically very closely related and shared much common culture.[22] But this is just the point: These wider unities were of the sort that are discovered by scholarly research. Not being embodied in a differentiated elite literary culture, they are less tangible— less easily made the objects of thought and action—than are such intellectualized literary complexes as Islam, Hinduism, and Christianity.

Traditional nonliterate Africa was not, however, entirely

or even largely "tribal" in the sense discussed earlier in this essay. We have argued elsewhere that much of the continent was occupied by societies that might be called "protopeasant" societies—societies that, although they lacked literary culture, nevertheless exhibited patterns of structural differentiation not unlike those characteristic of the traditional peasant societies of the Near East, Asia, and Europe.[23] Along the Guinea Coast, in the region of the Great Lakes, and in the southeast there were great kingdoms, many of which counted their subjects in the hundreds of thousands, or even millions and in which village communities of agriculturalists were bound together by elites made up of rulers and their administrative staffs and religious specialists. The latter devoted themselves full time to politics and religion and were supported by the tribute and taxes of the village folk. Particularly in the west, there were substantial urban populations engaged in trade and skilled crafts.

Nevertheless, there remained in traditional Africa, even in the larger kingdoms with their elaborate political hierarchies, a kind of egalitarianism that seems to have had two principal roots. One of these was the pattern of kinship and family structure, which over much of the continent rested upon exogamous unilineal descent groups. Although in the structure of the state persons might stand to one another in highly asymmetrical dyadic relationships of economic and political superiority and subordination, every person tended also to belong to one or more extended, solidary descent groups that cut across such hierarchical structures. Exogamy produced, in addition, a set of affinal ties knitting descent groups together and inhibiting subcultural differentiation among them. At the village level, rights in land characteristically were heavily concentrated in the hands of kinship or local groups. Thus, tendencies toward crystallization of rigid horizontal strata were checked, in spite of the frequent concentration of power and wealth in elite hands.

The other factor that tended to inhibit the development of a more rigid stratification was, as we have noted, the absence of literary religious traditions, which might have provided the basis for more clearly differentiated elite subcultures. However much the traditional African king or chief might stand above his people in terms of power and wealth, he shared with them an essentially common set of notions concerning goodness and beauty and the nature of the world. To be sure, during the nineteenth century, as a result of the early work of missionaries, there began to develop for the first time in many areas a semihereditary, culturally differentiated elite characterized by Western education, adherence to Christianity, and a style of life based upon Victorian taste. These tendencies, however, appeared too late to come to fruition, for they were shortly overtaken by modernizing forces that prevented the solidification of a gentry class and tended to spread the new culture through all levels of society.

These few examples, of course, far from exhaust the variety of traditional systems of stratification. They may, however, serve to indicate the wide range of settings in which the processes of modernization have developed. We must now turn to an examination of these processes.

Structural Modernization: Differentiation of Roles

In referring on previous pages to the process of modernization, we have mentioned at a number of points that one of its most characteristic features on the structural side has been the emergence of specifically occupational structures and roles as dominant features of society and as foci of social stratification. We must be clear about just what this means. Of course occupational roles, in the sense of specialized tasks within a division of labor, are nothing new in human history; these were common in all the traditional societies we have discussed. What is specifically modern is not specialization as such—although of course the development of modern technologies has been accompanied by a much greater degree of differentiation among occupational roles—but rather the very widespread separation of occupational roles from domestic life, and their location instead in specialized structures such as business firms and governmental bureaucracies.

Few historical changes can have been as far-reaching as this in their implications for social life. To Marx, more than anyone else, we owe our understanding of what it has meant. Where once nearly everyone did his daily work within his own or his patron's household—that is to say, in a social context in which he stood to his co-workers in a highly personal and total relationship of mutual responsibility—now the great majority move daily between household and job, between two social worlds that not only are spatially separated but, even more important, are in large measure normatively segregated and subject to different social rules. Even the small businessman, the farmer, and the private practitioner of a profession—persons whose work may still be carried out most nearly as an adjunct to the domestic group—are increasingly viewed by the society at large—and by the income tax laws! —as two persons: an employer and an employee. In this way the "self-employed" are assimilated to the dominant structural pattern.

All this has had fundamental consequences for social stratification. When work remained essentially embedded within domestic or wider kinship structures, it was but one among a total bundle of features upon which the position of the group in the stratification system depended. Even when occupational role was not legally or normatively ascribed, as it often was, in practice for the vast majority of persons it could be learned and practiced only within the domestic setting and hence was, de facto, hereditary. The development of distinct occupational structures—and also of extradomestic educational structures with the capacity to train persons for occupational roles— broke up this nexus—set occupational role free to become the principal focus and determinant of stratificatory position. Not completely, of course, for, as we have said before, so long as families persist as in some degree agents of socialization, they will influence the allocation of occupational roles; but now, to a very important degree, domestic units no longer *contain* the occupational structure, no longer determine the individual's place within it. Instead, the fate of the domestic unit itself, including its placement in the stratification system, depends upon the performance of one or more of its members within and according to the norms of an external occupational system that cuts across kinship.

This, in turn, tends to have political consequences which we must discuss in a later section: in politics, as in economics, the individual comes to be influenced less by local, particularistic ties—comes to be a member of a wider, more impersonal polity. Nor does this process of structural differentiation take place in isolation from cultural developments. Indeed, there is a very important specifically cultural dimension to the modernization of stratification that we must discuss in the next section. For the moment, however, we may concentrate upon the process of occupational differentiation itself.

The widespread differentiation of occupational from other structures, along with further differentiation among occupational structures themselves, occurred first in the Western world and is now occurring with varying speeds in the new states as one element in the overall process of modernization. It has not, however, occurred everywhere at the same rate and in the same way. We must ask ourselves how far the Western experience in this regard is being repeated, thus forming a reliable basis for prediction of the probable course of events in the new states, and how far the experience of the latter may be different in important respects. Again we are faced with a seemingly endless variety, out of which we can consider only some of the most important ranges of variation.

In the West, the differentiation of occupational from other structures came in the main as a result of the postmedieval rationalization and expansion of economics through the activities of private entrepreneurs. Its historical roots, of course, go back to the development in classical antiquity of the corporation—a structural unit having a legal "personality" distinct from those of its members. With increasing economic growth, this organizational form, which during the Middle Ages had persisted in the guilds, urban boroughs, and certain church bodies, was available for the creation of new kinds of economic enterprise: banks, trading companies and, ultimately, industrial concerns, drawing their leadership from existing merchants, gentry, and urban craftsmen and their workers from the latter and from the country villages.[24]

Throughout the early stages of this process, as Parsons has pointed out, persons at different levels within these business organizations stood in rather different structural positions with respect to them.[25] Participants in the new concerns were sharply divided between owner-entrepreneurs and employees, and it was the latter—the clerks and the new industrial proletariat—whose lives were now most clearly dichotomized between work and family, home and job. It was the worker who sold his labor to an external occupational structure in exchange for his family's basic subsistence. For the early capitalist—the owner-entrepreneur—the family-firm type of organization maintained the nexus between domestic and occupational structure. The firm was still the property of his domestic group. The full structural differentiation of the firm has only become complete during the late nineteenth and early twentieth centuries through the growth of the modern corporation, with its multiplicity of small stockholders and its hired management who, at least in formal structural terms, stand in the same relationship to it as do its industrial and white-collar employees.

Industry and commerce have not, of course, been the only fields for the differentiation of occupational structures in the West, though they clearly have in most cases provided the driving force in this process. The growth of government, an essential accompaniment of modern economic development despite the prominence of private entrepreneurship, has created large bodies of civil servants for whom the state is an occupational organization analogous to the firm. Practitioners of the learned professions, whose numbers have increased in response to the ever greater demand for specialized knowledge and skills, have also been drawn into modern occupational structures. Many have become salaried employees of business or government, but even "private" practitioners are affected. As Parsons has pointed out, one of the functions of modern professional associations has been to separate professional practice from the private, domestic interests of the practitioner, much as the structural separation of home and job does in the case of the employee of business or government.[26] The professional becomes, in a sense, an employee of his profession.

And of course agriculture has also, in the main, been reorganized, either in the direction of the large-scale industrial farm, employing a hired labor force, or toward the mechanized and highly capitalized family farm in which, though dwelling and workplace may remain spatially contiguous, the enterprise is managed in a rigorously "economic" way, the entire product being sold for cash, out of which the family derives an income with which, in turn, everything consumed is purchased. Indeed, in the case of agriculture significant phases of modernization took place in western Europe and the United States well before the great growth of industry. Rural folk had in many areas ceased to be peasants in the sense of semisubsistence cultivators bound to the gentry by political and economic ties of subordinate dependence. Many had by then become small-scale agricultural entrepreneurs producing for a cash market, or else employees of large-scale estate farmers. Wage work and an impersonal market were therefore not novelties to many who moved to the towns to take up jobs in the new factories.

In the new states, the differentiation of occupational structures has not, of course, gone as far as it has in Western countries. As a very crude measure of the difference, we may note that in 1950 only about one-quarter of the "economically active" male population of Asia and Africa were engaged in nonagricultural pursuits, while in the West the proportion ranged from about two-thirds to more than four-fifths.[27] Even these figures underestimate the real structural difference, for agriculture has, as we have seen, become a more modern occupation in the West. In most of the new states, the great majority of the population are not yet involved in modern, differentiated occupational structures, and the occupational system remains little differentiated within itself; most persons remain semisubsistence peasant cultivators, often producing for a market but nevertheless carrying out their productive work within a village context in which occupation remains embedded in kinship and community structures—in which workmates are kith and kin. To put the matter in terms of the pyramid image, the stratification systems of the new states remain much more sharply "peaked" and more "broad-based" than those of Western societies.

It is not, however, crude differences in the degree of occupational modernization that mainly concerns us here, for we cannot assume that the new states are merely less far along on a path identical with the one traveled earlier by the West. In important respects they are approaching modernization by different paths, and we must therefore examine qualitative differences in the *pattern* of occupational modernization, both among the new states and between them, taken together, and the West. In surveying some of these differences, we may look first at the elite and then at the "common man" level of society. We shall proceed topically, instead of area by area, in discussing this matter of structural modernization because differences in this regard do not correspond in any clear way with the sample areas we have chosen. When we turn to cultural modernization, we shall again proceed in terms of our three main examples.

Bureaucrats and Entepreneurs. First of all, as has often been pointed out, bureaucrats are more prominent, and entrepreneurs less prominent, in the elites of the new states than in those of the West—at any rate during comparable stages of modernization. There have been three main reasons for this: First, the early stages of economic modernization were mostly initiated, not by indigenous enterprise but rather by entrepreneurs from the West, where modernization was already well under way. We need not enter into a discussion of the famous problem, upon which Max Weber has shed so much light, of why this was so—why, that is, among all the traditional societies of the medieval period, it was in the West that modernization took place first. For our purposes we need only note that during the eighteenth and nineteenth centuries the West had vigorous entrepreneurs to spare for overseas enterprise, whereas in Asia and Africa such men were rare— though of course there was much variation in this respect.

(It is perhaps worth pointing out, however, that it is easy to overstress this contrast and to look, by way of explanation, for more profound cultural and structural differences between West and non-West than are in fact necessary to account for what happened. The advantage of initiative gained by Western peoples in being first may well have been of greater magnitude than the social and cultural peculiarities that made them first. There is doubtless something in the claim of non-Western nationalists who say that, although Western colonial enterprise may have contributed an initiative to overall economic development, it also inhibited the development of indigenous entrepreneurship simply by getting "in the way," quite apart from colonial policies favoring nationals of the metropolitan powers. Rather ironically, contemporary East Africans feel themselves excluded from business by entrenched Indian enterprise in somewhat the same way as an earlier generation of Indians in India felt themselves blocked by Englishmen!)

A second factor, related to the first, is that, being industrial latecomers with the Western example constantly before their eyes, and lacking a strong indigenous private enterprise, the new states have since independence tended to push development at a pace and in a fashion that required that much of the initiative remain in the hands of the state. The preindependence colonial governments, which tended to exercise a rather mercantilistic authority over the economies of the colonies, provided precedent for this way of doing things, which of course required expanded bureaucracies capable of the necessary planning and administration.

Finally, another result of the lateness of modernization in the new states is that modern commerce and industry themselves have come to them in later, more complex and large-scale forms in which the small individual entrepreneur is less prominent and the salaried executive more so than was the case in the West during comparable periods. This tendency is reinforced by the prominence in the economies of many new states of the large-scale production or extraction of raw materials for export. Even within "private business," therefore, many of the modern elite occupational roles are of the bureaucratic type, although of course as the economy expands, and in particular as the internal consumer market develops, there may arise new opportunities for individual enterprise in light industry and distributive trades.

All this is, of course, in the nature of a broad overview, and is subject to much local qualification and variation. India and Egypt, for example, have much more vigorous entrepreneurial groups than have, say, the African and most Southeast Asian countries, particularly if one excludes in the case of these latter countries such non-European immigrant merchant groups as Chinese, Indians, and Syrians. The former British dependencies in general, and India above all, are better supplied with trained civil servants than are other new states. Perhaps the most modern of all the states that have assumed sovereignty since World War II, in terms of the proportion of persons involved in modern occupational structures, is the Republic of the Philippines. On the other hand, some countries, like Indonesia and the Republic of the Congo (Leopoldville), came into nationhood with painful shortages of modern elites of all kinds. It is especially in this area of occupational modernization that differences in former colonial policies and practices make themselves felt. Britain's long, and relatively responsible (from the point of view of modernization), administration in India and the much briefer American administration in the Philippines left these countries with much more modernized occupational structures than did, for example, the long Dutch administration in Indonesia. It is in part for this reason that India, despite the apparently rigid nature of her traditional society, is today among the most modern of the new states.

Beyond such differences, however, a characteristic pattern remains: While there are developing in the new states the same broad types of modern elite occupations that appeared earlier in the West, the balance between the different groups —and in particular between bureaucrats and entrepreneurs— remains rather strikingly different.

Workers and Peasants. When we turn to the new industrial and commercial wage-labor force, we again find occupational roles broadly familiar to Western experience, but with important differences. To begin with, of course, this sector of the population remains small, by contemporary Western standards, in relation to the peasantry. But beyond this quantitative difference, the new wage workers, like the new elites, have come into existence under circumstances rather different from those in which their Western counterparts appeared. Like the new elites, they are mostly products of a more recent phase of modernization, in which the state has exercised greater initiative, or at any rate greater control, and in which technologically and organizationally more advanced—often larger-scale and more complex—forms have tended to be applied at the start. Although the governments of some new states—notably India—have for ideological reasons tried to encourage small-scale home industries, on the whole new states wishing to establish, say, a cotton textile industry, have equipped themselves with large factories and automatic machines rather than with spinning jennies. And governments, whether as state entrepreneurs or as custodians of the public welfare, have generally attempted, under the influence of modern welfare-state policies, to assure workers conditions of employment resembling as much as possible those of the modern West rather than those of the "dark, satanic mills" and Dickensian countinghouses of an earlier era.

Therefore, although the workers in the new states resemble their Western counterparts in becoming the occupants of full-time occupational roles played in differentiated occupational structures outside the family and local community, they have usually entered upon this condition under circumstances rather less productive of all those frustrations and anxieties that Marx subsumed under the term "alienation" than did the Western pioneers of industrial labor. There is an ample supply of alienated people in the new states; but industrial workers are not the most prominent among them, both because the industrial sector remains small and because workers tend to be relatively secure and prosperous in relation to their countrymen.[28]

Some of the political causes and consequences of these differences will be considered in the last section. Here we may usefully note one further area of variation: in the West, the early industrial labor force was in the main recruited from among persons for whom independent agriculture was not an alternative pursuit. The new factories were largely staffed by persons who had already become putting-out craftsmen or wage workers, either in towns or on the land, where wage work had gradually replaced the various forms of servile employment as the medieval manor was transformed into a modern "capitalist" estate. The Western worker of the eighteenth and early nineteenth centuries was usually, therefore, committed by sheer economic necessity to some form of wage employment. In the new states today, there are extremely great differences in the degree to which this is so. In some Asian and Near Eastern countries, even where land is held in some form of peasant proprietorship, overpopulation produces an "industrial reserve army" on a scale beyond even Marx's fertile imagination. One consequence, as Morris has pointed out for India, may be a labor force deeply committed to employment and urban life.[29] In many of the African countries, however, wage work competes for labor with individual cash-crop agriculture—often quite lucrative in cotton, coffee, and cocoa areas. The result is a widespread pattern of oscillation between farm and job, village and town, sometimes on a cycle of months or years, sometimes through daily "commuting," combining wages and cash-crop agriculture in whatever way the particular local circumstances make most profitable.[30] In such circumstances, a differentiated, deeply committed labor force is slow to develop; its absence, in turn, influences the degrees and kinds of industrialization that are possible.

We have already, in speaking of other sectors of the occupational system, said a number of things about agriculture in the new states. It is not quite accurate to suggest, as we did earlier, that agriculture represents simply a residuum of occupational traditionalism in societies the other sectors of whose populations are modernizing, for agriculture has not, of course, remained unaffected by the changes at work elsewhere. To be sure, there remain in many countries large numbers of free or tenant peasants engaged in what is essentially subsistence cultivation.

In many areas the plantation production of cash crops under the direction of either European settlers or enterprising indigenous gentry was an important early form of articulation with the international economy, and in some this remains true. In such cases country folk may come to form a kind of rural proletariat, depending upon wages for a livelihood but still living in varying degrees something like a village life. In other areas, including some in which plantation development was prominent earlier but has since independence been eliminated by land-redistribution programs, the independent cash-crop cultivator is the characteristic figure. In only a relatively few cases, however, such as the rubber areas of Malaya and the cocoa areas of West Africa, are independent cultivators coming to resemble modern farmers, systematically seeking to extract the maximum productivity from the land. More commonly, particularly where overpopulation is a problem, there is a tendency for peasant agriculture to become more and more labor-intensive in order to absorb the additional people—a tendency that might be characterized as "antimodern."[31] In general, then, it seems true that the agricultural populations of the new states remain the least influenced by modern occupational structures.

Schools. Thus far we have considered the modernization of the primary structure of stratification through the differentiation of new occupational structures. It remains to say a word about the secondary structure through which persons are allocated among roles.

As we noted earlier, normatively ascribed status—the allocation of occupational and other status-relevant roles in terms of kinship—was not so universal a feature of traditional societies as is sometimes assumed. Nevertheless, even in such comparatively open traditional societies as the Ottoman Empire, the relatively undifferentiated nature of the occupational system, and the scarcity of educational institutions capable of providing occupational training outside the family, meant that, in practice, occupational roles were learned by most persons within a kinship group. The development of extrafamilial educational structures, and of course the proliferation of occupational roles themselves, are largely responsible for the great increase in opportunities for mobility that comes with modernization, whatever the traditional setting in which the process occurs.

A number of factors have, however, combined to give schools and universities an even more important role in the modernization of the new states than they played in the earlier experience of the West. First of all here, as in the primary structure of stratification, the relative lateness of modernization has made a difference. The earlier, more primitive industries of the West were able to make more use of traditional craft skills, learned in the family or through personal apprenticeship. Early entrepreneurs were clever and ambitious artisans, merchants, and gentry, drawing more upon traditional skills and inventiveness than upon formal education.[32] Formal education played a role, particularly in the spread of basic literacy and in creating in the elite a greater receptivity to technological and social innovation, but it did not become the major channel of recruitment into managerial and industrial roles until relatively late. Government service, of course, was more closely related to formal education, but remained a relatively small sector of the occupational structure.

In the new states the transplantation from the West of relatively advanced forms of commerce, industry, and civil service, requiring greater and more specialized training, has given formal education a greater prominence from the start. The lack of educated persons has been viewed by governments as a major obstacle to more rapid development, and this has led them to invest heavily in educational expansion. In consequence, it is probably true that formal education has played a substantially more prominent role in occupational mobility in the new states than it did at comparable periods in the West. Whether this means that overall occupational mobility is greater in the new states—or at any rate in some of them —than it was in, say, late eighteenth- and nineteenth-century Western Europe is difficult to say, for we lack adequate data, but it may well be so. The allocation of occupation on the basis of education does not of itself, of course, mean equality of opportunity, for kinship groups may—always do to some degree—influence access to education. But this influence may well be less marked in many of the new states than at earlier periods in the West, for education in the new states, despite its missionary beginnings in many areas, is today much more the creature and creation of government than it has been in most Western countries until quite recently. The same popular demands that lead governments to expand education as a means to national development and individual opportunity also push them toward provision for equal access to it.

A further factor that tended to give greater prominence to formal education in the new states was the colonial setting in which the earlier phases of modernization took place. Quite apart from the intellectual content of their curricula, schools were the places where one learned the language and customs of the Europeans who dominated the new occupational structures and with whom, consequently, it was necessary to communicate effectively in order to succeed occupationally. Even with political independence and an increasing cultural indigenization of the new occupational structures, there has remained in most cases between them and the rest of the society a cultural gap, greater than that usually found in the West, where modern institutions are indigenous and hence clothed in familiar idiom, that the school plays a crucial role in bridging.

In some areas, the expansion of educational facilities in response to popular demand has run ahead of the growth and differentiation of the occupational system, with the result that large numbers of persons enter the labor market with expectations of employment that the occupational system cannot fulfill. The point here is not, as is sometimes suggested, that the content of education makes persons unfit for the jobs available to them; a secondary-school education does not of itself make a man less fit to be a truck driver or even a peasant farmer. The sense of grievance felt by the underemployed secondary-school or university graduate results, rather, from the fact that governments in the new states are held directly responsible for the welfare and progress of their people in a way that was less true in the West during comparable phases of modernization. In facing these responsibilities, governments find it easier to expand educational facilities than employment opportunities, and this results in a constant decline in the market value of education. In consequence, the educated underemployed or unemployed are in many of the new states a more serious source of alienation and political disaffection than are industrial workers.

Cultural Modernization: Religion and Science

These structural changes, centering upon the differentiation of occupational and educational systems, do not exhaust the processes of modernization that are at work in the social stratification systems of the new states. If we are more fully to comprehend these processes, we must also examine the changes that take place in culture—in the systems of belief and value by means of which persons relate participation in the new occupational structures to their aspirations for themselves and their countries. Indeed, there is an important sense in which the new occupational structures are not of significance to social stratification at all except insofar as this happens. The vertical dimension—the dimension of relative worth that we commonly regard as central to the very notion of social stratification—comes into being only insofar as persons interpret and evaluate roles in terms of some common culture.

This is not, of course, to say that the initiative for change lies wholly on the side of culture and that culture is the dominant force in shaping stratification systems. To say so would be to attribute to it an unwarranted degree of solidity and autonomy, and to ignore the pressure structural change can exert upon ideas. In actual societies there is rather a constant interplay between the structure of social relations, based upon proximate mutual understandings and expectations, and those more general common understandings concerning the larger meaning and worth of social relations that tend to develop in societies. Especially in societies of the complexity of those we are considering here, change may in varying degrees "originate" in either the sphere of ideological creativity or in the network of social relations. Compelling new ideas may call forth new kinds of social relations; new kinds of social relations, entered into by individuals with little thought concerning their larger meaning, may assume such magnitude that they challenge the existing consensus concerning the meaning and purpose of human endeavor. But seldom, if ever, can important changes be understood in either purely cultural or purely social terms.

In the modernization of stratification in the new states, however, structural changes have generally run ahead of cultural ones, for the new occupational structures we have been discussing were in large part introduced through the initiative of Western empire builders, entrepreneurs, and missionaries. New institutions were in many cases quite literally "transplanted," presenting members of non-Western societies with opportunities to participate in new roles in business firms, bureaucracies, plantations, mines and, perhaps most important of all, schools—structures whose affairs were managed in Western terms—before traditional cultures had had an opportunity to interpret and evaluate them. It is this element of abrupt confrontation, resulting from the relatively sudden expansion of Western power in the eighteenth and nineteenth centuries, that has led so many writers to use terms like "Western impact" and "Western challenge" in describing the modernization of the non-Western world.

There was, to be sure, an important element of this in the

modernization of the West itself, for societies and cultures never change all of a piece, even when the impulse for change comes largely from within. Traditional Western culture, too, felt itself "confronted" in the course of modernization by new and disturbing forces; traditional elites felt themselves threatened by "new men." And, in the non-Western world, the abruptness of the "challenge" varied a good deal with the time and circumstances of contact. In India and Indonesia, for example, the relationship with the West developed much more gradually and over a longer time than it did in Africa, where a fully industrialized West quite suddenly, in the late nineteenth century, burst in upon the previously more or less isolated interior. In Egypt and the other lands of the old Ottoman Empire, which had always been in relatively close contact with the West and which in most cases never became fully colonial, cultural engagement came to a much greater extent contemporaneously with structural innovation, or even preceded it in some respects. But because modernization occurred first in the West and was everywhere, to one degree or another, imported from the West to non-Western countries, the traditional cultures of the latter have all faced the problem of coming to terms rather abruptly with kinds of activities and social relations that were not only different from those familiar to traditional societies but that also had developed out of an alien tradition and came backed by alien power.

It is against this background that we must try to compare the movements of thought and ideology that have been associated with the emergence of modern occupational structures in the West and in the new states.

The West: Innovative Utilitarianism. In modern Western societies the new occupational structures have achieved a culturally dominant position in stratification systems in the sense that occupational performance has come to be generally accepted as the primary criterion of merit. This does not, of course, mean that there is anything like perfectly open recruitment to occupational roles or that nonoccupational criteria, such as patterns of behavior, speech, and style of life, often acquired through socialization in the family and hence of an ascribed nature, are not taken into account in persons' judgments of their own and others' status. These do indeed remain important features of the secondary structure and culture of stratification in the West, as we mentioned earlier. But at the heart of the modern Western culture of stratification there lies a commitment to the notion that the truly admirable man is the one who "does a job well," particularly an economically and socially useful job in one of the new occupational structures.

It is important to recognize that there are two distinct, though related, values involved in this commitment: equality of opportunity and productivity. While the first tends to be more prominent as a moral and political issue, the second is perhaps more fundamental as a characteristic of specifically *modern* Western culture, as Parsons and others have pointed out.[33] From the characteristically modern attitude that human life is subject to constant improvement through the application of intelligence and diligence,[34] the notion that talent should receive its opportunity to contribute to this process follows as a kind of corollary. But advancement according to merit can also be a feature of quite traditionalistic societies and can be applied in relation to quite traditionalistic ends, as we have seen in the case of the empire of the Ottoman sultans. Another well-known example is, of course, the traditional Chinese bureaucracy. It is the innovative utilitarianism of the modern West that is the most distinctive cultural counterpart and expression of its occupationally oriented stratification system and that underlies the high prestige within it of the entrepreneur and the engineer.

Much scholarship has been devoted to tracing the development of this element in modern Western culture. Max Weber has stressed the role of the Protestant Reformation in creating a spirit of "this-worldly asceticism" conducive to systematic, rationalistic devotion to a calling. An equally important and complementary development, clearly, was the deistic modus vivendi between Christianity and natural science that was arrived at during the seventeenth and eighteenth centuries. Although the notion that the truth is revealed not in God's word but in his work[35] did not by any means dispose of all the theological and philosophical problems posed by the existence within a single culture of these two bodies of thought, it did provide, and continues to provide, a tolerable personal solution for vast numbers of Western people.

In these terms it has been possible to believe not only that science and religion are compatible but also that the discovery of the laws of nature is actually a religiously sanctioned duty, a means of glorifying the Creator of the great ordered system of the universe. The application of science to practical technology could similarly be viewed as the fulfillment of the purposes of a rational and benevolent God. These ideas might even be extended beyond technology to society itself through the notion that the ultimate product of rationally ordered creation was rational man himself, destined by God's will to discover through reason the proper ordering of his society.[36] The Lutheran elimination of sacramental magic and the development of biblical criticism also contributed to the reconciliation of science and religion. Thus, a religious tradition continuous with the medieval past could take part in the formation of a new culture of stratification that admired and inspired the innovator.

Some such rapprochement between the religious ideas that move men most deeply and scientific technology is clearly required if modern occupational structures are to become fully "at home" in a society—if they are to become central to its stratification system in the sense of engaging the ambition and admiration of its members. Nowhere in the new states has such a reconciliation been completely achieved (nor, of course, has it in the West, though the process has doubtless gone further there), but everywhere the two sets of ideas seem to be at work upon each other. The attractions of modernity in terms of power and welfare appear to be too great to permit it to be rejected out of hand. But neither do traditional cultures and the traditional elites that sustain and are sustained by them simply melt away in the face of modern ideas and forms of organization. Nor are differences among traditions irrelevant to an understanding of the modernization of stratification. The triumph of modernity may indeed be in some sense inevitable in the long run, but the problems encountered along the way seem to differ rather markedly in different traditional settings, and these differences promise to influence the shapes that modernity will ultimately take in the various new states.

India: Syncretism. Perhaps the most interesting case is that of

India, with its apparent paradox of, on the one hand, traditional mysticism bound up with a unique social rigidity and, on the other, one of the most modernized occupational structures of all the new states. Part of the explanation, no doubt, lies in the long duration and peculiar depth of British influence, but this can hardly account for a situation in which so many leaders of the drive toward modernity have found it possible to draw inspiration for their efforts from precisely that religious tradition which has seemed to so many observers to be so inimical to the modern spirit.

Whatever other factors may be involved, part of the answer undoubtedly lies in the extraordinary pluralism of the Indian religious tradition, encouraged by the fragmentation of Indian society into countless endogamous groups and by its loose association with the central organization of the polity during several centuries of Mogul and British rule. The former provided an extremely rich and diverse body of cultural resources for reinterpretation in modern terms, while the latter freed higher culture from a too intimate, rigidifying involvement with a particular political structure, at any rate above the local village level, where the caste system was primarily rooted. Singer has pointed out that scholarly Western interpretations of Indian religion, including that of Weber, have commonly overemphasized the dominance, under Brahman leadership, of the otherworldly renunciation aspect of Hinduism, neglecting those religious traditions, more hospitable to economic enterprise, that were associated with the merchant castes.[37] In modern times, Gandhi has been able to draw from the Bhagavad-Gita inspiration for a movement that, if not specifically technological and economic in its aims— indeed, in some respects quite the opposite—has nevertheless been strikingly successful in harnessing traditional asceticism to the very this-worldly task of nation-building. Other modern intellectual and political leaders have found in the same tradition support for a full-scale attack on the problems of industrialization through socialist planning, leading Singer to propose, paraphrasing Weber, a study of "The Hindu Ethic and the Spirit of Socialism."[38]

One cannot, of course, expect to find in any of the new states a cult of the private entrepreneur of the sort that developed in the nineteenth-century West. As we have seen, the structural situation is all against it, as is nationalist ideology, which tends to associate capitalism with Western domination. The modern elites of the new states, like their economies, are inevitably "mixed"; entrepreneurs must yield much of the task of representing modernity to bureaucrats and politicians.

All of which does not, of course, mean that there remains no tension between Indian religion and cultural modernity. The magic and mysticism of popular Hinduism are still real enough. And within the body of modern Indian thought there are important strains between the more secular, technocratic planners and the Gandhians, for whom technological modernization can never be an end in itself and must often take second place to other values.[39] One has the impression, however, that, in one way or another, most Indians who occupy modern elite occupational roles have found ways of relating these activities meaningfully to personal and national aspirations that they feel are informed by Hindu tradition. Perhaps the very luxuriant diversity of that tradition itself reduces the need for more complete cultural synthesis, making it easier for modern entrepreneurs and civil servants to share high prestige in the eyes of the same public with representatives of traditional saintliness. What many observers of the Indian scene feel is, from a political standpoint, a dangerous tendency toward disunity may also be a valuable source of cultural flexibility.

In all the new states, the interaction between traditional culture and the ideas associated with technological and occupational modernization is complicated by the historical association of the latter with Western imperialism, to the struggle against which the new states owe their very existence. A satisfactory synthesis therefore requires some form of ideological separation of modernity as a national goal from its specifically Western associations. Here again the Indian tradition of diversity and syncretism appears to have made this relatively easy, enabling Indian modernizers to innovate while retaining a deep sense of national identity and continuity—indeed, allowing them to develop a certain sense of mission to "save the West from itself" by demonstrating to Westerners the proper uses of modernity. This attitude is common in the writings of Tagore and Gandhi and in the pronouncements of contemporary Indian political leaders.

Islam: Double-mindedness. The Moslem peoples of the Near East, on the other hand, appear to have found both the reconciliation of modernity which traditional culture and its separation from the humiliating association with Western domination somewhat more difficult. At first sight this seems rather surprising. The Islamic world certainly shares with the West more of the classical background of modern thought, both religious and philosophical, than did Hindu India, and medieval Islam itself was a good deal more rationalistic, less magical in content, than Hinduism. Indeed, orthodox Islam, with its austere monotheism and legalistic rigor, was doubtless the most rationalistic of all the traditional world religions. But the very closeness of the Islamic association with the West over many centuries and the particularly humiliating nature of the later phases of this association, involving the decay of Ottoman power and a peculiarly rapacious and degrading pattern of Western domination, with few of the redeeming features of responsible colonialism, seems to have left modern Islam in a posture of defensiveness from which it has found it difficult to contribute a substantial religious element to Near Eastern modernist thought. Gibb has characterized "the attitude of the vast majority of the orthodox *'ulamâ',*" the body of the professionally learned, as

a strict and unbending refusal to countenance any kind of truckling to the new philosophies and sciences. For them, these are all nothing but *ahwâ'*—velleities, caprices, unsubstantial imaginings of the rebellious human mind, or satanic devices to ensnare the heedless and foolish. A thousand years ago their ancestors met the assault of Greek philosophy in the same spirit and stood their ground. If Islam is a divine revelation, as they believe, history will repeat itself: the forces of materialsm, which the Divine Providence has permitted for a time to tempt and mislead the sick-hearted and the hypocrites, will surely be overcome. . . . It is not to be wondered at that to the generality of *'ulamâ'* the West stands for pure materialism.[40]

This is not to say, of course, that Islam has lacked modernist thinkers, merely that their success as synthesizers of the traditional and the modern has thus far not been so great as that of their counterparts in Hindu India. The case of the Egyptian Shaikh Mohammed Abdu, whom students of recent Islamic intellectual history speak of as the ablest and most influential of the modernists, is instructive in this regard. A student, and later a teacher, at the university mosque of al-Azhar who rose at the turn of the century to the office of Mufti of Egypt, Mohammed Abdu attempted in his own writings to reconcile Islamic theology with modern science, in a way rather reminiscent of eighteenth-century Western deism, and used his influence to press for the inclusion of scientific subjects in the curriculum at al-Azhar. He was however, unable to carry the Egyptian 'ulamâ' with him on either score, despite his eminence, and Gibb remarks that his influence has largely been confined to the educated laity. This imperviousness of the 'ulamâ' to modern thought has been reinforced by their cohesiveness as the official exponents of the *shari'a*—the body of sacred law, drawn from the Koran and the traditions of the Prophet, which Islamic orthodoxy has regarded as a full and sufficient rule for life.

At the same time, there has grown up in Near Eastern countries a separate modern, secular educational system that inherits much of the prestige traditionally enjoyed by learning in Islamic lands and that educates members of the new political and technological elites. The result has been a rather sharp bifurcation between traditional and modern elites, and a marked tendency on the part of the latter toward what Gibb calls "double-mindedness." In Turkey, the heartland of the Ottoman Empire (and not, of course, a "new state" in the strict sense), this tendency toward disengagement of serious Islamic thought from the problems of modernity has been carried to an extreme by a thoroughgoing secularization.[41] Popular piety, of course, has continued to play an important role throughout the Near East in nationalist and pan-Arab enthusiasm, and even most members of the modern elites (at least outside Turkey) seem to remain attached to Islamic belief in some form. But, cut off as it is by the intransigence of the 'ulamâ' toward serious concern with modern problems, professional theology contributes little to this personal piety, which consequently tends either to express itself in mysticism, sometimes drawing upon the traditions of sufism, or else to become a kind of religious veneer for political nationalism.

Nowhere in the non-Western world do the traditional religious cultures easily find common ground with modern scientific and social thought, or traditional elites with modern
ones—nor, we should remind ourselves, have they done so
in the West. Everywhere in the modern world there exists
among intellectuals in particular—but also among modern
elites of other kinds—a strong affinity for secular ideologies
that are more easily reconciled with modernity. Still, everywhere, East and West, the religious cultures of the medieval
past and the religious systems that informed them continue,
even when specifically religious commitment has been lost and
traditional elites swept aside, to play an important role in
giving modern men a sense of identity and historical continuity—a sense of national and personal purpose and self-
esteem that is of particular importance in a period of heightened national self-consciousness. When new elites take their
places beside the old, or even displace them, the new men, so
long as the rupture is not total, can draw upon the sentiments
embodied in the traditional stratification systems in support
of their own positions.

Looking at the new states of Asia and the Near East, and at
the West itself, it is deceptively easy to become impressed by
the alienation of modern elites from traditional culture or by
the shallowness of their allegiance to it; to appreciate how
important it still is in those areas, it is instructive to turn, by
way of contrast, to the new states of Africa that lack such
traditional cultures—lack, that is to say, traditional literary
cultures based upon world religions.

Africa: The Search for Continuity. Those African countries
that lie to the south of the Sudan belt and the Ethiopian highlands—that is to say, beyond the reach of premodern Islamic
and Christian influence—have great difficulty relating themselves to the traditional African past. Having acquired their
boundaries through European diplomacy, they are often extremely heterogeneous ethnically and linguistically. Underlying cultural unity certainly exists over large areas of the
continent: For example, the speakers of Bantu and related
languages, who occupy a very large part of sub-Saharan Africa,
are very closely related historically and share many elements

of common culture. But, not being embodied in supertribal
literature and religion, these common elements are difficult
for elites to utilize in the creation of common cultures for the
new states. Culturally and linguistically akin though they often are, the traditional states and tribes tended in the past,
and tend today, to confront one another as sovereign entities.
The positions of their traditional elites—the kings, chiefs,
and religious practitioners—always rest upon loyalties that
from the point of view of the new states tend to be divisive.
It is therefore not surprising that in many African countries
the system of stratification reveals a particularly sharp cleavage between traditional-tribal and national-modern elites and
that "the tribal question" assumes great political prominence.

Rather paradoxically, the more the traditional elites succeed in modernizing themselves, the more divisive their influence becomes, for this merely serves to associate the desire
for modernity with traditional state and tribal loyalties, thus
sapping their peoples' loyalty to the wider society and polity.
An excellent example is provided by the Kingdom of Buganda, which forms the geographical core and contains between one-quarter and one-third of the population of the
soon-to-be independent British protectorate of Uganda. The
Baganda are among the most modernized of Africa's peoples;
they enjoy a high level of education, have a relatively advanced and prosperous agricultural economy, and a government that is relatively modern and efficient, being served by
a corps of quite well-trained civil servants. Baganda physicians, lawyers, and teachers have taken their places alongside
the chiefly hierarchy, itself now manned by educated persons,
to form a single elite in the eyes of the people. But all this has
merely served to make the kingdom more "indigestible" from
the point of view of Uganda as a whole. Most Baganda, viewing the traditional kingdom as the natural vehicle for modernization, have stubbornly refused to give their loyalty to a
wider national unit.[42] Similar tendencies have been exhibited
by such West African peoples as the Ashanti, the Yoruba,
and the Bakongo.

One consequence of this pattern has been to present modern African leaders with particularly difficult problems in
"cultural management"—in the creation of bodies of ideas

and beliefs that would persuasively express a sense of nation
hood and legitimate their own leadership in the drive toward
modernity. The new elites' common culture, and even their
very language of communication with each other, are often
acquired in mission schools and are taken directly from the
West as the Smythes have noted in their study of the Nigerian
elite.[43] But this tends to be an ideologically unsatisfying situation, both because it provides no symbols in terms of which
the elite may relate themselves to their people and because it
tends to perpetuate a sense of dependence upon the West,
particularly galling to Africans who have experienced four
hundred years of Western negrophobia. The new states of
Africa and their modern elites must therefore perform a
rather staggering feat of cultural creativity: They must, in
addition to solving the problems of modernity, create a sense
of national unity and self-respect without the resources of
unifying tradition with which their Asian and Near Eastern
counterparts have had to work. Such vague conceptions as
"negritude," "African personality," and "African Socialism"
represent early responses to this problem as does President
Nkrumah's attempt to create a synthetic Ghanaian culture by
combining symbols drawn from various traditional tribal
cultures.

It is perhaps worth pointing out, however, that this lack of
traditional roots also has its positive side. If the Africans lack
the cultural resources of tradition, they also are unencum-
bered by it. If they can solve the problems of continuity and
cohesion, their very rootlessness may enable them to respond
more flexibly to the problems of modernity and to maintain
societies that are more open.

The Politics of Equality

We may now return to the problem with which we began:
the relationship between stratification and politics in the
process of modernization. Politics—the distribution of the authority to make binding decisions—is not the same thing as
stratification, as we noted earlier, but is related to stratification
in important ways. As we have seen, political values and roles
are part of the culture and structure of stratification, and political processes influence the distribution of persons through
the stratification system. But the relationship is a reciprocal

one; the pattern of politics is itself influenced by stratification, and it is this aspect of the matter that we will explore in this final section.

From the point of view of the uses and limitations of the Western experience of modernization as a guide to an understanding of contemporary events in the new states, this aspect is of particular interest, for what we may call the "politics of equality" have been a central feature of the modernization of the West in a way that has deeply influenced our thinking about what modernization in the generic sense means. Equality and inequality, in their various meanings, have been key concepts in our thought about recent Western political history, and we tend, almost without thinking, to cast them in a similar role when we consider the affairs of the new states. We may appropriately ask ourselves, however, how accurate the parallel really is—how far the circumstances that made stratification the kind of issue it has been in the modernization of Western politics are present in the new states today.

The politics characteristic of modern societies tend toward egalitarianism in three ways: First, they tend to be populistic. Political participation—membership in the civil society—is widely diffused. It is in principle a property of every adult person. The legitimacy of political acts rests upon the degree to which they may be represented as reflecting the "will of the people." There are, of course, societies that are modern in the sense of being highly industrialized and possessing modern occupational systems but in which effective power is held by a tiny political elite. But even these modern totalitarian regimes are populistic in ideology, claiming that their actions reflect the "real" or "objective" popular will unclouded by "subjective considerations," and are concerned to demonstrate this by securing the symbols of popular approval through manipulation and coercion. They differ from traditional authoritarianisms precisely in feeling the necessity to require their people to participate by actively consenting to political acts; traditional authoritarianisms required only that the people obey.

Second, modern politics, whether liberal-democratic or totalitarian, are egalitarian in the sense that one of the principal objects and justifications of politics is assumed to be a constant improvement in the social and material welfare of the common man. Material inequalities are justified on the ground that they provide incentives for extraordinary effort—effort that will be more productive of general material welfare than greater immediate material equality would be. The imposition of material hardships, as in the "forced-draft" industrialization programs of the Soviet Union and Communist China, are justified on the ground that they will result in great future comfort and well-being for the masses. Traditional authorities, too, often assumed the burden of promoting the national wealth and power through military conquest and the manipulation of trade, but modern polities are expected to do more: whether through state planning or laissez-faire (or, more commonly, of course, through some mixture of the two) they assume responsibility for promoting constant progress through technological and social innovation.

Finally, modern politics is egalitarian in that the state, again whether it is totalitarian or liberal-democratic, assumes responsibility for furthering equality of opportunity—responsibility for creating conditions, including most prominently widespread educational opportunities, which will allow talent to find its own place in the occupational system. There have, as we have seen, been traditional societies in which elites were relatively open to talent, but the undifferentiated nature of the occupational systems and the smallness of the elites in such societies made equality of opportunity highly theoretical for most of their members. Only in modern societies is it possible for the placement of most persons in the occupational system to be a matter for aspiration and choice, and only in such societies, consequently, can the state assume the burden of encouraging mobility for all.

All these features of modern politics follow more or less directly from the processes of structural differentiation and cultural modernization that we discussed in previous sections. All three aspects of egalitarianism just listed—populism, utilitarianism, and equality of opportunity—are logically related to the cultural commitment to progress through science and technology. The structural differentiation of occupational systems draws ordinary persons to some degree out of the matrix of local and kinship ties and makes them available for participation in a wider polity. Schools and the occupational structure itself provide vehicles for personal and group ambition and progress. All this seems generic to modernity everywhere.

Modern polities are thus characteristically populistic, progressive, and friendly to mobility, but they differ in the degree to which they are liberal-democratic or totalitarian. The new states aspire to modern egalitarianism in the senses discussed above, though they do not yet enjoy the conditions for its full achievement, and most of them also aspire—or at any rate began by aspiring—to liberal democracy. It is therefore of interest to recall some of the ways in which political egalitarianism, democratic liberalism, and totalitarianism have been related in the history of the West and to ask how far these relationships are or are not paralleled in the contemporary development of the new states. Again we must draw up an outline that greatly simplifies events but may have the virtue of serving as a model for comparative purposes.

The West: The Democratization of the Estates. The traditional societies out of which the modern West grew were "highly stratified" in several senses. The elites were small and the common people were many. Wealth was highly concentrated in the hands of the feudal aristocracy, as also was political participation. The polity as a whole was highly decentralized, since sovereignty was distributed, along with rights in land, among a network of aristocratic lords and vassals, but, as between this landholding aristocracy and the peasants, authority was highly unilateral, the peasants often occupying a status of legal unfreedom and having recourse to no justice beyond that of the lord.

So far there is little here that is unusual in the general range of peasant societies. The legal details of European feudalism are not, of course, repeated elsewhere, but the pattern of a large, dependent peasantry supporting a small political and economic elite is common to peasant societies everywhere. Beyond this, however, there was in traditional Europe another kind of inequality that has not been so common elsewhere: Between the peasantry and the aristocracy there developed a cultural differentiation that became very marked. This was not merely a differentiation between "high culture" and "folk culture"; literary culture was pursued not so much by the lay aristocracy as by the church. Rather it was a differentiation between the culture of the peasantry, rooted in the cycle of agricultural life, and that of the mounted knight, the cavalier. The culture of chivalry, centering upon the glorification of military prowess and status honor, drew upon religion, as also did that of the peasant villages. But the two subcultures drew from medieval Christianity different ideals, and integrated these into quite different styles of life and views of the world. Between the two there was a hereditary gulf; aristocratic and peasant status and culture were "in the blood," in principle immutable. What was an appropriate model of virtue for the noble was not an appropriate one for the peasant—in fact, was forbidden to him.

Of course this is an oversimplified picture. Besides the peasantry and aristocracy there were the clergy and the merchants and craftsmen of the towns, both in some degree open to mobility. And there were not just two great status groups, but several lesser ones as well. Both aristocracy and peasantry were subdivided in significant ways. Finally, the estates were, of course, crosscut by vertical ties of personal loyalty. But the fact of elaborate cultural differentiation, associated with self-conscious hereditary status, remains.

Next, we may ask: Through what processes have these traditional, highly stratified Western societies become the modern, relatively egalitarian ones of today? The modernization of the West was, first of all, preceded—perhaps it would be better to say "introduced"—by a period of political centralization and expansion of trade. The latter resulted in a growth in the numbers and wealth of the merchants and craftsmen in the towns, the former in the strengthening of the patrimonial element in the medieval state at the expense of the feudal. Both increased the opportunities for mobility. Then, in the eighteenth and nineteenth centuries, the modernization of agriculture and the growth of urban industries produced an increasingly large class of wage laborers, no longer tied to persons of higher status as personal dependents. These changes also further increased the numbers and wealth of the entrepreneurial class. All this was accompanied by increasing demands for wider political participation and state intervention on behalf of welfare and wider educational opportunity—in short, for those features of political egalitarianism that, we suggested earlier, are typically modern.

But what, in the course of all these changes, became of the cultural stratification so characteristic of the traditional West, and how does this relate to the growth of political egalitarianism? Certainly the cultural stratification did not disappear; its descendants are still with us in the form of the modern class cultures described by Richard Hoggart, Nancy Mitford, and William Lloyd Warner, and, of course, by countless novelists.[44] Particularly since the decline of differential political rights, and the rise in general affluence, these subtle differences of speech, behavior, and style of life are in many ways the most tangible aspects of stratification, the sweetest fruits of personal success and the bitterest of failure.

It seems not unreasonable to suggest, as of course many others have suggested, that this cultural stratification has in important ways conditioned the modernization of politics in the West. What seems to have happened was something like this: As the hereditary estates of traditional Europe were gradually transformed into the much more fluid classes of today, the traditional cultural differentiations were carried over into modern life to form the basis for modern class cultures and modern class consciousness in politics—not, of course, without undergoing important transformations. Peasant culture must have contributed importantly to the new urban proletarian cultures that formed one of the bases for the working-class solidarity expressed in trade-union and socialist movements.

This is not, of course, to suggest that economic and political grievances were not also important, along with the break in the personal tie between superior and subordinate and the separation of working life from domestic life, in producing a sense of alienation in the working classes. It does seem likely, however, that the sense of solidarity that directed working-class energies in part into labor and socialist movements instead of into individual striving for mobility—a solidarity that also, of course, made individual mobility more difficult, since there was solidarity above as well as below—also owed something to this cultural differentiation. Richard Hoggart argues persuasively that the contemporary erosion of English working-class culture by the mass media, in addition, of course, to the achievements of the welfare state, tend to rob the working class of its leadership and sense of community.[45] It is also significant that the period of greatest class consciousness and of the greatest strength of socialist ideology in the American labor movement coincided with the period of mass immigration from abroad into urban industries—the period when the American working class was most differentiated culturally from the other segments of society. Thus, for a certain period, ethnicity played a role in American stratification somewhat analogous to that of class culture in Europe.

The traditional aristocratic culture, too, had a further career, interacting with the burgeoning bourgeois culture of achievement in various ways to produce the cultures of modern Western elites. In general, as mobility came to be more and more a matter of wealth, the bourgeois culture of sober, competitive striving and the aristocratic culture of cultivation and noblesse oblige became successive steps in the careers of successful families, even in the United States where there was little direct continuity with the traditional system of estates.[46] Thus, in different ways both "lower" and "higher" class cultures and class consciousness conditioned the movement toward egalitarianism.

The political institutions within which the politics of equality developed in the West were also shaped by the stratification system of the medieval past. Indeed, the stratification system might be said to have provided the framework for the medieval state. In the medieval parliaments, representatives of the estates—nobility, clergy, and urban burgesses—held established rights and obligations vis-à-vis their kings. In particular the larger vassals, the barons, enjoyed as individuals substantial autonomy within their fiefs, and as members of corporate bodies exercised constitutional checks upon royal power.[47] During the period of centralization at the end of the Middle Ages, these institutions were threatened by the growing power of the kings and their patrimonial bureaucracies. In England they survived the attempted absolutism of the Stuarts and the upheavals of the Cromwellian period, and under the settlement of 1688 a constitutional pattern was arrived at that recognized the authority of parliament and established a framework for representative government.

Thus it was possible over the centuries, through the extension of the franchise, to absorb into what had begun as an aristocratic institution an ever widening circle of political participants. Medieval local government bodies, based upon the shires and boroughs, also survived to become modern representative local governments. These accommodations were both stimulated and faciliated by the increasing openness of the English aristocracy, which was thus able to maintain the tradition of responsible aristocratic political leadership while admitting to its privileges and responsibilities increasing numbers of recruits from below.[48] Thus was created the modern British "establishment"—diverse in its social origin but nevertheless a "status group" in the sense of being united by a feeling of common tradition and purpose, including, most importantly, a devotion to both equality and liberal democracy.[49] The occasional challenges to its modern legitimacy on the ground of insufficient devotion to equality would seem to be the price of a constitutional and social structural continuity that nourishes liberal democracy.

The difference in the manner in which these processes developed in England and France has been regarded by many of the most perceptive students of political modernity in the West as a kind of natural laboratory in which to observe the relationship between equality and political democracy. In France the continuity with traditional constitutional institutions based upon the estates was much more severely interrupted. By the end of the eighteenth century, as Tocqueville shows, centralization had gone so far throughout most of the country that neither national nor provincial assemblies were capable of revival.[50] The independence of both the nobles and the burgesses had been destroyed, though the former retained their privileges and exclusiveness and hence attracted the envy and hatred of both the latter and the peasants. The alternative to autocratic centralism, therefore, was not the reestablishment of the traditional constitution, as Burke had urged[51]— this, Tocqueville says, was no longer possible. The alternative was populistic centralism, and in the revolution France was the scene of the first experience of what Talmon calls "totalitarian democracy."[52] Large masses of people were politically activated by a millennial egalitarian ideology enunciated by dedicated leaders. All mediating political structures, in terms of which constitutional adjustments in the direction of equality might have taken place, having been destroyed previously by royal encroachment, the leaders ruled by acclamation. "Nothing had been left that could obstruct the central government," says Tocqueville:

but by the same token nothing could shore it up. That is why the grandiose edifice built up by our kings was doomed to collapse like a house of cards once disturbances arose in the social order upon which it was based.[53]

The necessity for a radical break with the past in the pursuit of equality, instead of its gradual accommodation within continuing political institutions, left French society deeply divided into mutually hostile segments, a situation that ever since has tended to make stable democratic governments difficult.

Elsewhere in Europe and in the European settlements overseas there were other variations in the pattern of development of the politics of equality out of the highly stratified societies of the past, variations we need not trace further. Enough has been said to make the major point that concerns us; namely, that both the pattern of cultural stratification and the related political structure the West inherited from its peculiar medieval past deeply influenced the manner in which the politics of equality developed in the West.

To sum up rather crudely: The ascriptive and culturally differentiated stratification of the estates both stimulated and directed the rising egalitarian sentiments of individuals and groups. The different patterns of interaction between this drive toward equality and the political democratization of the medieval political framework seem to have produced in the West varying degrees of attachment to liberal democracy. We clearly should not expect that the politics of equality will develop in the same manner—that the same elements will play the same roles—in societies in which the traditional background is different in major respects.

The Politics of Equality in the New States. The Ottoman Empire, which provided the immediate historical setting for the development of the politics of equality in the Near East, differed radically from traditional Europe, both in its political structure and in its pattern of stratification, as our earlier out-line will have made clear. It was more egalitarian than tradi-tional Europe in the sense that there was more mobility into the higher levels of the political structure. But the highly centralized and autocratic nature of the state, upon which this mobility depended, precluded the development of a con-stitutional balance of powers within the body politic. Occu-pational and ethnic corporations did, to be sure, enjoy sub-stantial internal self-government, but these were not bound together in any framework of mutual responsibility for the polity as a whole. Neither was a group consciousness and sense of common responsibility for the whole lodged in a group of great families; the latter existed but they had no constitutional place. Even a solid social and cultural legitimacy seems to have been denied them. These qualities of a politically re-sponsible status group were found rather in the two great arms of the Ottoman State—the imperial administrative ser-vice (including the janissary military forces) and the judicial-religious body, the 'ulamâ'. Both were, in what Gibb calls the "Golden Age" of the empire—the sixteenth century—aristoc-racies of education and training rather than of birth, and their legitimacy as the administrators of Islamic universalism rested at least in part upon that fact.[54]

When, therefore, during the later period of the empire, the central authority weakened and tendencies toward hereditary oligarchy developed in the administrative service, these ten-dencies, instead of producing a responsible, legitimate hered-itary aristocracy, appeared rather as a corruption of a pre-viously more open society and an affront to religion. The association of this oligarchy with increasing European domi-nation during the period of decay served to further discredit it. Attempts at reform and the reassertion of central authority by the sultans and their viceroys in Egypt during the nine-teenth century served only, under the conditions then pre-vailing, to increase European influence. They also sometimes served, as for example did Mohammed Ali's oppressive pro-gram for forcing the commercial cultivation of cotton in Egypt, to stimulate populist and antiregime sentiments among the people.[55] Finally, the idea of nationality, perhaps spread from Europe where it was at the same time undermining the legitimacy of the Hapsburgs, gave focus to these resentments and anxieties.[56] The result was the dissolution of the Ottoman realm into a series of nation-states, often with an interlude of European administration.

In this setting, the politics of equality have tended to be expressed in ethnic nationalism, often backed by Islamic religious sentiments, and in antagonism to the remnants of Ottoman rule, to oppressive landlords, to the cosmopolitan foreign business interests that grew up during the last century of the empire and, of course, to European domination. With the defeat of these forces, however, the nationalist movements find difficulty in organizing effective constitutional polities, for Near Eastern societies tend to lack internal differentiation along lines that might find expression in parliamentary party organization. (It is of some interest in this regard that perhaps the most successful constitutional regime in the area is that of Lebanon, where the diversity of religious groups has provided a political framework.) There is no tradition of a cohesive, responsible, legitimate aristocracy; proletarian movements, as so often in the new states, are led by intellectuals and are more expressive of nationalism and intellectual alienation than of independent class interests. The 'ulamâ' having thus far rejected the very idea of modernity, are in no position to provide a responsible lead in coping with its problems. In these circumstances, political energy tends in many cases to be directed outward into international affairs—into, for example, the pursuit of Pan-Arab unity—at the expense of attention to the problems of internal modernization.

The most successful mode of political organization in the area has been the military regime, backed by the civil bureaucracy. It is perhaps not far-fetched to see here an element of continuity with the past.[57] Like the administrative service of the empire, these are often open status groups: united by common education, outlook, and discipline, and open to mobility. They also contain the largest available body of persons with the technical knowledge relevant to the tasks of modernization.

India presents an entirely different picture. Where the Near Eastern polities are formlessly and sometimes somewhat aimlessly populistic, modern India, as we would expect from her traditional stratification system, is intricately crisscrossed by lines of differentiation along which political energies flow with vigor and purpose. Traditional Indian society was of course even more highly stratified than was the medieval West, in the sense that a greater number of closed groups were recognized and the structure of inequality was more fundamentally underwritten by religion. But the highly local nature of most of the castes, and their divorce, at least in recent centuries, from the central organization of the polity, prevented the development of a single national hierarchy of broad strata on the Western pattern. Their even more closed, corporate character made it difficult for modern egalitarian tendencies to express themselves in intercaste mobility, although of course the growth of a modern secularized group standing outside the caste structure has provided a field for individual movement. For the majority who remained within the caste framework, the politics of equality have been expressed instead through "caste associations"—regional groupings of related castes—which compete for political power within the parliamentary electoral framework and which promote the economic and social interests of their members.[58] Sometimes the associations operate independently of the national parties, sometimes within their state and local branches. By drawing upon the tradition of local caste struggles for position within the classical four-*varna* scheme, they are able to call forth traditional sentiment and solidarities in support of such modern goals as improved educational and occupational opportunities for their members.

Students of contemporary Indian society seem rather sharply divided concerning the meaning of these caste associations for the political future. The Rudolphs see in them a useful way of linking traditional and modern political processes and of articulating the aspirations of millions of village folk with an inevitably distant national politics.[59] Harrison, on the other hand, sees in their growth a threat to the cohesion of a country already deeply divided by linguistic and regional loyalties—loyalties the associations tend to express and to reinforce.[60] In comparative perspective, the caste associations would seem in any case to provide an element that is relatively rare in the polities of the new states: a structure of political pluralism in terms of which large numbers of persons can pursue the politics of equality—can participate in the political process in ways that are effective and satisfying to them—but that at the same time tends to prevent the excessive concentration of power and public attention upon the center. It also makes possible the continued separation of the official agents of modernization—the civil service—from direct participation in political controversy. The fact that such pluralism also entails a certain loss of unity is perhaps merely the Indian version of one of the enduring dilemmas of democratic society, expressed by Abraham Lincoln in his message to the special session of Congress in 1861:

Is there in all republics this inherent and fatal weakness? Must a government of necessity be too *strong* for the liberties of its own people or too *weak* to maintain its own existence?[61]

The problem for India, as is was for the United States a century ago (though, of course, the actual culture and structural elements involved are different and, hence, so also must the solution be), is to find a political modus vivendi that protects the integrity of the central government without stifling pluralism.

When we turn to the new states of Africa, we find it extraordinarily difficult—even more so than in the case of the Asian states—to distinguish enduring features from transitory ones. The oldest of the African countries (Ethiopia and Liberia, of course, excepted) has been sovereign for less than a decade, the others for far shorter periods. We may, however, take note of some features that seem likely to condition the politics of equality in Africa for some time to come, whatever the fate of particular governments and sets of national boundaries.

First of all, the new African states are in most cases "nations" in only the most tentative sense. Lacking traditional bases for a sense of national unity, they tend to be congeries of traditional societies in varying stages of modernization, held together by the leadership of elites whose common culture is largely alien to the traditional cultures and discontinuous with them. The politics of equality, and indeed such political self-awareness of any kind as may be said to transcend the boundaries of the traditional societies, have thus far consisted in the main of the assertion of the dignity of things generically African, as against Western domination.

This sentiment is profound and widespread, for Western domination has, in Africa even more than elsewhere, often taken forms that were particularly damaging to indigenous peoples' sense of integrity and self-esteem. This has been particularly true for members of the elites who have experienced Western racism overseas or in local European colonial circles. During the period of nationalist agitation, all kinds of local (and sometimes incompatible) discontents and ambitions could be fused with these elite grievances. But such diffuse sentiments are more readily utilized in the organization of independence movements than in the continuing political life of sovereign states. With the achievement of independence, there emerges the problem of finding or creating structures within the social fabric of the various states in terms of which to channel the politics of equality.

At present there appears to be a tendency for the single strong party—the vehicle for the successful drive to independence—to dominate the politics of most of the new states through centralized governments. Such parties and governments in the short run, draw strength both from their successful defiance of the colonial regimes and from their inheritance of the latters' institutional assets: relatively disciplined bureaucracies, armies, and police forces. In addition, large parts of the populations of many of the African states are as yet hardly politicized at all in the modern sense, having passed directly from the paternalistic rule of the European district officer, or *commandant du cercle,* to that of his equally paternalistic African successor. At present, therefore, the dominant parties can count upon the political quiescence of a large proportion of their countries' people as well as upon the enthusiastic support of most of the politically articulate. Over the long run, however, the economic modernization of these countries, which is the common goal of all the new regimes, will tend to draw the peoples of the backward areas into political participation, and the unity derived from the period of agitation for independence will wane. The question of the legitimacy of the regimes, in terms of more diverse and deeply held values, will then tend to come to the surface.

It seems very likely that the future politics of most of the African states will be dominated by the problems of the role to be played in their affairs by their constituent traditional societies—the "tribes." In the absence of national cultures that might be represented by, and help to legitimate, national elites) it is not, of course, out of the question that such may be created in time by gifted and responsible elites), the alternatives would seem to be two: on the one hand, a continued unity and centralization, increasingly maintained by authoritarian means: and, on the other, the evolution of constitutional arrangements, of a broadly federal sort, in which traditional solidarities might be represented and contained. In particular the possibility of something like stable, liberal democratic regimes in the African setting would seem to depend upon development of the latter sort.[62]

Conclusions

In this essay we have attempted a preliminary comparative sketch of the modernization of social stratification and politics in the West and in some of the new states. It is, of course, the merest outline of what a serious study of the subject would be, but it has enabled us to explore what appear to be some of the major ranges of variation and, perhaps, to reach a standpoint somewhat outside the peculiarities of the Western experience. It may be useful to summarize here some of our tentative conclusions:

1. There is a complex of features of social stratification and politics—what we have called the "politics of equality"— that may be said to be generically modern.

2. The particular form this complex will take in any given society is, however, influenced to an important degree by the traditional structure and culture of stratification within which it develops.

3. The form the politics of equality will take in the new states is also influenced, both structurally and culturally, by the circumstances of the encounter with the West.

4. The development of the politics of equality in a relatively liberal democratic direction depends both upon the existence of legitimate and responsible national elites and upon the channeling of popular political energies through pluralistic structures. In various instances these latter have included class, caste, associational and, perhaps, tribal structures. Perhaps the most interesting research task suggested by this preliminary survey is the further exploration of the variety of structures that may serve in this way.

PART 2
BUGANDA: A CASE STUDY

7

Social Stratification in Traditional Buganda

One hundred years ago, the king of Buganda, the Kabaka, ruled a land stretching some one hundred and fifty miles around the northwestern side of Lake Victoria, the largest of the great chain of lakes which runs north and south along the highland spine of eastern Africa. It was a prosperous, vigorous realm with perhaps a million—perhaps more—inhabitants: cultivators of the fertile, well-watered lake-shore soil and fishers in the lakes and sluggish, papyrus-choked rivers. In many respects the kingdom was maritime (or lacustrine); in the rolling hinterland, criss-crossed by swamps and streams, travel was often slow and precarious, but on the lakes and rivers large planked canoes driven by paddlers could transport fighting men or trade goods swiftly and securely over a wider area—which is perhaps why the kingdom seems to have spread around the lake shore more readily than it spread inland. But there was much movement by land as well. A network of roads, built and maintained by corvée labour provided by the king's chiefs and sub-chiefs, connected the scattered village communities with the capital. Gangs of workmen and companies of militia warriors moved back and forth across the country, doing the work and fighting

Reprinted by permission from Lloyd A. Fallers, ed., *The King's Men: Leadership and Status in Buganda on the Eve of Independence* (London: Oxford University Press, 1964). Dr. Fallers was assisted by F. K. Kamoga and S. B. K. Musoke. Mentions of the Appendixes in the text and the footnotes refer to the original publication of *The King's Men;* the Appendixes are not included here. For a map showing the peoples of Uganda Protectorate, see chap. 3, p. 44.

the battles of a king whose will was increasingly pervasive and increasingly directed towards national expansion. '*Kabaka afugira wala*', the Baganda boasted: 'The Kabaka rules far and wide.'

Much more than most African kings, the Kabaka not only *reigned*, but also *ruled*—actively and powerfully. Most traditional African kingdoms were not highly centralized polities; in most, the king was in some degree a *primus inter pares*, merely the most eminent and powerful among a group of hereditary rulers, each having an independent legitimate authority rooted in the locality and people over which he ruled. In such a polity, the headman or chief, while in one of his aspects an administrative subordinate of the king, also held another role: that of representative of his people to the king. Very frequently this rootedness of the holder of intermediate authority in the territory and people he ruled, and hence his capacity to represent as well as rule them, derived from his position in a unilineal descent group—a solidary group of persons related in either the patrilineal or the matrilineal line. In many African societies, descent groups and territorial groups were closely linked; the headman or chief was the leader and representative of both. As recent studies have made clear, this construction of the polity out of territorially based lineage building-blocks was often more a matter of political theory than of genealogical fact; most members of a community or chiefdom might not be actual biological lineage-mates in the appropriate line of descent, but political thought found ways—through various forms of fiction and the 'rearrangement' of genealogies—to treat them as if they were.[1] Thus the typical African kingdom was governed under a kind of traditional constitutionalism in which authority was diffused and checked, and consent was obtained, through a hierarchy of corporate groups, theoretically based upon descent, acting through their senior members as headmen or chiefs.

Such polities tended towards either decentralization or fragility. The first tendency is well illustrated by the Ashanti confederacy of Ghana, an aggregation of matrilineal chiefdoms in which, at each level, the chief's or headman's office, symbolized by the stool, was the property of, and its occupant responsible to, one or more corporate communities of kin.

R. S. Rattray explains how it was that this structure could unite three-quarters of a million persons into a powerful defensive alliance capable, for example, of fighting the 'Ashanti Wars' against the British during the eighteen-eighties and -nineties, and yet remain for most purposes a loose confederation of essentially self-governing communities:

> Every one of those subordinate stools (i.e. chiefdoms) . . . possessed a history, a tradition, a genealogical tree and an organization which was an exact replica of those possessed by the paramount stool. The smallest of these stools was as jealous of its traditions as the greatest, and but for the dangers of the age in which these amalgamations took place, would possibly have continued to remain more or less insulated. It was only the quest of common safety, summed up in the words 'unity is strength', that made the Ashanti accept a form of government that superficially might seem to savour of an aristo-cracy. He kept this aristocracy, however, and allowed it to function as such, only on the very rare occasions of great emergency. Rulers and ruled well understood this to be the case. The tribal or national danger having been averted, each unit went back to the manage-ment of its own affairs. . . .[2]

The other tendency—the tendency towards fragility—appeared most prominently when polities of this kind attempted to go beyond defensive alliance to the active pursuit of some common goal—usually national expansion through conquest. Thus a gifted leader like the famous Shaka could for a time weld many corporate patrilineal groups of Southern Bantu together to form a powerful, aggressive Zulu nation. But ultimately, Max Gluckman has argued, such centralization could not endure in the absence of fundamental structural changes:

> . . . Shaka stated quite clearly that to build a nation he had to destroy the tribal organization. . . . Yet in this objective not even he could succeed. . . . He built his kingdom so rapidly that he had to leave untouched those chiefs who surrendered to him voluntarily. He also had to reward his close supporters, and his only means of doing so was to give them land and followers. They became county chiefs, each with his own army, and the old tribal system reasserted itself. When one of the county chiefs died, his son succeeded him. Shaka was aware that his subjects' loyalty to his chieftains was a danger to his own rule and the stability of his empire. . . .[3]

At some time in the past, Buganda, too, may have been a polity of this kind—an aggregation of smaller polities tenuously bound together by defensive alliance or by heroic leadership. According to legend, the most important political offices were at one time held by the heads of, and on behalf of, patrilineal clans and lineages. In more recent times, unilineal descent groups continued, as they still do today, to govern inheritance and succession in the domestic sphere; but more and more, through processes which are described in the following chapters, the government passed out of their hands and into the hands of chiefs who were appointed by the Kabaka and loyal to him alone—a kind of proto-bureaucracy. By the middle of the nineteenth century, the kingdom was governed by a corps of chiefs who owed their positions largely to the personal grace of the Kabaka, who might appoint, dismiss and transfer them at will. Every young man aspired to a career in the service of the Kabaka, around whom was woven a cultural tissue of arbitrary fierceness and power. A chief might one day stand at the pinnacle of wealth and influence, the ruler of a large district and the recipient of lavish tribute from his people and estates from his king; next day, having incurred the monarch's disfavour, he might be stripped of property and office, lying in stocks, the object of scorn and physical tortures of a most imaginative kind. As we know, absolute power does not exist. There were checks in the form of advice and pressure from subordinates and kinsmen. But consent and legitimacy were secured, not so much by constitutional restraint upon the Kabaka, as by a nation-wide psychic and material 'pay-off' in the shape of the spoils of war. The whole kingdom had in the late nineteenth century come to be organized for expansion and plunder at the expense of neighbouring peoples.

The Neo-traditional Kingdom

Today there is still a Kabaka's Government, recognized and granted a wide measure of autonomous authority by the British government of the Uganda Protectorate and by its successor, the new national government. The material manifestations of the Buganda Government and the activities of its members have been transformed. It occupies a large and elegant new building at one end of a wide, tree-lined boulevard, at the other end of which is situated the Kabaka's modern palace. Inside the building are the most modern offices, fitted with type-writers, filing cabinets and telephones, and occupied by the Ministries of the Treasury, Justice, Education, Health and Natural Resources. In another part of the building is a legisla-tive hall in which sits the modern Buganda parliament, a largely elected body. In the districts outside the capital there are, again, offices manned by functionaries employed on civil service terms and engaged in the tasks associated with modern government. The present Kabaka, Mutesa II, is immaculately tailored, Cambridge-educated, and speaks flawless English.

Along with all this change there is also continuity: the government building is called the *Bulange* after the traditional audience-hall of the Kabaka; the parliament is called the Great Lukiiko, after the traditional gathering of the chiefs to pay homage; the administrator in charge of the county of Buruli carries the title of the *Kimbugwe*, the traditional keeper of the king's umbilicus, which in the past had great ritual significance. Do we see here fundamental change, with only superficial continuity? Or are the deeper currents those of continuity, with change only on the surface?

In the field of religion, too, there has been both change and continuity. Traditional religion centred upon the cults of gods, ancestors and nature spirits. Communication through spirit possession with these beings, all of whom were capable of influencing man's life on earth, was the principal form of religious activity. Ordinary persons sought communication with the spirits in order to cure a disorder, to secure children or to further their political careers. The Kabaka sought it on behalf of the nation, particularly to secure supernatural support in war.

Today most of this has passed away and the vast majority of Baganda are Anglican or Roman Catholic Christians, with a strong minority of Sunni Muslims. The Christian churches are all but legally established. The Kabaka is crowned in the Anglican cathedral and there is an agreement whereby major posts in the government are shared out among the three religious groups. Both Anglican and Roman Catholic churches have largely Ganda clergies, including bishops. There is no doubt at all that the churches have entered deeply into Ganda life—have become Ganda churches. Most importantly, perhaps, the leading members of society, in a traditional sense, are pillars of the church. Chiefs and wealthy landowners often have reserved for them special pews in the little country churches which they have built. There are, of course, thousands of merely 'nominal' Christians, just as there are in Europe and America, and there is also a similar secularizing tendency among young intellectuals and politicians, but an objective observer would probably say that, while Baganda are typically tempted, and sin, in rather different directions from Westerners—because they live in a different social and cultural milieu—they probably, on the whole, sin no more frequently. For example, there are important remnants of the past in the shape of a social system which encourages polygyny and a tradition of 'pagan' magic, and Baganda often yield to both. This, however, only makes the Baganda more exotic sinners than Westerners, not more frequent, or more profound sinners, for they remain Christians in a real sense all the while.

Closely associated with religion in the field of cultural change is education, for the missions which brought Christianity also founded Western-type schools. The response to Western education—and to technical training of all kinds—has been enthusiastic from the very beginning. The problem for the missions and for the government has always been to provide sufficient schools to satisfy the demand. Again, the leading members of society—the Kabaka and his senior officials—are generally well educated and they make great efforts to see that their children are even better educated. Furthermore, a good many of the *élite* have for half a century been educated in the very type of institution best calculated to produce the maximum socialization impact—the English 'public school' type of boarding school, after which the schools of Buganda were modelled. The leading Buganda Government officials and the leaders of the most important political parties are overwhelmingly 'old boys' of the two *élite* boarding schools—one Anglican and the other Roman Catholic.

Finally, there has been a radical transformation of the economy. In traditional Buganda, the average family engaged in subsistence agriculture, growing plantains for its staple food and perhaps producing a specialized handicraft product—pottery or bark cloth or iron hoes—for exchange with its neighbours at the weekly market. Much of the circulation of goods and services was incidental to the exercise of political authority; that is to say, jurisdiction over land and people were one, and the political hierarchy was supported by taxes and tribute in goods and services levied upon the villagers.

Today the average Muganda is a cash-crop farmer, growing cotton or coffee for money with which to buy an ever-expanding range of imported goods. Often he holds freehold title to his land, and he very frequently hires by the day migrant foreign workers from nearby Rwanda and Burundi to supplement the family labour force during the busy season. He responds to the market in much the same way as a midwestern American farmer and tends to be coldly instrumental in his approach to agricultural problems. For example, during the political crisis of 1953–5, when the Kabaka had been exiled by the Protectorate government and when relations between the Baganda and British political officers were extremely bad, British officers of the Agriculture Department reported practically no disruption of their normally good relations with farmers. Agriculture, the Baganda felt, was a matter with which politics should not be allowed to interfere.

Thus, Baganda are, in many ways, extremely 'acculturated' and the leading members of society are the most acculturated of all. There are here no culturally conservative, traditional chiefs pitted against a group of young, Western-educated, commoner politicians. Baganda do not see or practice politics in these terms, as so many African peoples do. Rather, Ganda society has acculturated, as it were, from the top down, and hence the new culture tends to have universal legitimacy. Indeed, from the point of view of the Baganda, this new culture, which includes many Western ideas of government, Western education, Anglican and Roman Catholic Christianity, the motivations appropriate to a money economy—all this has become *their* culture in a fundamental way. They have, so to speak, 'naturalized' the foreign elements and thus kept a sense of cultural integrity and 'wholeness' through a period of radical change. In order to understand how this has been possible, we must glance back at the circumstances of Ganda-European contact under which the present neo-traditional kingdom came into being.

The creators of the new Buganda were the young chiefs who

had achieved high office under Kabaka Mwanga in the
eighteen-eighties and -nineties. We may recall that in traditional
Buganda, at any rate by the nineteenth century, most of the
important political offices had ceased to be hereditary. Most
officials were appointed by the Kabaka and the most important
recruiting ground for chiefs was the corps of pages—young
boys who were sent to the palace to serve him. A quick-witted
boy would catch his master's eye and be given a subordinate
post—the first step toward the higher reaches of power if he
continued to serve loyally and intelligently. This meant that
within the traditional system there was room for the wholesale
replacement of personnel. An entirely new group of men could
take power without violating the system, and this is indeed
what happened.

First the Arab traders, and then the Christian missionaries,
established themselves at court and began to proselytize among
the pages. Why traditional Ganda religion did not oppose this
with greater vigour is a question which we need not pursue
here, except to say that the Kabaka regarded all religion in an
essentially instrumental way and hence encouraged competition among Christianity, Islam and the traditional cults in
the hope of deriving maximum benefit from all of them without
committing himself to any. The result was a struggle for
ascendancy among factions of young chiefs, aided by the Arabs
in the case of the Muslims and by the Europeans in the case of
the Christians. The Christians won and a British Protectorate
was ultimately declared.

Thus it happened that a new set of chiefs, committed to
Christianity and progress, came to power at a time when the
fundamentals of the Protectorate relationship between the
British and the Baganda were being worked out. Because they
had been recruited from traditional sources and because the
traditional system provided for recruitment through achievement, they did not look upon themselves as revolutionaries in
the sense that they were basically altering political arrangements; rather they were Christianizing and improving a king
and kingdom to which they remained essentially loyal. (We
know something about how they saw these events because
several of them wrote memoirs.) Although they were at times
made aware of British power in a way which indicated quite
clearly that the Protectorate was not really an arrangement

arrived at between equals, still it took a form which allowed them to believe that they had secured the benefits of association with Britain with a minimum of political interference. How this extraordinary process occurred will be described subsequently.

The Baganda have not, however, been alone in their relationship with Britain. Rather, the neo-traditional kingdom formed the core, first of a Protectorate, then of a nation, which also included other peoples. Buganda is the core in the sense that the political arrangements upon which the Protectorate rested were originally entered into in the eighteen-eighties and -nineties by the British and the Baganda and only later, and in most cases with considerably less consent, were extended to the penumbra of tribes which later made up the Eastern, Western and Northern Provinces. A good deal of this added territory was, in fact, conquered jointly by the British and the Baganda.

Buganda is also the core of the country in another, and more contemporary, sense. Buganda has contained both the capital and the commercial centre of the Protectorate and consequently the new political and economic institutions and facilities which have grown up during the association with Great Britain have their locus there.

Thus the Baganda, the pivotal group in Uganda, have contributed to the country a powerful impulse towards modernization but have also remained intensely chauvinistic and reluctant to merge themselves into a wider Uganda nationality. The other peoples of Uganda tend to regard the Baganda with a mixture of admiration and resentment. Among their Bantu-speaking cousins in southern Uganda, admiration tends to predominate, while among the Nilotic—and so-called 'Nilo-Hamitic'—speaking peoples of the north, resentment is perhaps the stronger element. Everywhere, however, there is reluctance to solve the problem by accepting Ganda domination, for the Baganda have been emulated in their peculiar progressive isolationism by neighbouring peoples, often with the active encouragement of the British Protectorate Government.

The crisis which faces contemporary Buganda, then, is simply this: with the achievement of the universally desired goal of self-government, they must choose whether to seek their political future alone—an alternative which, because of their central position in the country, is so hazardous as to be hardly a realistic alternative at all—or else to give up the isolation from their neighbours which, among other factors, has made possible their unusually smooth acceptance of modernity. They must cease to be Baganda first and last and accept a new identity in the company of their neighbours.

This and the following chapters constitute a study of social stratification in the Kingdom of Buganda, traditional and modern. "Modern" does not, however, mean 1973. The research upon which this study rests was completed in 1957 and the book in which it originally appeared was published in 1964. The terms "today" and "contemporary" may therefore be taken to refer to 1957. To give an adequate account of the turbulent intervening years would require a book in itself, but I present the bare facts:

Uganda became an independent state in 1962 under a coalition government in which the stronger partner, in terms of parliamentary seats, was the Uganda Peoples' Congress, representing areas outside Buganda, the weaker being the *Kabaka Yekka* ("the king alone," or Buganda monarchist) Party. The opposition was formed by the Democratic Party, associated with the Roman Catholic church. Mr. Milton Obote, a Lango from northern Uganda and leader of the U.P.C., became prime minister and the Kabaka was elected president. This coalition lasted two years, after which relations between Buganda and the central government steadily deteriorated, while Prime Minister Obote moved increasingly toward personal rule. In May 1966, the central government launched its military forces against the palace and the Kabaka's government. Many Baganda were killed or imprisoned, though the Kabaka himself escaped to die in exile in England. The monarchy was abolished and Buganda was divided into administrative districts.

Mr. Obote held power until January 1971, when he was overthrown by General Idi Amin, his own chosen instrument for control of the army. Many imprisoned Baganda have been released, and for the moment other interethnic tensions have become more prominent. Buganda's relations with her neighbors—crucial to the long-term future of Uganda—remain in a state of suspension.

'Social stratification' is of course a complex phenomenon, involving a number of aspects which have been emphasized in varying degrees by the many social scientists who have concerned themselves with it. For Karl Marx and his followers it has meant primarily the distribution of control over the means of production—the distribution of economic power. William Lloyd Warner, on the other hand, has interested himself mainly in the *culture* of stratification—the differentiation in styles of life among groups judged by themselves and others to be 'higher' or 'lower' on an evaluative scale.[4] Again, Glass, Bendix and Lipset, and the investigators of the National Opinion Research Center, have centred their attention upon the prestige-ranking of occupations and upon the frequency of inter-generational occupational mobility.[5] In view of this wide range of interests and emphases among students of the subject it may be useful, as we set out to describe stratification in a non-Western society, if we outline briefly at the beginning what we shall mean by it.[6]

We shall assume that stratification has two main bases in the very nature of social life. First of all, social inequality is a *moral* phenomenon. All human communities have values and consequently their members evaluate one another differentially in terms of these. Each has some conception of the 'admirable person' against which its members may measure their own and others' conduct. However, and this we take to be the second fundamental basis for stratificatory phenomena, human communities are never simply homogeneous collections of like beings; even the simplest of them have 'structure' in the sense of a division of labour by sex, age, generation and kinship, and in most communities other distinctions are recognized as well. The degree of such division of labour or 'social differentiation' is closely, though of course not exclusively, related to the degree of technological complexity. The most elaborate differentiations of persons on the basis of age and kinship are found in non-industrial societies, but the prodigious array of occupational specialities found in modern Western societies is only possible because of their relative technological sophistication. Now the existence of social differentiation means that the value system, in terms of which persons evaluate one another, must also make distinctions. If different tasks are allocated to men and women, parents and children, chiefs and people, the value system must take account of this by providing, not merely an image of the 'admirable person', but also images of the 'admirable woman', the 'admirable son', the 'admirable chief', and so on. These clusters of more specialized moral expectations we usually call 'roles', and societies differ widely in the numbers and kinds of roles they recognize. But the matter does not end there, for the value system not only enables persons to evaluate one another according to the adequacy with which they perform roles; it also goes on to the differential evaluation of roles themselves. Thus modern American society grants particularly high prestige to the entrepreneur, whereas in traditional China the scholar was the person most admired.

Thus stratification has both cultural and structural roots; to study it we must examine both the pattern of social differentiation and the way in which roles are thought about and evaluated. But this is still not all there is to stratification, for if roles are differentially evaluated, and thus differentially desirable, then society must assume the task of deciding how roles are to be allocated. Its freedom of choice in the matter will be limited both by the number of the more desirable roles available and by the distribution among persons of the qualities necessary for their adequate performance. And if society—or those who act on its behalf—is to retain the allegiance of its members, it must justify its choice ideologically. Thus, after inquiring about the degree and kind of social differentiation and the ways in which social roles are evaluated, we must go on to determine how persons are selected for roles—whether on the basis of merit, for example, or on the basis of descent—and what various persons and groups in the society think about this process of selection. Further, we may ask how far persons playing similar roles are seen by themselves and others as constituting relatively discrete groups and how far the members of such 'status groups', in so far as they exist, share common distinctive sub-cultures.[7] Do peasants or priests or chiefs, that is to say, form relatively closed groups with distinct ways of life and feelings of common destiny? Are they, in the Marxian sense, 'class conscious'?

Thus, to understand the 'dynamics' of stratification we must examine the interplay among ideology, social differentiation and the process of allocation of persons to roles. The task of describing the consequence of the encounter with the West for social stratification in Buganda then falls naturally into several parts. First, we must determine the ways in which outside forces have reshaped the system of roles available to the person who would win the respect and admiration of his fellows. Direct Western influence, and local processes of change resulting from Western influence, have brought new roles and altered old ones; roles have been re-evaluated and have thus come to have changed value as determinants of social rank. Having examined these changes in the system, we shall then inquire into the ways in which roles are filled today, as compared with the late nineteenth century, in order to determine how far contact with the West has increased or decreased social mobility in Buganda. In this chapter and in Chapter 8 we address ourselves to the first problem; the second will be taken up in Chapter 9.

In describing the process of social differentiation—the development of new roles—there are again two dimensions which may usefully be distinguished. There are, on the one hand, the ideas by means of which the Baganda think about power, wealth and honour and which express their values regarding the legitimate distribution of these things. On the other hand, there is the actual structure of social roles—the standardized social relations in which persons are involved. In more stable societies these tend to be closely related; actual social relations tend to reflect (though of course never completely) categories of thought in the common culture. In rapidly changing societies, however, they may become quite widely separated. Both ideas and structure have, of course, changed during the past seventy-five years in Buganda, but it seems useful to keep them distinct when considering the process of change. Structural change represents the adaptive response of Baganda to the opportunities and pressures brought by Western missionaries, business men and colonial officials who have brought opportunities for them to become Christian priests, cash-crop farmers and political party leaders —all new roles which were not present in traditional society. Moving into these roles is for individual Baganda a matter of immediate, personal adaptation to changed circumstances. At the same time, there takes place rather more slowly a process of adaptation in the shared system of ideas of the Baganda by which these new roles are interpreted and evaluated culturally, are fitted into the total scheme of belief and value by which Baganda live. We shall not argue that either of these processes is in any sense 'more fundamental'; we shall assume, however, that both have some 'potency' in the total process of social change—that ideas on the one hand and the actual structure of social relations on the other interact to shape the future of Ganda society.

Traditional Cultural Definitions

Central to traditional ideas about stratification in Buganda are the word *mukopi* and its antonyms. A *mukopi* (pl. *bakopi*) is simply a person of no particular distinction; the word denotes a residual category of persons who are *not* something else. It is often today translated as 'peasant', and this is correct enough in a residual sense, for the vast majority of Baganda did and do live by the produce of the small agricultural holding. Agriculture is not, however, part of the actual meaning of the word. A fisherman—*muvubi*—is also a *mukopi*, as is a *mukomazi* (bark-cloth maker) or a *mubumbi* (potter.) In fact, as Wrigley has noted, few Baganda men took much part in traditional agriculture, cultivation being considered primarily women's work. The wives of fishermen, bark-cloth makers, potters and other craft specialists cultivated the plantain gardens, which supplied the staple food, as well as the plots of annual crops. The word *mulimi*—'cultivator'—has probably come into popular use quite recently to denote the man who makes his living cultivating the recently introduced cash crops, cotton and coffee.

A *mukopi*, then, is an undistinguished, ordinary person as distinct from the various types of important persons. One way to be distinguished from a *mukopi* is to be a *mulangira*, a 'prince' or descendant of a Kabaka.

The prince, in the eyes of the Baganda, derives his special position, not so much from being a member of a royal group or class, as from his association as an individual with the *nnamulondo*, the royal stool, and the other signs of kingship. The Kabaka, that is to say, is not a *primus inter pares*, a prince among princes. As Richards' account of Ganda political values in

The King's Men makes clear, he is the unique, despotic pinnacle of Ganda society. [8] He is *ssemanda*, the 'charcoal fire of the smith', who can forge the kingdom as the smith forges iron. He is *ssegwanga*, 'first in the nation'; *ssaabasajja*, 'first among men'; and *ssaabataka*, 'first among clan heads'. He is *mpologoma*, 'the lion'; and *namunswa*, 'the queen termite', who, Baganda say, feeds upon her subject termites. The uniqueness of the Kabaka is emphasized by the fact that the princes, unlike members of commoner clans, do not have a collective totemic symbol. Rather, they have only the totems of their mothers, who belong to various commoner clans. The kingdom belongs, not to the princes as a group, but to the Kabaka.

Among princes, particular distinction attaches to being a *mulangira ow'engoma*, a 'prince of the drum', a son or grandson of a Kabaka. Only such a person was traditionally eligible for the throne. Princes more distantly related in the patrilineal line to the ruling Kabaka are *balangira abamabundugu*, 'princes who have dropped away', or *balangira abakopi*, 'peasant princes'. There is little in the way in which they are treated to distinguish these latter from peasants; their style of life is the same and they have no special privileges. They may receive some small degree of extra deference, but enjoy no economic or political advantages. There remains, however, even in the case of very distant princes, a residue of royal eligibility which is recognized in the great reluctance of kings to appoint princes to important chieftainships. Princes of the drum were closely guarded, and even sometimes killed, in order to guard against usurpation, for there was no rule of seniority among siblings and each was therefore a possible focus for revolt. [9] The fact that even the peasant princes, theoretically ineligible to succeed, were kept out of positions of power, indicates that even they were not entirely without the quality of potential kingship.

Another way to be distinguished from a *mukopi* is to be a *mwami*—a person who rules. Where the distinction between *mukopi* and *mulangira* is one of ascribed status at birth, the distinction between *mukopi* and *mwami* emphasizes instead achieved status, for most of the positions of substantial power in the kingdom tended, particularly during the later part of the nineteenth century, to be open to the talented man upon appointment by the Kabaka. The Prime Minister (*Katikkiro*), the king's officers (*batongole*) and most of the territorial chiefs (*bakungu*) were royal appointees, chosen in most cases from among the hundreds of boys who were sent to the palace to serve as pages (*bagalagala*) to the king. The idea of a successful career as a reward for effort and talent is expressed in the phrase *kukulakulana mu bwami*—'to rise in chieftainship'. Aspiration to social mobility is central to Ganda life and it is rewarded by the *kitiibwa* (honour) which is the accompaniment of success.

Another distinction which Baganda make, and upon which they elaborate, concerns the difference in manners between the sophisticated man at the capital and the 'country bumpkin'. The latter, the Baganda say, *atalina mpisa*, lacks 'proper habits' or *politesse*. He is *wa boggo*, a person of rough, intemperate speech. His opposite is *muntu mulamu wa mu bantu*, a 'person with proper social manners', who knows how to speak and handle himself at court. Although a *mukopi* need not be rough-hewn and unsophisticated, in practice Baganda believe that these qualities are likely to be characteristic of *bakopi*. There is a phrase, *mukopi be kopokopo* (the latter word is merely an adjectival reduplication, for emphasis, of the root—*kopi*), which describes the utterly undistinguished man, the very quintessence, so to speak, of *kopi*-ness.

All of this elaboration of differences in power and sophistication, however, should not lead us to believe that the Baganda are (or were traditionally) divided into self-conscious classes or status groups. Indeed, nothing is more alien to Ganda culture than the conception that men may be arranged into discrete and internally homogeneous strata. Three elements should perhaps be distinguished here; the idea of strata, objective cultural differentiation by strata, and self-consciousness of common interests on the part of members of strata. All of these elements are involved in the corporateness which characterizes a status group (*Stand*) in Max Weber's sense and all of them may, of course, be present in varying degrees in particular societies. All are relatively undeveloped in Ganda society. Both the idea of strata and the self-consciousness of common stratum membership are, as far as we can determine, very weak. There is no convenient way of expressing in Luganda the idea of a stratum and there apparently was little, if any, 'class consciousness' in traditional society.

The terms *mukopi, mwami* and *mulangira* do, perhaps, refer to status groups in a minimal sense, but they carry very little connotation of common interests and are very loose categories. Perhaps we should call them 'status categories', in contrast to 'status groups'. Cultural differentiation was traditionally limited to differential possession of material wealth and to the differences in courtliness of manners mentioned above. Neither manners nor the consumption of goods and services, further-more, were culturally elaborated to the point where they could be correctly handled only by persons familiar with them from childhood. A successful person could easily learn the consumption patterns and manners appropriate to a great chief. There is no Luganda equivalent to the Western notion of the *parvenu* —the person who has risen through ability but is unable to master the subtle differences between gentlemanly and un-gentlemanly behaviour.

This is not to say that Ganda society lacks corporate groups of any kind, but only that these are not features of the strati-fication system. In the sphere of kinship and clanship, there is a clear conception of the solidary patrilineal unit with common

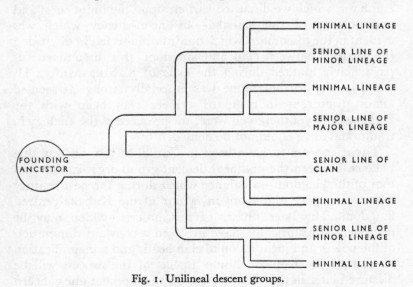

Fig. 1. Unilineal descent groups.

rights and interests. All Baganda are divided among some forty patrilineal, totemic clans (*bika*), the exact number depending upon the interpretation of certain marginal cases. Each clan has its head (*mukulu* or *jjajja*), a descendant of the founding ancestor, and each is divided into a descending series of segments: major lineages (*masiga*, 'hearthstones'), minor lineages (*mituba*, 'fig trees'), and minimal lineages (*nyiriri*, 'lines'). Each of these segments also has its head. Within each segment, there is a senior line, known as the *kasolya* ('roof'), the members of which are sometimes spoken of as *balangira* ('princes'). (See Fig. 1.) This latter terminological analogy between clan and kingdom is carried further in the practice of speaking of the clan head as a Kabaka, or, more cautiously, as 'being like a Kabaka'. Descent-groups were in no sense ranked, although members of a clan which had provided a prime minister or a queen-mother might derive from that fact a good deal of self-satisfaction and material benefit, as well as a measure of prestige.

It is interesting, if inconclusive, to speculate about the historical implications of the analogy between the structure of the clan and that of the kingdom as a whole. There is unquestionably an inconsistency between this idea and the emphasis, which we discussed earlier, upon the uniqueness and omnipotence of the Kabaka—an inconsistency which was evident in the discomfort which our informants felt in discussing the analogy between clan and kingdom; this discomfort was particularly marked during the exile of Kabaka Mutesa II, when loyalty to the throne was especially strong. It seemed almost traitorous to compare a mere clan head with the Kabaka, and yet there you were; the presence of the analogy in traditional ideas could not be denied.

There appears to have been in Ganda society an unstable balance between the unilineal descent group organization and that of the kingdom—a balance which during the past century has swung more and more in favour of the Kabaka-centred kingdom. The later phases of this process, which may be documented historically, have involved a constant diminution of the power and jurisdiction of clan heads and a magnification of that of the Kabaka. Some aspects of the process will be discussed later in this chapter, but for the moment our concern is rather with the ideas governing unilineal descent.

It is in the unilineal descent system that one finds the idea of corporateness and its corollary, the idea of collegial equality, elaborated. While there is, as we have said, seniority within the unilineal descent group, nevertheless there is also corporate solidarity. The *butaka*, the burial ground in which are the graves of the ancestors, is 'ours'—a common possession. Decisions concerning succession, which still today are legally the province of descent groups, are made in council, not by the heads of segments acting unilaterally. Within the patrilineal segment, collateral equality is expressed in the extension of kinship terms to all members of the same generation. Thus, 'my father's brother' is also 'father' and his son is 'brother'. Collaterality may also be expressed by the phrase *ba lubu lumu* which may mean, among other things, 'of one generation'.

Outside the descent-group sphere, these conceptions of corporateness, collaterality and collegiality seldom appear. In the kingdom at large, Baganda seem to conceive of each man as having an independent relationship with the Kabaka or with some other superior—preferably the former. We have said that there is no conception of solidary classes or status groups, and it is interesting that in the organization of the state there apparently was traditionally no conception of *levels* of organization. One level, that of the ten great territorial divisions, had a name —*ssaza*; beyond that there were simply superiors and subordinates with ranks and titles. These were, in order of rank: *mumyuka* ('second in command'), *ssaabaddu* ('head of those who serve'), *ssaabagabo* ('head of the shield bearers'), *ssaabawaali* ('head of the slaves'), *musaale* ('the arrow') and *mutuba* ('fig tree'). The *ssaza* chiefs were ranked according to this scheme, as were their subordinates and, in turn, their subordinates' subordinates. Today the state organization has been rationalized, with the *ssaza* ('county') units divided into units called *magombolola* ('sub-counties'), and these in turn into *miruka* ('parishes'). Chiefs at the same level are sometimes spoken of as being of *lubu lumu* ('the same generation'; see above) or *ddaala limu* ('the same step on the ladder'), but apparently this is a new conception. The traditional view saw men as being arranged, not in levels or ranks, but simply in dyadic relations of subordination and superordination. This is not, of course, to suggest than an emphasis upon dyadic relations of subordination and superordination is incompatible with conceptions of status level and stratum solidarity; in medieval Europe, as also, no doubt, in many other peasant societies, both existed. The point is simply that in Buganda *only* the dyadic conception of inequality was important. We may note in this connexion that the Great Lukiiko, the king's council which has today become a collegial and largely elected legislative body, was traditionally nothing of the sort. It was formerly a gathering of the king's chiefs and officers to pay homage. The word itself comes from the verb *kukiika*, 'to pay homage'.

Not surprisingly, there is a good deal of terminology in Luganda for talking about dyadic relations of subordination and superordination. A superior is *mukama wange*, 'my lord'; and a subordinate is *muddu wange*, 'my servant', or *muweereza wange*, 'my emissary'. These terms, which emphasize the personal tie between the individuals concerned rather than simply differences in rank, are almost universally used today, in all phases of Ganda life—in modern economic and political relations as well as in more traditional contexts. A *mukopi* seeking land or a man ambitious for wealth and power 'attaches himself in loyal dependence to a superior' (*kusenga*). It is through such ties of a patron-client nature, Baganda believe, that a person gets ahead in the world. A popular proverb says, *Omuddu awulira y'atabaza engule ya mukama we*: 'The obedient servant carries his master's crown into battle.' Faithful service is rewarded by the opportunity to acquire wealth and glory. A master seeks in his servant *bwesige* ('loyalty'), and *buwulize* ('obedience'). Conversely, a servant seeks a master who is *ow'ekisa* ('kind') and who is *ayagalibwa abantu aba waggulu* ('favoured by his superiors').

Such, in brief, are traditional Ganda ideas concerning social stratification, the ideas in terms of which Baganda evaluate their fellows. We may next examine the concrete structure of the traditional kingdom to see how these ideas were carried out in everyday behaviour.

The Structure of Traditional Stratification: Two Sample Areas

It will perhaps be useful if we take our examples to illustrate the traditional structure of stratification from two contrasting areas of the kingdom. This will provide the reader with some idea of the range of variation which existed and will at the same time illustrate the process of political centralization which was under way in Buganda even before European influence made itself felt. By taking one of our sample areas from the ancient heartland of Buganda and another from the recently conquered 'marches', we can observe some of the consequences of the military expansion at the expense of the neighbouring peoples which characterized so much of the period just prior to the entry of Europeans.

The county of Busiro (see map insert in *The King's Men*) is part of the original core of the kingdom which, according to legend, coalesced around the founding Kabaka, Kintu. (The present Kabaka, Edward Frederick William Walugembe Mutesa II Luwangula, is Kintu's thirty-fourth successor.) The county of Buddu, on the other hand, only became a part of Buganda during the reign of Jjunju, the twenty-sixth Kabaka. The different positions of the two areas in the historical expansion of the kingdom may be seen in Fig. 2 and the genealogy of

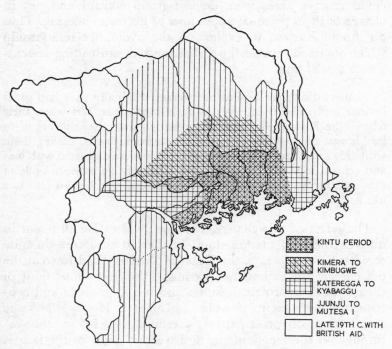

KINTU PERIOD

KIMERA TO KIMBUGWE

KATEREGGA TO KYABAGGU

JJUNJU TO MUTESA I

LATE 19TH C. WITH BRITISH AID

Fig. 2. The growth of the kingdom.

the royal line given in Appendix A provides a key to the relative times involved.[10] It is impossible to assign absolute dates to events prior to the arrival of the first Europeans in the eighteen-sixties, although the fact that most of the royal burial-places are known suggests that archaeology may one day be able to supply an accurate time-scale.

From the point of view of our interest in traditional stratification, the importance of this range of variation is that it is associated with variation in the relative 'strengths' of the two great principles of social differentiation in Buganda which we have already mentioned, namely, ascription through unilineal descent on the one hand and achievement in the service of the Kabaka on the other. The historical trend seems to have been from the former to the latter; Baganda believe, and there is no *a priori* reason to doubt them, that over the centuries the Kabaka moved from a position of *primus inter pares* among heads of patrilineal descent groups to that of a despotic monarch who could remove areas from descent-group control and put in charge of them personal appointees of his own choosing. Thus Sir Apolo Kagwa, in explaining the avoidance relationship which obtained between the Kabaka and certain leading descent-group heads, says:

. . . others didn't see him at all because originally they had great honour and ruled themselves in their own areas. But when their fellow, the Kabaka, became more exalted than they, he began to lord it over them and to drive them out of their lands, leaving them with only small areas. For that reason, they were disgusted with him and refused to visit him, saying: 'We shall not go to see a bully of that sort, for we were formerly his equals but now he just treats us like *bakopi*.'[11]

The effect of this change, however, was rather different in different parts of the kingdom. In the old core area, in spite of what Sir Apolo says, the Kabaka obviously had to treat the descent groups with some circumspection, for here most of them had their principal estates and burial-grounds and consequently here their influence was greater. Fig. 3 shows the distribution of principal clan estates (*butaka bw'akasolya*) throughout the kingdom. In Busiro alone seven of the largest clans have their principal estates, while those of most of the

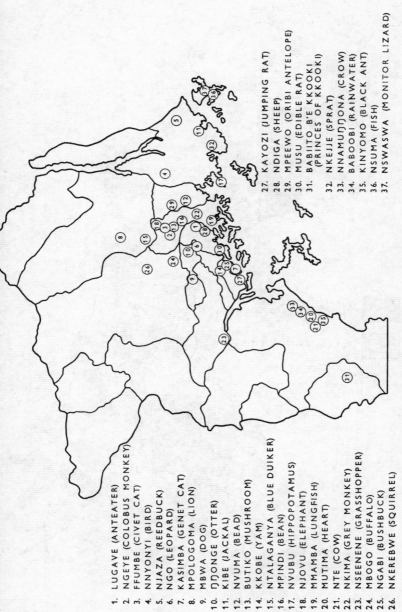

Fig. 3. The distribution of principal clan estates. (From Nsimbi, 1956.)

1. LUGAVE (ANTEATER)
2. NGEYE (COLOBUS MONKEY)
3. FFUMBE (CIVET CAT)
4. NNYONYI (BIRD)
5. NJAZA (REEDBUCK)
6. NGO (LEOPARD)
7. KASIMBA (GENET CAT)
8. MPOLOGOMA (LION)
9. MBWA (DOG)
10. ƉƉONGE (OTTER)
11. KIBE (JACKAL)
12. NVUMA (BEAD)
13. BUTIKO (MUSHROOM)
14. KKOBE (YAM)
15. NTALAGANYA (BLUE DUIKER)
16. MPINDI (BEAN)
17. NVUBU (HIPPOPOTAMUS)
18. NJOVU (ELEPHANT)
19. MMAMBA (LUNGFISH)
20. MUTIMA (HEART)
21. NTE (COW)
22. NKIMA (GREY MONKEY)
23. NSEENENE (GRASSHOPPER)
24. MBOGO (BUFFALO)
25. NGABI (BUSHBUCK)
26. NKEREBWE (SQUIRREL)
27. KAYOZI (JUMPING RAT)
28. NDIGA (SHEEP)
29. MPEEWO (ORIBI ANTELOPE)
30. MUSU (EDIBLE RAT)
31. BABIITO BE KKOOKI (PRINCES OF KKOOKI)
32. NKEJJE (SPRAT)
33. NNAMUƉƉONA (CROW)
34. BABOOBI (RAINWATER)
35. KINYOMO (BLACK ANT)
36. NSUMA (FISH)
37. NSWASWA (MONITOR LIZARD)

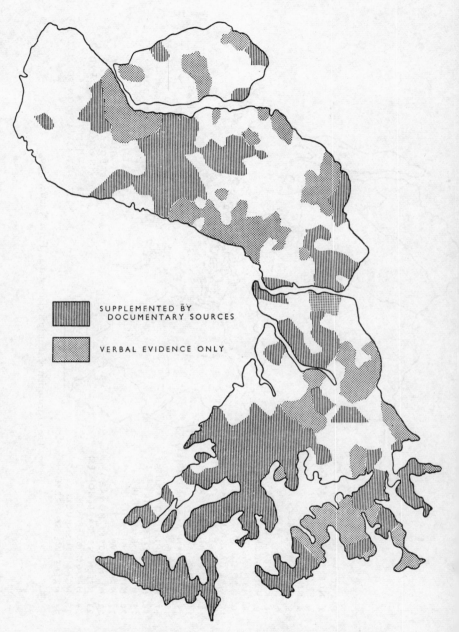

SUPPLEMENTED BY
DOCUMENTARY SOURCES

VERBAL EVIDENCE ONLY

Fig. 4. Areas held by descent-group heads (*bataka*) in Busiro in 1884.

others are located in nearby parts of adjoining counties. In Buddu, on the other hand, although five clans have their principal estates there, none of these is a 'true' Ganda clan. Their ties tend to be with the neighbouring Nyoro-speaking peoples to the west and relatively few of their members live in central Buganda. In arranging for the administration of such an area, relatively recently conquered from Bunyoro, the Kabaka was much less restrained by the position of descent-group heads, for here there was no tradition of past equality.

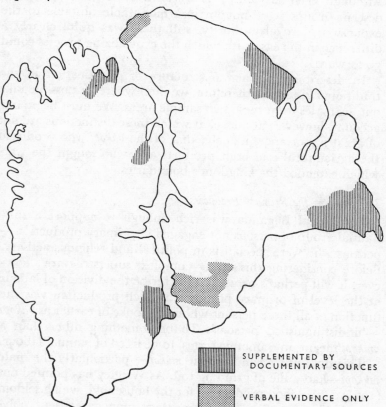

SUPPLEMENTED BY DOCUMENTARY SOURCES

VERBAL EVIDENCE ONLY

Fig. 5. Areas held by descent-group heads (*bataka*) under the *Katabalwa* in Buddu in 1884.

The difference may be seen in Figs. 4, 5, 6 and 7, which show the areas controlled in the eighteen-eighties by descent-group heads and by appointees of the Kabaka respectively, on the one hand in Busiro and on the other hand in the area of the *Katabalwa*, the most important subdivision of Buddu. Although not a complete county, the area of the *Katabalwa* is roughly equal in size to Busiro. (The study upon the results of which these figures are based is described in Appendix B.) The details will be discussed later, but for the moment we need only note the contrast between the two areas as regards the relative influence of descent-group heads and appointees of the Kabaka. Although even in Busiro, as we shall see subsequently, the descent groups were not an insurmountable obstacle to the expansion of royal authority, still there was quite clearly a difference in the ease with which the centralizing process could go forward.

In describing the actual structure of stratification in the traditional kingdom, therefore, we shall wherever possible take our examples from these two sample areas. We must begin our account, however, at a level at which these distinctions are not of great importance, namely, that of the *bakopi* who produced the agricultural and craft products and who fought the wars which extended the kingdom's boundaries.

The Bakopi: the Primary Producers

Traditional Buganda was rich enough to support a substantial group of persons not engaged in primary production—persons who were specialists in political and religious activity. Before considering this rather complex 'superstructure', however, it will perhaps be useful to describe the division of labour at the level of primary production. Such production was the function of all those persons whom we spoke of earlier as *bakopi* —'undistinguished persons'. To be something other than a *mukopi* meant, in economic terms, to be freed of manual labour.

This does not mean that the *mukopi*—particularly the male *mukopi*—had a life of grinding toil. As Wrigley has pointed out (1964), the food production for the household, which seldom contained more than one elementary monogamous or polygynous family, was, and is today, in the hands of the woman, with her short-handled iron hoe. The main focus of her energies was the *lusuku*, the banana garden, which produced the raw material for the staple, a mash of steamed green fruit. The banana garden was a woman's world and she was proud of it.

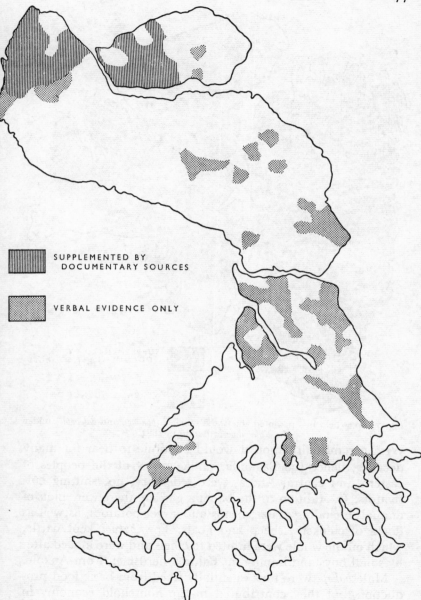

Fig. 6. Areas held by appointed chiefs and officials (*bakungu* and *batongole*) in Busiro in 1884.

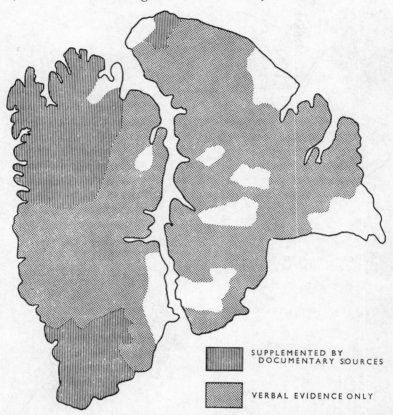

SUPPLEMENTED BY
DOCUMENTARY SOURCES

VERBAL EVIDENCE ONLY

Fig. 7. Areas held by appointed chiefs and officials (*bakungu* and *batongole*) under
the *Katabalwa* in Buddu in 1884.

With careful cultivation it would continue to bear for many
decades; hence the Baganda, unlike many of the peoples of
eastern and central Africa, were sedentary, not shifting cultivators. In addition to the banana garden, there were plots of
annuals including maize, beans and sweet potatoes, as well as
flocks of chickens, sheep and goats. Few *bakopi* kept cattle,
which on the whole were limited to chiefs and were looked after
by small boys and immigrant Bahima herdsmen from Ankole.

Male *bakopi* were thus essentially freed from basic food production, but they contributed to the household economy in
other ways. Men hunted and fished and made the banana beer
which was almost as much a staple as was the steamed fruit.
They also built and repaired houses and made bark-cloth, the

fabric which was formed by pounding and drying the inner bark of the fig tree. The cloth was used for clothing, bedding, burial wrappings and for partitioning houses. In addition to these common crafts, many men also engaged in the more specialized crafts—smithing, pottery-making and canoe-building. Surplus produce and craft products were exchanged at the markets which were regularly held under the supervision of officials of the Kabaka.

But *bakopi* men probably contributed as much to the support of the non-productive superstructure as they did to their own households. As we shall see, there were regular collections of food and craft products by the chiefs and officers of the Kabaka, but beyond this there were substantial demands upon men's time and labour to maintain roads, to build the residences of the Kabaka and the chiefs, and to provide manpower for the army. The organization of these activities will be discussed later; here it is sufficient to note their magnitude in the context of the household supply of labour.

The demands for military service must have increased as conquest and expansion reached a crescendo in the nineteenth century. Kasirye lists sixteen major campaigns during the reign of Kabaka Suna II (1832?–56) and no fewer than sixty-six during the twenty-eight-year reign of Mutesa I (1856–84).[12] Although elements of a standing army were developed towards the end of the traditional period, the bulk of the troops continued to be militia. Men who did not go to war were subjected to a special tax.[13] Stanley, who made rather careful estimates of the strength of the various units, arrived at a total of 125,000 fighting men, exclusive of camp-followers and non-Baganda levies, for the army with which he saw Mutesa I attack the Buvuma Islanders in 1875.[14] He estimated the population of the kingdom at nearly one million—probably a fairly accurate figure. For those who lived along the shore of the lake or on the islands, there was service in the canoe fleet which made up the navy of the Kabaka. The campaign against Buvuma referred to above was in part a naval action and Stanley therefore had an opportunity to assess the strength of the fleet. There were present on that occasion 230 war canoes, of which the largest was 72 feet in length. Stanley estimated that they carried a total of between sixteen and twenty thousand men, including the crews of paddlers.[15] Military campaigning must thus have occupied a substantial part of the energies of the *bakopi*.

So also work on the roads and on the residences of the great must have kept them away from their villages a good deal of the time. Each chief was required to maintain, with labour supplied by the people of his area, a road from his headquarters to the capital or to one of the roads leading to the capital. Judging by the difficulty with which roads are kept in repair today, particularly during rainy seasons, this activity must have consumed a good deal of labour, although of course the absence of wheeled vehicles in traditional Buganda makes ancient and modern road-maintenance problems not really comparable.

Even more demanding, one would judge from available accounts, were the drafts of labour to work on the capital and on chiefs' headquarters. Ganda buildings, to be sure, were not substantial. They were beehive-shaped structures built of poles and reeds lashed together, and were thatched from pinnacle to base. (The mud-and-wattle walls, which are today a universal feature of the houses of those unable to afford brick, are apparently a later introduction.) The traditional buildings did, however, require a good deal of labour, both because they were rather intricately made and because they frequently had to be rebuilt, either because of fire and termites or because the occupants had simply decided to move. Indeed, the mobility of the Kabaka and his chiefs is a striking feature of traditional Buganda and is probably associated with the growth of royal power. In a country with only the most rudimentary means of communication, the monarch can most effectively make his authority felt by actually moving from place to place. Medieval English kings, with their writs and seals, nevertheless found constant itinerating a necessity of political communication; the lack of writing made it even more so for the kings of Buganda.[16] Suna and Mutesa I were constantly moving back and forth across the country, directing military operations, consulting oracles and putting down dissidents.[17] All of these movements required temporary camps to be built for the Kabaka and his retinue. Also, the 'permanent' capital was frequently moved. Mutesa seems to have moved ten times and to have had a new capital constructed on each occasion.[18] If Kagwa's accounts of the size of the capital are not grossly exaggerated, this will have required very large amounts of labour. The palace enclosure alone, according to Kagwa's sketch, contained more than five hundred huts, but this was only a part of the total capital complex; the latter also included the 'town houses' of the chiefs, who were required to be in almost constant attendance at the court.[19] To Speke, who visited Mutesa I in 1862, the capital at Banda appeared as 'A whole hill—covered with gigantic huts, such as I had never seen in Africa before'.[20] To Stanley, twelve years later, the new capital at Rubaga was '. . . a hill covered with tall conical huts, whose tops peep out above the foliage of plantains and bananas, and lofty fences of cane'.[21] Stanley adds that the 'audience hall' (*bulange*) was twenty-five feet high, sixty feet long and eighteen feet wide.[22] The country establishments of chiefs, though on a much less elaborate scale, were nevertheless substantial, and all this required much labour on the part of *bakopi*.

Such, in brief, was the division of labour by means of which the *bakopi* supported both themselves and the large group of persons who did not engage in primary production. We may now examine the structure of this latter group, recalling the several bases of differentiation from *bakopi* status which we have already discussed.

The Bataka: *Heads of Clans and Lineages*

We have already mentioned the segmentary structure of patrilineal descent groups. It is important to be clear about the geographical distribution and functions of these groups and their heads for two reasons: first, because while the *pattern* of unilineal descent in Buganda is one familiar to Africanists, the function of descent groups in the Ganda polity had by the nineteenth century come to be very different from that of descent groups in most African kingdoms; and, second, because the position of the *bataka*—the heads of clans and lineages—has continued to provoke controversy in modern Buganda and it is therefore useful to understand as clearly as possible what the situation was at the time of first contact with outside influences.

It is important to note, first of all, that in the nineteenth century the clans and lineages of which the *bataka* were the heads were not in any sense territorial communities. The constituent lineages of a particular clan were likely to be widely scattered and even small local communities were seldom, if ever, communities of lineage-mates. Although unilineal descent groups had, and still have, structures of authority in connexion with their particular functions, they have never in recent times been the basic building-blocks of the state. The state is rather made up of units in which authority follows lines of personal patronage and clientship; descent is, in principle, irrelevant. The basic mode of affiliation in the state is described by the verb *kusenga*—to attach oneself by choice to a superior as his loyal dependent. Descent gives one an indispensable social indentification and a group membership, above all for purposes of succession; it does not necessarily give one a place of residence or a political allegiance—none, that is, more specific than one's allegiance to the state as a whole. As we shall see in Chapter 9,

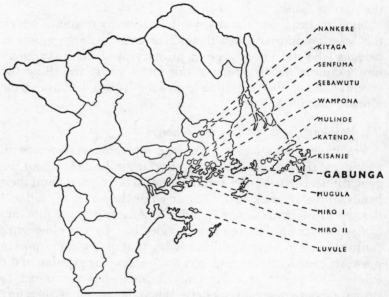

Fig. 8. Distribution of the principal estates of the maximal lineages (*masiga*) of the Lungfish clan.

however, descent groups did have opportunities to function rather like rudimentary political parties in national politics. When a new Kabaka or chief took office, his mother's patrilineal kinsmen often received major appointments.

An example will perhaps make clearer the spatial distribution of unilineal descent groups in Buganda. The Lungfish clan is one of the 'original' (*bannansangwa*: 'those who were found') Ganda clans and is generally believed to be the largest. The distribution of the principal estates of its major lineages (*masiga*) is shown in Fig. 8, from which it is apparent that the clan lands do not form a compact block. As is the case with all the old clans, most of the major lineage estates are located in the central part of the kingdom, but within this central area they are widely scattered. The estates of the minor lineages (*mituba*) which make up a major lineage (*ssiga*) may, however, form a contiguous block of territory, as is the case with the *ssiga* of the *Nankere* shown in Fig. 9. The map shows the *kasolya* ('roof', or principal) estates of the seven constituent

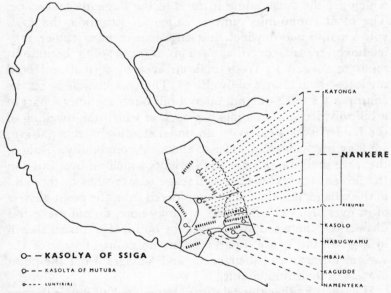

Fig. 9. Estates of the major lineages (*mituba*) of the maximal lineage (*ssiga*) of the *Nankere*.

minor lineages and also indicates the degree of segmentation into minimal lineages (*nyiriri*) which exists in two of its minor lineages—the principal minor lineage, within which the major lineage headship descends, and one other, that of the *Kayonga*.

The lines on the map indicating minimal lineages do not attempt to show the locations of their estates within the minor lineage area.

In the example of the area of the *Nankere*, it is perhaps worth noting in passing the anomaly of the small minimal lineage (*lunyiriri*) of Kibumbi, which is conceived of genealogically as being of the same depth as the entire major lineage (*ssiga*) of the *Nankere*. According to tradition, Kibumbi was the father of the first *Nankere* and his descendants, presumably through other sons, ceremonially dress the *Nankere* when he succeeds to the office. Despite its depth, however, Kibumbi's descent group continues to be thought of as a minimal lineage (*lunyiriri*).[23]

We have referred to the lands which are associated with clans and lineages as 'estates'. These estates are, in many cases, *mitala* (sing. *mutala*), low hills surrounded by swampy land which are the outstanding features of the Buganda landscape. The local community unit is called in Luganda the *kyalo* (pl. *byalo*), a word which has customarily been rather misleadingly translated 'village'. This is misleading because it tends to suggest to Westerners an area of agricultural land nucleated by a cluster of dwellings. The Ganda *kyalo* is, on the contrary, a stretch of land, often a hill but sometimes a part of a hill, divided into holdings, on each of which the dwelling of the holder is located. With an understanding of this pattern, we may use 'village' to refer to the local community. 'Estate', then, we shall use to refer to the rights which an overlord—in the present context a clan or lineage *mutaka*—has in the land of the village; it is the village considered from the point of view of its overlord. (The Baganda, we may note, do not make this distinction; the word *kyalo* serves for both.) The places shown in Figs. 8 and 9 are 'estates' from the point of view of the various lineages and their heads and 'villages' from the point of view of their inhabitants.

However, neither this relatively large block of major lineage land—known as Bukerekere after the area within it which forms the principal estate of the major lineage—nor any of the minor lineage subdivisions is, or was traditionally, populated in the main by members of the lineages in question. Any person was free to attach himself to (*kusenga*) the *mutaka*—the head of the clan or lineage and master of the estate. Conversely, by no means all the members of a lineage lived on the land which formed its principal estate. Although many members would, in fact, live on the lineage land, others would go elsewhere to 'seek their fortunes' by attaching themselves to other *bataka* or to chiefs' or king's officers. The pattern of land rights was greatly altered by changes introduced in 1900 and it is consequently extremely difficult to discover how far in earlier times the relationship between a *mutaka* and a tenant who was his own lineage mate differed from that which obtained between a *mutaka* and a *musenze* ('settler', a non-kinsman). Mukwaya, who has surveyed this whole subject, concludes:

> His position as a peasant was more or less the same whether he lived under a kinship head or any other type of chief. But his security of tenure and freedom from molestation and petty irritants were greater if his chief were a clansman. This feeling sometimes gave rise to wholesale movement of large sections of the population as clansmen followed a successful member of their clan in his progression from bigger to bigger chieftainships.[24]

The *butaka* estates were, therefore, 'clan lands' and 'lineage lands' only in the sense of providing the headquarters of the head of the clan or lineage and the religious centre for its members. The focus of religious sentiments was the burial ground in each estate in which were preserved the graves of important ancestors. The rest of the estate was, in principle, available to be allocated to anyone by the *mutaka* in accordance with the *kusenga* pattern, although lineage-mates would no doubt not be evicted to make land available for this purpose.

The *mutaka*, then, played two roles: on the one hand, he was a *mwami*—an overlord of an estate and its inhabitants; on the other hand, he was the leader of a scattered community of patrilineal kinsmen. The process of progressive centralization to which we have several times referred involved a shift in the relative emphasis given to these two roles; it involved a diminution in the functions performed by *bataka* in the government of the kingdom as a whole, limiting their authority more and more to the domestic affairs of their unilineal descent groups. An extended discussion of these two roles of the *bataka* would be out of place here, but we must outline their main features.

The central concept in the concerns that brought clan- and lineage-mates together under the leadership of their head was *busika*—a word which combines the meanings of 'inheritance' and 'succession'. *Busika* refers to any property or office which may be transmitted through descent, but more fundamentally it refers to the whole idea of patrilineal continuity through time. Thus, while a *musika*—an 'heir' or 'successor'—takes the deceased person's property, it is more important that he in many ways succeeds to his social status generally, becoming in *loco parentis* to his children for jural and ritual purposes. [25] If the deceased occupies an hereditary office in the clan, the *musika* takes his place to such an extent that he may speak in the first person of an action taken by a predecessor in office one hundred years earlier. The spatial loci of this idea of patrilineal continuity are the graves of ancestors located in the *butaka* lands of the clans and lineages. It is as guardian and arbiter of the interests and sentiments which cluster about this idea that the *mutaka* functions in the internal life of the clan or lineage.

It is, first of all, the responsibility of the clan head and his hierarchy of lineage heads to maintain possession of the burial grounds and to see that the graves are kept in a proper state of repair. [26] Traditionally there was an ancestor cult which involved propitiation of deceased members of the clan or lineage and communication with them through spirit possession. While much of the formal practice of the ancestor cult has lapsed in the face of almost universal conversion to Christianity or Islam, still the sentiments derived from it remain and form the basis, for example, of the dissatisfaction felt by many Baganda with the new freehold form of land tenure which was introduced in 1900. Many burial grounds were either given to non-clansmen by the chiefs who presided over the 1900 land settlement or, more frequently, were shortly thereafter sold to non-clansmen by improvident clan and lineage heads. In such cases graves may be untended and overgrown with weeds, a situation which is offensive to even the most pious Christians and Muslims. Anxiety about the loss of these burial grounds (*butaka* proper) has been one of the main sources of movements of opposition against the policies of the Uganda and Buganda Governments since 1900. The 'Bataka Party', although it has never consisted mainly of clan or lineage heads, has consistently mobilized, along with other sentiments, the diffuse feelings of outrage felt by many Baganda at the violation of clan and lineage burial grounds. There were, however, threats to clan and lineage possession of burial grounds even before the recent changes in land tenure. As the process of centralization of control in the hands of the Kabaka went forward during the nineteenth century, former clan and lineage estates were some-times given as benefices to kings' chiefs and officials. This made for a self-conscious, and rather defensive, awareness of 'clan interests' even before the changes which were introduced in 1900.

Aside from being the visible symbol and guardian of clan or lineage interests, the head was responsible for the administration of the *corpus juris* which governed succession. The principal occasion for the exercise of jural authority was the ceremony called *kwabya olumbe* ('removing the state of mourning') which ended the period of mourning for the dead. Whether the deceased was an ordinary peasant requiring a successor to look after his widow and children or the head of a lineage whose successor would occupy the office, the correct person had to be selected and installed. This done, death, as the name of the ceremony suggests, was banished and the spirit of the deceased was appeased. Sometimes an unsuccessful candidate for succes-sion would refuse to accept the decision, which would then be challenged before the head of the next most inclusive patrilineal unit. Another common subject for litigation was the status of units in the hierarchy of descent groups; the head of a minor lineage which had grown large might refuse to accept the authority of the major lineage head, claiming for his unit the status of an independent major lineage. At each level, the head sat in judgment together with the heads of subordinate segments as a sort of chairman of the bench.

The *bataka* were not in former times, however, merely leaders in the internal affairs of descent groups. According to tradition, they have from the beginning been associated with the kingship; indeed, as we have mentioned, tradition suggests that early in the kingdom's development they held the major positions of authority, the Kabaka occupying, perhaps, a *primus inter pares* position. For example, the *Kisolo*, head of the Otter clan, was Prime Minister (*Katikkiro*) to the first Kabaka, Kintu.[27] The

Walusimbi, head of the Civet Cat clan, is said to have preceded Kintu in Buganda and to have been the Prime Minister of Kintu's successor, Kabaka Cwa Nabaka.[28] A. H. Cox has shown how, according to tradition, most chieftainships were hereditary during the early period.[29] Two clans, the Lion and the Leopard, even claim to have descended from early kings and thus to be related patrilineally to the royal line.[30]

Clans and lineages, furthermore, have traditionally had ceremonial duties to the Kabaka which bound them to the throne. For example, the *Nankere*, the head of the major lineage within the Lungfish clan whose estates are shown in Fig. 9, was in charge of the 'maturation rite' (*kukuza*) which each new Kabaka passed through.[31] The *Mugema*, head of the Grey Monkey clan, formally installed the new Kabaka and was also, until recent times, hereditary chief of the central county of Busiro. Other *bataka* had such duties as guarding the royal stool, and commanding the canoe fleet.

Gradually, however, through at least two distinguishable processes, the independent authority of the Kabaka grew at the expense of that of the *bataka*. First, the Kabaka acquired a degree of control over the succession to clan and lineage headships. Thus, many lineages seem to have originated from royal appointments in the following way: the Kabaka might appoint a member of an existing lineage to an official post in some other part of Buganda and as a mark of favour might grant him an estate in that area. Gradually the estate would come to be known as *butaka* and the descendants of the chief would claim the status of an independent minor or major lineage. According to one account, it was in this way that the line of the *Gabunga* came to hold the office of admiral of the canoe fleet and ultimately displaced an older line as head of the lungfish clan.[32] It was natural in such a case, where the office in question was one of critical military importance, that the Kabaka should continue to exercise a good deal of influence in the selection of a successor. In recent times it has been accepted that the Kabaka is *ssaabataka*—chief of all *bataka*—and that all successors to clan and lineage headships must be presented to him for his approval.

A second way in which the Kabaka extended his control was by simply displacing clan and lineage heads from areas ruled by them. As time went by, larger and larger areas passed by royal grant out of the hands of *bataka* and into those of the appointed chiefs and officials—the *bakungu* and *batongole*.

The Bakungu *and* Batongole: *Kings' Chiefs and Officials*

Our understanding of traditional political offices is often obscured by the course which social change has followed in Bugunda. If British overrule had brought a sharper break with traditional political institutions, present-day memory of the pre-1900 situation would probably be clearer than it is. As it happened, British influence acted to reform, rather than to overthrow, the traditional structure. Traditional offices and terminology were carried over, but with changed functions and connotations; the result is that Baganda themselves often have little sense of the profound change which their political institutions have undergone and thus often read into the past present-day functions of offices and meanings of terms.

At no point does this difficulty present itself more prominently than when we attempt to understand the position prior to 1900 of the two main kinds of appointed officials of the Kabaka—the *bakungu* and the *bami ab'ebitongole* or *batongole*. In the first place, the term *bakungu* has tended to fall into disuse, although present-day Baganda generally identify it with the chiefs of the modern Buganda Government, particularly the county (*ssaza*) and sub-county (*ggombolola*) chiefs. This corresponds roughly with traditional usage. The officials known as *bakungu* traditionally were the *ssaza* chiefs and their leading subordinates, who formed something like a hierarchy of territorial governors.[33] Traditional history suggests that many of the offices held in recent pre-colonial times by *bakungu* were once hereditary in patrilineal descent groups and that they gradually came to have more the character of an appointive proto-bureaucracy through extension of royal authority over their recruitment. Cox has shown how, in the various accounts of traditional history, the *ssaza* chieftainships are, one after the other, taken out of the hands of particular descent groups.[34] Even at the end of the nineteenth century, however, the territorial hierarchy of *ssaza* chiefs and their ranked subordinates (*mumyuka, ssaabaddu, ssaabagabo*, etc.) was a mixture of hereditary and appointed officials, although the appointed element had come to predominate. Three *ssaza* chiefs were still hereditary and Nsimbi gives four instances in which this was also true of ranked subordinates of *ssaza* chiefs.[35] Even within a single county the hierarchy might be mixed; an hereditary *ssaza* chief might have a *mumyuka* appointed by the Kabaka and an hereditary *ssabaddu*.[36] Today all territorial chieftainships are appointive and their occupants tend to be spoken of simply as '*bami ba Kabaka*', 'chiefs of the Kabaka'.

The term *batongole* has undergone a more complete transformation. Today's *mutongole* is a subordinate to a landlord or to a parish (*muluka*) chief—the lowest rung on the official ladder (see account in Southwold, 1964)—whereas his pre-1900 namesake (more often, it seems, called '*ow'ekitongole*', although the difference is probably not important) was an officer of the Kabaka or of a chief who might, particularly in the former case, be a person of very great importance. The root—*tongole*—means 'a responsibility carried out on behalf of a superior'. '*Butongole*' is land ruled on behalf of someone else. To be sure, the appointed *mukungu* also ruled on behalf of his superior, the Kabaka, and in fact there may well have been no sharp distinction between the two types of official.[37] On the whole, however, the officials spoken of as '*batongole*' appear to represent a more recent and more widespread extension of royal prerogative. They were often directly responsible to the Kabaka and independent of the *bakungu* chiefs. Some were, as Nsimbi says, royal favourites or national military heroes whose estates represented rewards.[38] Other were officers responsible for providing specialized services to the royal household and the state. Today the estates and titles of many traditional *batongole* have been assimilated to the official structure of the Buganda Government along with titles and areas of jurisdiction formerly associated with *bakungu*.

As this latter point suggests, there has in modern times taken place, in addition to change in the meanings of terms, a general rationalization of the whole political structure. Lines of authority have been clarified and jurisdictions redefined to produce a neat, pyramidal structure with consistent levels of organization of the sort characteristic of modern bureaucracies. The traditional system was much more ragged, full of overlapping jurisdictions and lines of authority, for the Buganda Government of the nineteenth century had not yet taken on the functions which make greater rationalization of organization essential.

The changes which British overrule have brought to the government of the Kabaka will be considered at great length in the following chapter. Here we have meant merely to explain why, after we have attempted to describe the traditional *bakungu* and *batongole*, there will persist a certain vagueness in our understanding of their roles in traditional society. A clearer picture is probably no longer recoverable.

We have attempted to recover as much as possible by reconstructing, as accurately as surviving documents and the memories of living men will allow, the position of these two types of official in the two sample areas mentioned earlier in this chapter—the *ssaza* of Busiro and territory of the *Katabalwa* in the *ssaza* of Buddu. (See Appendix B for a description of the methods by which these data were gathered, Figs. 6 and 7 for maps showing the estates of *bakungu* and *batongole*.)

According to traditional history, Buddu was taken from the neighbouring kingdom of Bunyoro in the time of Jjunju, the twenty-sixth Kabaka.[39] Jjunju retained the Nyoro administrative divisions and titles previously held by Nyoro princes and chiefs; he simply substituted his own Ganda *bakungu* chiefs and arranged them according to the Ganda ranking system. The *Katabalwa* became *mumyuka*, the *Kagolo* became *ssabaddu*, the *Kajeerero* became *ssabagabo*, the *Bugala* became *ssabawali* and the *Mukudde* became the officer (*mutongole*) in charge of the Buddu estates of the *Nnamasole* (Queen Mother).[40] The *Ppookino*, previously a Nyoro prince, became chief over the whole of the new *ssaza*. Within the area of the *Katabalwa*, many estates were held by *batongole*, some of whom were appointees of the Kabaka, while others were personal followers of the *Katabalwa* himself. In the former category were, for example, the *Kakiiza*, the officer in charge of the royal herds in the area. Several estates, in addition, were held by military captains, also classed as *batongole*. The estates of the *Katabalwa* himself were very extensive, covering 69 of the 219 villages under his jurisdiction. Still other estates were held by officials (*batongole*) of the *nkuluze*, the treasury, and of the Queen Mother. Altogether, 188 villages were held by *bakungu* and *batongole*, leaving only 31 in the hands of hereditary *bataka*.

The predominance of appointed officials and the relative

neatness of the hierarchy in the area of the *Katabalwa* is presumably a result of the greater freedom of the Kabaka to make political arrangements afresh to suit his own liking in a newly conquered area. In contrast, in the heartland *ssaza* of Busiro, which has been part of Buganda since the dawn of traditional history, hereditary *bataka* predominated and there was a veritable jungle of overlapping and interdigitating authorities, the cumulative result of centuries of *ad hoc* adjustments. To begin with the most prominent anomaly, the *ssaza* chieftainship itself was held, not by an appointed *mukungu*, but rather by a hereditary *mutaka*, the *Mugema*, head of the Grey Monkey clan. This was one of three hereditary *ssaza* chieftainships which survived into modern times and its continued existence is attributed to the great prestige of the *Mugema*, whose ancestor is said to have rescued the infant Kimera, the third Kabaka, from danger in Bunyoro. The *Mugema* was consequently spoken of as the 'parent' of the Kabaka and enjoyed a good deal of political immunity, although there is ample evidence that this immunity was a source of royal irritation.[41]

Under the *Mugema* were two principal *bakungu* chiefs appointed by the Kabaka: the *Senkezi*, the *mumyuka*, who ruled the area north of the river Mayanja Kato, which divides Busiro at its narrowest point, and the *Makamba*, the *ssabaddu*, who ruled the part south of Mayanja Kato. It would appear, however, that neither the *Senkezi* nor the *Makamba* exercised within his 'jurisdiction' the kind of over-all authority enjoyed by the *Katabalwa* in Buddu. At the end of this chapter we shall attempt a functional overview of the traditional polity, indicating the authority of various officials *vis-à-vis* the main tasks of government. For the moment, it will be sufficient to note that the estates of the *Senkezi* and the *Makamba*, whose size presumably gives some indicating of their holders' authority, were a good deal smaller than those of the *Katabalwa*; and also that there were in Busiro many more *batongole* and hereditary *bataka* who were probably largely independent of the ranked *bakungu*.

We have already noted the concentration of principal estates of large, important clans in Busiro (Fig. 3) and have discussed in some detail the structure of one of them, the Lungfish clan. While the *bataka* had lost much of their independent authority to the appointees of the king, and while the king had come more and more to influence their succession, still they enjoyed great prestige, deriving both from their hereditary positions within the clans and from their association with the Kabaka. The head of the Lungfish clan, the *Ggabunga*, exercised great power as commander of the royal fleet on Lake Victoria, and his estates and those of his lineage heads covered a great part of southern Busiro, in the territory of the *Makamba*. The *Kibaale*, who had some of his estates within the area of the *Senkezi*, was head of a major lineage of the Oribi Antelope clan and the steward of the royal household, with authority over the servants and wives of the Kabaka. Also in the area were the *Walusimbi*, head of the Civet Cat clan, and the *Ggunju*, head of the Mushroom clan, as well as many other *bataka*, large and small. In addition to the heads of these 'commoner' clans and lineages, there were also 'princely *bataka*', heads of lineages descended from past kings, who often were settled near the many royal tombs which gave Busiro its name (*masiro*: 'tombs').

Proximity to the capital, which was usually located either in Busiro itself or in neighbouring Kyaddondo, made Busiro a convenient location for estates of appointed *batongole* in whom the ruling Kabaka had a personal interest or who supplied special services to the palace. One large area in the north of the *ssaza*, for example, formed the estate of the *Musonyi*, who was responsible for supplying clothing to the Kabaka. Another official estate (*kitongole*), consisting of seven villages, was called Kikebezi and was the estate of the suppliers of firewood to the palace. Many others were held by military captains or by the military commander for Busiro, the *Bulusi*. Again, relatives of the ruling Kabaka—his mother, sisters and in-laws—had estates which were put in the hands of their own *batongole*. A notable instance of the lack of neatness and consistency in the traditional political hierarchy is provided by Busamba, the estate of a *mutongole* called the *Kasamba*, who was not part of the Busiro structure at all, but rather was a subordinate of the *ssaabaddu* of the neighbouring county of Bulemeezi, even though Busamba lay entirely within Busiro.

The position of the *bakungu* and the *batongole*, then, varied a good deal from place to place; they were sometimes not entirely distinct from each other and *bakungu* were often interlarded with hereditary *bataka* in the hierarchy of ranked territorial chiefs. This over-lapping is illustrated diagramatically in Fig. 10. Everywhere, however, the two types of appointed officials represented a progressive strengthening of central control by the Kabaka and a concommitant decline in the political importance of descent groups. The political functions of clans and lineages were progressively confined to their own domestic affairs, principally the adjudication of inheritance and succession.

Before leaving the subject of traditional Ganda political structure it may be useful to pause briefly for some comparative remarks. First of all, it will be apparent to Africanists that, as we noted in the introduction, the traditional kingdom was not

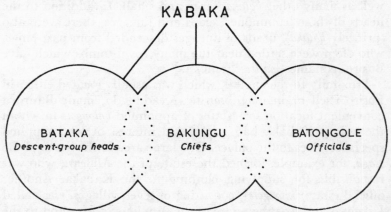

Fig. 10. The over-lapping of the three categories of office holders.

a typical African state. Most African polities of sufficient size, power, and complexity to deserve the name 'kingdom' were in structure 'segmentary' or, to use Southall's useful term, 'pyramidal'.[42] That is to say, they were relatively decentralized polities in which the structure of the kingdom was duplicated within each of its major divisions or segments. Each segment—and there were frequently several levels of segmentation—was a kingdom in miniature, owing only a conditional allegiance to the larger unity of which it formed a part. This was the case, for example, in Ashanti and in the southern Bantu states. The chiefdoms which made up the Ashanti confederacy formed a single unit only sporadically, usually only for military purposes, and within each chiefdom there was again a similar decentralization.[43] Among the Southern Bantu kingdoms, the Zulu achieved the greatest degree of centralization through the creation of a system of military regiments, based upon age and cross-cutting the constituent segments; but this was not sufficient to overcome the inherent tendency towards segmentation and the king's authority declined.[44]

Perhaps the clearest expression of the difference between these states and Buganda lay in the ability of the Kabaka to control appointments to positions of authority over territorial subdivisions. Unlike the subordinate chiefs in the more segmentary kingdoms, whose positions rested upon some combination of descent and the consent of the people over whom they ruled, the chiefs of the Kabaka were increasingly responsible directly and solely to him. Legitimacy, instead of rising pyramidally, so to speak, through a series of heads of increasingly inclusive units to the king, went in Buganda directly from the people to the king, who then in turn conferred it upon a hierarchy of subordinates. The kingdom as a whole could thus become an object of explicit and continuous government in a way which was impossible in a more pyramidal state. Of the African kingdoms of which we have adequate descriptions, Dahomey seems to have been most like Buganda in these respects.[45]

In Africa, the tendency of states to take a decentralized, pyramidal form resulted from the prominence in their social structures of unilineal descent groups. Most commonly, the segments of which the political pyramid was composed either were themselves actual or fictional descent groups or else were formed around such groups by affiliating to them non-related persons.[46] In either case, the unilineal descent group was the basic building block of society; it provided a foundation for local corporateness and autonomy which stood in the way of greater centralization and royal despotism. Highly centralized states like Buganda could develop only by suppressing this autonomy and, as we have seen, such a tendency has been the dominant theme in recent Ganda political history, at any rate until outside intervention. One is reminded here of Max Weber's discussion of feudalism and 'patrimonialism' in medieval European history—the struggle between the centralizing efforts of kings, expressed in their attempts to build up bodies of patrimonial retainers responsible to themselves alone, and the decentralizing tendency of subordinate authorities to become locally rooted hereditary lords. [47] The structural bases of decentralization are of course different: in Africa the corporate unilineal descent group; in Europe the local dynasty, with its own vassalage built up through subinfeudation and its loyalty to the aristocratic estate. But, while these differences are important, we may recognize at the same time that the Kabaka, and perhaps the king of Dahomey, occupy a place in history in some ways analogous to that of the European monarchs of the 'age of absolutism'.

Priests, Mediums and Diviners

Like most Bantu, Baganda believed that there were supernatural forces or beings of several kinds which were capable of influencing the lives of men. [48] Some of these were non-human, but the most important, again in characteristic Bantu fashion, were spirits of the dead. Baganda distinguish between *mizimu*—the ghosts of dead persons—and *balubaale*—spirits which, like the *mizimu*, are anthropomorphic and are believed to have once lived on earth as persons, but which now form a sort of pantheon of gods with particular spheres of interest. Perhaps the best way of putting the distinction is to say that ghosts are the spirits of ancestors—persons known to be related to persons still living—while the gods, even though once human, are not thought of as kinsmen of living persons. The most important ghosts were those of past kings, going back to Kintu, the legendary founder of the nation. Among the more prominent gods were Mukasa, associated with fertility, fishermen and Lake Victoria (the Buganda name for the lake is *Nnalubaale*: fem. 'Great God', or perhaps 'Mother of God'); Kikuba, the guardian of the western frontier and hence patron of war against the Banyoro; Nende, guardian of the eastern (Busoga) frontier; Musisi, the earthquake god; and Kawumpuli, the god of plague. The total pantheon was very large, the major national gods such as those just listed grading off into a host of minor local spirits associated with particular rocks or rivers or trees.

The other principal type of supernatural force was that embodied in fetishes—manufactured objects believed to possess magical power of a non-anthropomorphic sort. Most commonly these consisted of cow or buffalo horns filled with magical substances—hence the general use of the term *jjembe* ('horn') for any kind of fetish. The most powerful fetishes were those of the Kabaka, but possession of them was widespread.

The major emphasis in Ganda religion was not upon the ritual reaffirmation of existing institutions but rather upon instrumental magic. The one exception was the kingship; there were ceremonies, fully described by Roscoe, which emphasized the king's despotic powers at the time of his coronation and others which reinvigorated him and secured for him the support of his ancestors. Apart from this, the particular structure of society received little ritual support. As we have seen, the society was a relatively fluid one and was becoming even more fluid through the extension of the authority of the Kabaka in the appointment of officials. Particular territorial and kinship groupings of persons were increasingly subordinated to the needs of the central government. Correspondingly, in Ganda religion regular ceremonial celebrations associated with particular features of the substructure of Ganda society were becoming relatively less important than rituals which had as their object the acquisition of supernatural support for the nation as a whole in its wars and raids against neighbouring peoples and for individuals in pursuit of their personal needs and aspirations. Thus, while Baganda believed in the continued influence of ancestors in the affairs of their descendants, there was apparently no regular, public ritual complex associated with the structure of unilineal descent groups. Again, the relations between particular offices in the state were not supernaturally sanctioned. The one national public ceremony was the coronation, and on this occasion officials and descent groups were indeed ritually associated with the kingship. This was not, however, a very *sacred* ceremonial; the gods were not called upon to sanction particular patterns of right and duty between king and people or between king and officials. The rites were simply an affirmation of the king's authority and an exhortation to him to expand the power and boundaries of the kingdom. The gods and other supernatural forces were more prominent in a different context, namely, that of supernatural aid for particular purposes, national or individual.

The basic form of religious activity was spirit possession. Both gods and ghosts might be propitiated with gifts of food or beer by ordinary, uninitiated persons, but serious communication with spirits required that an established medium (*mmandwa*) be possessed and thus induce the spirit to speak through him or her. Possession took place in a setting of constant drumming, singing, shaking of gourd rattles (*nsasi*) and drinking of banana beer. When the spirit descended upon the medium—'caught him by the head' (*yamukwata ku mutwe*)—he rose up, making violent, shaking movements, stared wildly about him, and perhaps sang for a bit. Then he spoke with the voice of the spirit to whatever problem had caused the séance to be held, and finally collapsed in a state of exhaustion. Mediums were chosen by the ghosts or gods for whom they spoke. They fell ill physically or mentally and might run about on all fours like animals or tear off their clothes and climb trees. When, through the help of an established medium, they recognized and yielded to the spirit, they were cured of the symptoms and thereafter might themselves practise as mediums.

Against the background of this very brief account of traditional belief and practice we may consider the position in nineteenth-century Ganda society of specialists in religious activity.

Perhaps the most prominent religious specialists were the persons attached to the two types of national religious centre—the *masiro* (tombs) of dead kings and the *biggwa* (temples) of the major gods. The former were patterned after the palace of the living Kabaka and, indeed, a king's tomb was sometimes spoken of as a *lubiri* (palace), the suggestion being that the dead king was still present; he had merely retired, so to speak, to the position of 'elder statesman', leaving his successor in active control of the state. The physical manifestations of the late Kabaka were his jawbone and umbilicus, relics which his successor had caused to be elaborately decorated with beads and cowries. During his lifetime the umbilicus, known as the king's 'twin' (*mulongo*) had been kept by the *Kimbugwe*, an official second in rank to the *Katikkiro* whose duties were those of a personal advisor. An excellent description of one of the tombs, which are today maintained by the Buganda Government, may be found in John Taylor's *The Growth of the Church in Buganda*.[49] In charge of the tomb was the *Nnalinnya*—the sister of the king who during his life had been his 'official sister' (*lubuga*). The chief wife (*kaddulubaale*), and a number of other wives as well, also continued to live in the tomb enclosure, maintaining the essentials of a royal household. When these women died, others from their lineages were chosen to succeed them. The dead kings' importance lay in the fact that they maintained an active interest in the welfare of the state, and particularly in its military success. A reigning Kabaka might ask advice of his predecessors, or the latter might volunteer advice through their mediums. The 'wives' and 'sisters' of the deceased king might be possessed by his spirit, but the principal medium was a commoner who was 'called' in the manner indicated above.

The temples of the main gods also resembled royal palaces and they themselves might be spoken of as kings. There is, indeed, some indication that they may have represented earlier dynasties of earthly rulers.[50] Again there were the physical relics, in this case often, apparently, mummified bodies or parts of bodies.[51] One or more priests (*kabona*) were in charge of each temple, but these were temporal officials; as in the case of the king's tomb, there was, in addition, a medium who had been chosen by the spirit to be its mouthpiece. The various gods seem to have been loosely associated with particular clans, but the connexion appears to have been limited to the selection of priests from the clan in question. Mediums and supplicants might be of any clan.[52] The national shrines of the major gods were large-scale affairs and their activities centred upon the Kabaka and the Central Government.[53] Even the major gods, however, had smaller, local shrines attended by local mediums who dealt with the needs of the humbler members of society.

The numbers and importance of the religious functionaries attached to temples and royal tombs are extremely difficult to estimate. Probably the tombs of all of Mutesa I's twenty-nine predecessors were maintained in some form, while Kagwa's account suggests that there were at least some dozens of temples of the gods.[54] Estates seem to have provided at least the more important centres with economic support. The lands attached to king's tombs formed part of the *butaka* lands of the princely lineages descended from them. Speke tells of encountering, on his journey in 1862 along the west bank of the Nile near Jinja, an area 'dedicated in some mysterious manner to Lubari (Almighty)' and exempted 'from the civil power'.[55] Speke calls it a 'church estate'.

In addition to the religious specialists attached to these more important centres, there were many more local practitioners, many—perhaps most—of whom were part-time specialists after the manner of the village smiths, potters and other craft specialists. Those who survive today tend, as Taylor says, to be 'general practitioners', but nineteenth-century Baganda seem to have distinguished, at least in principle, among diviners (*balaguzi*), herbalists and bone-setters (*basawo*), and sorcerers (*balogo*). Here again, spirit possession was a principle form of action, the spirits summoned including those of gods, ghosts, local natural features and man-made fetishes.

We may sum up the position of religious specialists in nineteenth-century Ganda society in the following terms: the dominant form of religious action—instrumental magic for state or individual ends—was consonant with the fluid and despotic character of the polity. And like the rising group of state officials—the *bakungu* and *batongole*—the principal religious practitioners—the mediums—were individually 'called', rather than being hereditary, although of course the source of the call differed, being in the one case the temporal ruler and in the other the god, ghost or fetish.

The Palace and the Capital

Nineteenth-century Buganda was a crescent-shaped land stretching some one hundred and fifty miles around the northern shore of Lake Victoria from the Nile in the east to the Kagera in the southwest, near the present-day Uganda-Tanganyika border. Along most of this arc, territory which was undisputably Ganda extended back from the shore fifty to sixty miles. Beyond, to the north and west, lay Buganda's traditional enemy, the kingdom of Bunyoro, at the expense of which the boundaries of Buganda were constantly being extended. On the east and southwest were two clusters of smaller kingdoms collectively known as Busoga and Buhaya (or Buziba) respectively; here the Kabaka was recognized as an overlord, to whom tribute must be paid to discourage raiding. The population of Buganda proper probably numbered about one million, that of the tributary states perhaps a million more.[56]

The nerve-centre of this kingdom and empire was the Kabaka, sitting in his palace enclosure (*lubiri*) in the capital (*kibuga*). As applied to most African kingdoms the phrase 'nerve-centre' would be misleading, for African polities of comparable scale were seldom so highly centralized. Nineteenth-century Buganda, however, was actively and continuously administered from the centre and consequently it is of some importance to examine briefly the sort of central organization which made it possible for the Kabaka to maintain active control over a territory one-quarter of the size of England without written communication and with no means of travel on land beyond the human foot. [57]

Sir Apolo Kagwa has left a good deal of quite detailed information about the physical layout of the capital and the palace enclosure in the diagrams which he prepared for Roscoe's *The Baganda*. Projecting Sir Apolo's drawing on to a modern map, it is clear that the capital occupied an area at least two miles by three miles, and quite possibly extended a good deal further. [58] At the highest point was the palace enclosure, which Roscoe says was an oval measuring one mile by one-half mile. [59] Within this enclosure lived the Kabaka and his wives, pages, servants and slaves; within it also were the various audience halls in which state business was conducted. Outside the enclosure, stretching away in front and to the sides, were the town houses of chiefs and officials and the huts of their servants and retainers. It is of course useless to attempt to establish with any accuracy the numbers of persons accommodated within the palace and the capital; one has the impression, however, from Kagwa and Roscoe and from the accounts of travellers such as Speke and Stanley, that the population of the palace enclosure must have numbered several hundred at least, while that of the capital perhaps amounted to some tens of thousands.

The capital was not a 'city', if by that term one means a permanent aggregation of persons leading a differentiated way of life which might be called 'urban' as over against the 'rural' life of the countryside. In nineteenth-century Buganda, and even today, when the modern city of Kampala has grown up around the old capital, the urban-rural distinction seems inappropriate, as Wrigley has noted previously. It was and is so, in spite of the large aggregation of population, because the capital as a unit had no permanent population and no functional independence of its own. Mobility tended to prevent the growth of distinct urban and rural cultures just as it restricted the development of self-conscious status groups. No one identified himself as belonging to the capital; instead Baganda always thought of themselves as belonging to their counties of origin. One remained a *munnabuddu* or *munnabusiro* (a man of Buddu or Busiro), even though one might have resided in the capital for many years.

The capital-dweller maintained a foothold in the countryside —usually a holding of land from which he might draw supplies of food—and consequently there was constant circulation of persons. In addition, the capital itself was moved every few years and this, too, discouraged the growth of local urban identification. Indeed, Buganda as a whole creates a striking impression of spatial fluidity; unlike many of the peoples of eastern and central Africa, the Baganda had in their permanent banana gardens the means for a highly sedentary life, but their culture and society dictated instead constant mobility. Messengers sped along the well-kept roads carrying information and orders to and from the capital; armies and groups of labourers moved more slowly across the country fighting wars, putting down revolts, repairing roads and erecting buildings; dozens of relatives and retainers followed each official as he was transferred from place to place in the service of the Kabaka. In a very large number of cases these movements resulted directly or indirectly from orders emanating from the capital.

The capital, then, was primarily a control centre and its organization is best understood in that light. One function of the organization within the palace, of course, was to serve the personal needs of the Kabaka, although the principal household officials did not, apparently, actually live inside the enclosure.[60] Much of the space inside was occupied by the houses of the king's many wives, organized in sections, each under the control of a titled 'chief-wife' (*mukyala*). Under each chief-wife were several ordinary wives (*basebeyi*) and slave-concubines (*bazaana*). Thus the royal household was rather like a microcosm of the kingdom and the two spheres were linked by an arrangement whereby each wife received, on behalf of the Kabaka, taxes from a particular chief.[61] The other main occupants of the palace were the pages (*bagalagala*), under their chief, the *Ssaabakaaki*. All these persons

—wives, concubines and pages—served the personal needs and comfort of the Kabaka, but they also were instruments of royal control. Marriages were links between the Kabaka and political favourites and the royal fathers-in-law were often rewarded with gifts and office. Affinal links with the Kabaka were eagerly sought after, for in the next generation the lineage of the Queen Mother (*Nnamasole*) would be even more richly rewarded as 'parents' of the king. The corps of pages also played a vital part in the political structure beyond the palace enclosure. Made up of sons and other dependents sent by chiefs, lineage and clan-heads and officials to 'seek their fortunes', they formed a pool of eager talent from whom the Kabaka might, on the basis of direct personal observation, choose men to serve him as chiefs and officials. The 'department (*kitongole*) of the pages', as Baganda call it, was in a very real sense a 'school for chiefs', providing a common background of training for all those who would later serve the king.

Outside the palace enclosure were the shrines occupied by the most important mediums when visiting the Kabaka, the residences of the palace officials, and the compounds of the *Katikkiro* (Prime Minister) and all the other chiefs and officials appointed by the Kabaka. Although the latter were appointed as administrators of territorial divisions of the kingdom, they in fact spent a very large part of their time at the capital attending court and hence the affairs of the territories under their control were almost always in the hands of deputies (*basigire*, literally 'entrusted persons'). In traditional Ganda thought, it was necessary for chiefs to be constantly at the capital in order to indicate their loyalty. A chief who remained at his own headquarters was suspected of plotting against the Kabaka. Thus chiefs were hostages, so to speak, for their own good behaviour. There was also another reason for their constant presence at the capital. The non-routine tasks which the Kabaka required of his servants were largely of a military nature and chiefs wanted always to be available for command of a raiding expedition, success in which would bring favour and promotion.

We have now surveyed the main dimensions of social differentiation in nineteenth-century Buganda. Before going on to consider how these have been altered by recent processes of change, it may be useful to sum up from a functional perspective by examining the way in which the various tasks of government were carried out.

The Organization of Adjudication, Taxation and War

The three principal activities which went to make up 'ruling' (*kufuga*) for the Kabaka of Buganda were *kusala emisango* (adjudicating, literally 'cutting', disputes), *kusoloza omusolo* (levying taxes) and *kugaba olutabalo* (waging war). By glancing briefly at each of these activities, we can see in action the various parts of the state structure which have been described.

Adjudication was a political act; that is to say, adjudicating disputes among his subordinates was part of a superior's general superordination and it expressed this superordination as well as settling the matter at issue. Furthermore, as was true of other aspects of political superordination, the authority exercised in adjudication was *personal*. In 'cutting' a dispute, a chief, in addition to in some sense 'applying the law', abstractly conceived, emphasized the litigants' personal dependence upon himself. There was, no doubt, a substantial element of 'rule of law' in Ganda adjudication, but there was also much personal authority. Thus an appellant, wishing to carry his case to the next highest level, accused, not the one who had allegedly wronged him, but rather the judge who had found against him.[62]

'Judges' were not, of course, specialist law officers; every person in authority, from the humblest *mutongole* to the Kabaka, was judge over those under him. There was, however, a rather elaborate set of procedures which marked litigation off as a special activity. What we know of all this comes from the observations of Roscoe and from Kagwa's account.[63] British administration has too deeply influenced both procedure and substantive law to make present-day observation an accurate guide, though even today enough of the traditional pattern carries over to give a distinctively Ganda style to litigation. An accuser came before his superior and paid a fee in order to lay his complaint. The superior, acting as judge, sent out an emissary to bring in the accused and each party was given an opportunity to state his case, standing before the 'bench' and throwing down small sticks to record the points in his argument. The judge then restated the case for each side, giving the principals an opportunity to correct him. Finally, after collecting fees from both parties, he gave judgment. A further 'expression of thanks for winning' (*kintu kya mpozensinge*) in the form of livestock, cowry shells or bark-cloth was expected of the successful litigant. The unsuccessful party might appeal from each judge to his political superior until he reached the court of the *Katikkiro*, known as the *ggombolola* (a term since given to the chiefs subordinate to county chiefs). Beyond this, appeal lay to the Kabaka himself and, finally, to the ordeal of drinking an infusion of an intoxicating herb (*madudu*), the successful litigant being the one who could withstand its effects.

At the higher levels, much litigation appears to have arisen from the conflicting ambitions of chiefs and officials. A favourite means of securing advancement was for one chief to accuse another to the Kabaka of treachery or incompetence in the hope that the latter might give him (the accuser) *carte blanche* to seize the alleged miscreant's office and property—to 'eat him up' (*kumulya*), as the saying went.[64] Such cases were dealt with juridically in formal pleading before the Kabaka and they provide the clearest illustration of the political character of much adjudication in traditional Buganda. Adjudication, in such cases, was also management and control of the political hierarchy itself, an expression of the king's control over the whole of the state machinery. This juridical mode of control extended, not only to relations among the *bakungu* and *batongole* appointed by the Kabaka, but also to the affairs of the hereditary *bataka*, for the king was also *ssaabataka* (chief of the clan heads) and thus an appellate judge in clan disputes. His authority to adjudicate disputes concerning relations of superiority and subordination among clan and lineage heads must be reckoned among the most important centralizing influences in the Ganda polity.

Taxation was another centralizing influence, for it enabled the Kabaka to control the distribution of goods and services among his people. Its aim was not the accumulation of wealth, for commerce seems to have been relatively undeveloped. Rather, the purpose of the quite high levels of taxation was to provide the Kabaka with surpluses from which he could reward his favourites. The circulation must have been quite rapid, for the buildings shown on Kagwa's chart of the palace as constituting the treasury (*nkuluze*) would hold only a small part of the goods collected in a single year.[65]

Again our main source of information on nineteenth-century practice is Kagwa.[66] According to him the levy, which presumably took place annually, included one in every twenty head of livestock, a vessel of simsim, a vessel of white termites and a bark-cloth from each homestead.[67] Specialists were taxed in dried fish, hoes, baskets, pots or whatever products they provided. Those who did not serve in the militia were subject to a special additional tax, while bachelors, chiefs and persons who had just established themselves on new land were exempted. Collections were carried out by special emissaries (*babaka*) of the Kabaka, who were given hospitality by the chiefs as they made their rounds. Tributary states sent their contributions directly to the capital.

The 'payoff' to the king's chiefs and officials began at the collecting stage, where they received definite shares according to a rather elaborate system. In the example of the collections of bark-cloth for a single county for one year described by Kagwa, the county chief and his subordinates received 60 per cent., the collector for the county 12 per cent., the *Katikkiro* 8 per cent., the palace officials 4 per cent. and the Kabaka the remaining 16 per cent. Eighty-four per cent. thus went to the king's servants. But material rewards for loyal service did not end there. From the goods remaining in the treasury, it was the custom for the Kabaka to make free and unexpected gifts to guests or favourites, and these were regarded as tremendous rewards, being indicative of special royal favour. Kagwa notes that a person who had been thus favoured left the court 'accompanied by great pomp, as everyone had witnessed his growth in favour at the king's court'.[68]

Perhaps the greatest and most general rewards for service to the Kabaka and the nation, however, came as a result of participation in wars and raids. One function of the military organization was, of course, defence against attack, but by the second half of the nineteenth century, Buganda seems to have been perpetually on the offensive.

Once again Kagwa provides us with the clearest picture.[69] Together with Stanley's description of the campaign against Buvuma in 1875, it gives us what appears to be a remarkably complete account of Ganda military organization in its most aggressive period.[70]

The nature and purpose of Ganda warfare is perhaps best indicated by reference to the phrase *kugaba olutalo*—'to wage war'. Literally, it means 'to give war', rather as, in English, a hostess 'gives' a party. '*Kugaba*' means to 'distribute largesse' and this was, indeed, the spirit in which the Kabaka made war. Having decided after discussion with the leading chiefs that war was called for—usually because some tributary group had failed to pay—he summoned all his chiefs to the palace by causing the great war drum—called *ntamivu*, 'the drunkard'— to be beaten. He then publicly chose one of the chiefs as the 'recipient' (*mugabe*) of the war—the general—and charged him with the task of despoiling the enemy. This was the greatest benefit which the Kabaka could bestow, for success would bring wealth, promotion and glory. Kagwa quotes the speech of fealty with which a chief who had been selected responded to the charge—a speech very similar in pattern to that repeated in the king's presence to this day by newly appointed Buganda Government civil servants. Brandishing his staff like a spear and performing a little war-dance, the general declared:

I am Kimoga, son of Kungu of the oribi antelope clan. I will not flee from the enemy, but will fight with my whole strength which I have demonstrated to you and will kill him or be killed.[71]

This was not empty boasting. It is clear that when inspired both chiefs and warriors were capable of great—even reckless— personal bravery.[72]

The organization of the army followed very closely that of the state. Each chief or official was required to muster as many fighting men as he could from among his people; if Stanley's estimates based upon observation of the Buvuma campaign are accurate, a national war might turn out a large part of the able-bodied adult male population.[73] War was thus a national undertaking. Towards the end of the nineteenth century, there developed a 'royal guard' under a corps of permanent military captains; this seems to have been composed of musketeers, as contrasted with the spear-armed militia, and the title of its commander, the *Mujasi* (from the Kiswahili *Mjasiri*: 'brave one'), suggests that it was formed under coastal Arab influence.[74] The bulk of the army, however, continued to be composed of peasant militia. Areas along the shore of the lake provided units in the canoe fleet, overall command of which was in the hands of the *Ggabunga*, head of the Lungfish clan. The fleet was mainly a transport force for conveying warriors among the islands and along the coasts.

The object of war was to plunder the enemy's land of cattle, wives and children and induce him to pay regular tribute. It is significant that nearly half of Kagwa's account of the 'customs pertaining to war' is devoted to the system of sharing the spoils. Various shares were allotted to the general, the chiefs and officials commanding bodies of troops, and the fighting men themselves. Before returning from the expedition, the general formally counted the cattle and slaves taken and selected the best to make up the king's share. These were carefully guarded during the return journey. In addition, there were special shares for the commanders of the troops of the *Katikkiro*, the *Nnamasole* (Queen Mother) and the *Lubuga* (the king's 'official sister'). The booty was rather widely shared. In an illustrative case provided by Kagwa, where the expedition took some 14,000 slaves, half were given to the warriors who had actually captured them.[75]

Upon the expedition's return to the capital, there was a formal accounting before the Kabaka. Before a gathering of the army drawn up in front of the palace, the general reported upon the military success of the campaign, the amount of plunder captured and the conduct in battle of members of the force. Each commander led his men before the Kabaka and was required to account for his performance. Each advanced in turn to a great pot of beer which had been placed before the king and asked whether he had not been brave and whether he might not now drink. To those who had fought bravely, the army shouted 'Drink!' but to those who had faltered the reply was 'We saw that you were afraid; do not drink!' Cowards were punished by being burnt alive or by being made to go about in women's clothing. Chiefs who had proved weak or cowardly were dismissed from office and the heroes of the campaign often took their places.

War was thus the focus of what had perhaps become, in the nineteenth century, the master value in Ganda culture—the aggrandizement of the nation and the king. That it was a *popular* value which vindicated much of the arbitrary cruelty with which the Kabaka ruled, and not merely an ideology of the élite, is indicated by the acclaim which apparently greeted the brave individual warrior within his own family. There was a special ceremony with which a father might honour a son who had covered himself with glory in the national interest. The father slaughtered a sheep for a feast, thanked the gods for giving him a brave son, and throughout the ceremonial meal waited upon the son as a servant.[76] Organizationally, as well, warfare represented the clearest working-out of the pattern towards which the whole polity was moving: an institutional system in which positions of honour were open to talent, in which ability and diligence were quickly rewarded and failure was quickly punished.

8

The Modernization of Social
Stratification

As a result of nearly one hundred years of increasingly intimate
contact and exchange with the modern Western world, the
pattern of social differentiation which we have described has
changed substantially. It will be our task in this chapter to outline these changes so that, in the chapter following, we may
consider social mobility in Buganda against a known background. If we wish to understand the influence of Western contact upon mobility, we must first know how, during recent
generations, the system itself, within which persons are differentially mobile, has been changing.

The most obvious difference between nineteenth-century and
present-day differentiation is of course quantitative; there are
today very many more distinct roles in Ganda society than there
were three-quarters of a century ago. To a very large extent,
furthermore, this proliferation has taken place in the occupational sphere. Where in the eighteen-eighties there were no
more than, say, a dozen, at most, distinguishable occupational
roles (essentially those discussed in the previous chapter), today
there are probably hundreds. To be sure, some of the new roles
which exist within the borders of Buganda are not yet occupied
by Baganda. Many positions in government service requiring
specialized training are occupied by Europeans, while the great
majority of the business men, and even of the skilled artisans,

Reprinted by permission from Lloyd A. Fallers, ed., *The King's Men*:
Leadership and Status in Buganda on the Eve of Independence (London:
Oxford University Press, 1964). Dr. Fallers was assisted by S. Elkan,
F. K. Kamoga, and S. B. Musoke.

are Indians. Even taking these facts into account, however, the number of new occupational roles available to Baganda becomes ever greater and the number occupying them increases steadily through the 'Africanization' of the civil service and the entrance of Baganda into new forms of business enterprise and professional practice. What are the consequences for a society of this sort of proliferation of occupations?

Occupational Role and Modernization

At this point it may be useful to digress briefly to consider the place of occupational organization in the processes of economic and social modernization—processes which have been at work all over the world during the past two centuries. These processes have not, of course, operated everywhere in the same way and at the same rate. In Western Europe and North America they have been the results of centuries of mainly internal development; in much of Asia and Africa, on the other hand, they have come much more quickly, often under the influence of—and in reaction to—Western colonial or quasi-colonial domination. It would be rash indeed to assume that these different paths toward something which we can define broadly as 'modernization' are leading to precisely the same destination: a uniform and universal modern society and culture. As the example of Japan has shown, there is little reason to expect such a result even if industrial economies and populistic politics succeed in taking root everywhere. Nevertheless, there does appear to be a certain logic to the process of modernization. Modern and modernizing societies appear to share important common features and among these is an emphasis upon occupational differentiation, with consequences for both economic organization and social structure.

Now, the most obvious relationship between occupational role and modernization is of course in the technological domain. The technological-scientific explosion of recent centuries has, quite simply, provided the materials for many more technical specialities, and hence for many more distinct occupational roles, than were hitherto possible. From a social and cultural point of view, however, this technical specialization is the least significant aspect of the matter. More interesting is the apparent tendency for modern societies to give generally greater prominence to occupation in *social* differentiation as well. In the modern United States, for example, where this tendency has perhaps been carried farthest, we tend to locate a person socially by asking his occupation. Our first question, upon meeting a person for the first time, is: 'What does he do (for a living)?' with the implication that this is the most salient piece of information we could have about him. From it, we feel, we can predict with fair accuracy his income, attitudes and general style of life.[1] Social stratification and mobility in modern societies are investigated primarily in terms of the ranking of occupations.[2]

There is, apparently, a sense in which occupation is socially and culturally more important in modern than in non-modern societies. Clearly one root of this greater importance is the progressive separation of occupational structures from other structures—notably those of family and kinship—so that a sphere that was once 'embedded' in kinship comes to have a life of its own. In non-modern societies, occupational roles are more often performed in structures of the 'family firm' type or in the context of other particularistic relationships of the patron-client variety. The kinship group, or the group formed by the family of the patron and those of his clients, is also the work group, so that the economy, on the production side at least, is a household or manor economy. But in the modern West, as Marx and many others have emphasized, more and more work —and a larger and larger proportion of occupations—has been carried out in organizations based upon neither kinship nor any other kind of particularistic tie. Such organizations—modern business firms and government bureaucracies alike—merely purchase the individual's labour; they are the owners of the tools with which he works and of the goods and services which he produces. For its part, the family, which was once the occupational as well as the domestic unit, now becomes much more purely domestic and is linked with the occupational system only through one member—usually the husband-father.[3] When the salary or wages from the job of this member become the sole source of livelihood for the family, then occupation has, indeed, acquired an independence of the family, and in fact a certain dominance over it. The family's chances of acquiring those qualities which confer higher rank tend to be heavily determined by the occupational performance of the breadwinner.

This has been the Western pattern, and it is important to recognize that the development of the relationship between kinship and occupation in the modernization of non-Western countries may not prove identical. Apparently in Japan it has been possible to organize modern industrial occupations in part in terms of kinship or quasi-kinship ties.[4] Even where this is possible, however, the occupational system retains a certain dominance because in most cases the kinship groups involved cannot ultimately control the resources upon which their economic fate depends.

In modern societies, then, occupational role tends to confer status upon its occupant and upon the kinship group dependent upon him. In part this is a question of the money income from the job and the status-symbolic goods and services which it will purchase, but, beyond this, occupational roles and clusters of occupational roles have tended in the modern world to elaborate sub-cultures of their own, including value systems, argots and feelings of solidarity. The occupational label, as Hughes has put it, becomes a 'combination of price tag and calling card'— a place in the stratification system and the major field for the public expression of the self.[5] Individual occupations develop sub-cultures and are the objects of evaluation, and the same is true of the clusters of occupations to which modern Westerners tend to apply the term 'class'. Thus 'working class' and 'middle class', 'white collar' and 'blue collar', are broad groups of occupations similarly evaluated in the stratification system and sharing similar sub-cultures. Mobility between these 'classes' involves learning new sub-cultures and acquiring new loyalties; it is achieved, fundamentally, through occupational mobility.

But the difference between modern and non-modern societies with respect to the place of occupations is not simply that occupation and rank are generally more closely related in the former than in the latter. In traditional India, occupation and rank were perhaps more closely related than they have been at any other time or place. The difference lies, rather, in the *way* in which the two are related. In modern societies, one's occupation tends to determine one's place in the stratification system. In non-modern societies, on the other hand, one's place in the stratification system tends to determine one's occupation. To put it in another way, in non-modern societies rank is a matter of diffuse status in which occupation is merely one of the elements. Thus, the Hindu villager is, first of all, a member of his caste, a diffuse status group; from this follows an appropriate occupation, along with other features, such as ritual and marriage patterns. The same was true, though of course to a lesser extent, of the members of the 'estates' of medieval European society.

There are, however, two rather different ways in which occupation may come to be bound up with diffuse status in non-modern societies. The commonest way, or at least the way most familiar to Westerners, is through status ascription. If status is inherited, then all those features, including occupation, which go to make up status tend to form a single bundle of ascriptive characteristics. The Indian or medieval European peasant inherited an occupation, or permissible choice of occupations, along with a set of political rights and obligations and a whole style of life. It is this form of involvement of occupation in diffuse status which most readily occurs to Westerners, because their own recent social and ideological history has been so concerned with the issue of social mobility. Western reform movements have to a great extent been concerned with freeing occupation from the nexus of ascribed status and thus providing the possibility of occupational mobility through individual achievement. There have, however, been other non-modern societies, of which Buganda is probably not the only example, in which the involvement of occupation in diffuse status derived, not from status ascription, but rather from the sheer simplicity of occupational differentiation itself. Thus in Buganda *mukopi* and *mwami* were diffuse statuses in the sense that they were very unspecialized and implied general inferiority and superiority. A *mukopi* was an agriculturalist or fisherman who was inferior and who obeyed. A *mwami* was a king's official or chief, a man of honour (*kitiibwa*) who ruled. That was all. There was, as we have seen, a good deal of mobility, both upward and downward, but the division of labour was simply too rudimentary to allow occupation as such to emerge as a distinct social and cultural field.[6]

Another, and related, deterrent to the emergence of occupational role as an independent basis for social differentiation was the enclosure of such division of labour as existed in the network of personal relations of superiority and subordination. 'My lord' (*mukama wange*) and 'my man' (*musajja wange*) were roles of *general, personal* obligation and responsibility which did not admit of much distinction between 'private' and 'professional' life.

Modernization has therefore not meant to the Baganda, as it has to so many non-Western peoples, primarily a breaking of the bonds of ascribed status. Individual achievement through effort and ability is nothing new to the Baganda; indeed, we shall have seriously to consider in the next chapter whether the effect of Western influence has not been to reduce, in some respects, the fluidity of Ganda society. Modernization has, on the contrary, meant for the Baganda primarily a great proliferation and de-personalization of available occupational roles and hence an incipient elaboration of occupation as a basis for social differentiation. In the remainder of this chapter we shall inquire: which new occupational roles have become available to Baganda; how many Baganda have become the occupants of such roles; and to what extent and in what ways has Ganda culture responded to this situation by making occupation a major basis for differentiation and cultural elaboration?

Changes in the Vocabulary of Stratification

As we shall see, many Baganda now occupy modern occupational roles in the sense that they have 'jobs' in modern-type organizations and derive from these jobs their major incomes. There are today, albeit in small numbers, Baganda who are civil servants, members of the learned professions, business men, modern farmers (as contrasted with peasants), politicians and publicists. We must discuss each of these new occupations in turn, but it may be useful if we first say something about the general features of the new system of ideas pertaining to stratification which seems to be emerging.

The development of modern specialized occupational roles has meant, inevitably, a decline in the relative importance of such diffuse status classifications as *mukopi* and *mwami*, and the language has begun to recognize this. Chiefs, for example, as we shall see, are coming to have some of the characteristics of modern civil servants; the word *mwami*, consequently, is coming to mean, not just any person of power and standing, but rather a person who is employed by the Buganda Government to do particular kinds of work. At the same time, a quite different usage of the word has also developed: it has come to mean something very similar to the English 'Mr.'. Thus, in both the written and the spoken language, Samwili Mukasa will, on formal occasions, be called '*Omwami* Mukasa' or, in writing (as in addressing letters), '*Omw*. Mukasa'. This usage, is, to be sure, more common in contexts where Europeans are involved. Baganda still tend in everyday speech to refer to persons by clan or Christian name in situations where Englishmen or Americans would use 'Mr.' But the new usage is by no means limited to European-Ganda situations; it is, for example, very commonly used in the Luganda press. There has also developed, following English practice, a use of the word *mukyala* (or *Omuky*.) to mean 'Mrs.'. Originally, apparently, the word was used only for the senior wives of powerful persons—persons traditionally spoken of as *bami* (pl. of *mwami*).

Significantly, the term *mukopi* has come to be pejorative. In the ordinary canons of polite behaviour today, everyone is entitled to be *Omw*. and has the right *not* to be called a *mukopi*. The word *mukopi* is still, to be sure, a very common one, but one would today tend not to call a person a *mukopi* to his face and one would tend, in a political speech, for example, to prefer instead the modern expressions *bantu ba bulijjo*—'ordinary people'—or *bannakyalo*—'villagers'—in speaking of 'the people'. Another modern way of referring to the rustic is to speak of him as *simuyigirize*, 'uneducated'. All these changes in usage away from the direct expression of inequality reflect, of course, the recent development of populistic politics in Buganda.

In place of the diffuse status categories *mukopi* and *mwami* there is developing a new vocabulary for talking about the new forms of social differentiation. The new peasant cash-crop farmer, for example, is called *mulimi*, 'cultivator'. An unskilled wage labourer is *mupakasi*, the word used in the past to refer to a head-porter. The army of white-collar menials who man the offices of business concerns and government departments are called *kkalaani*, the Kiswahili word for 'scribe', while another

Kiswahili word, *ffundi*, is used as a generic term for artisans of various types. The coinage or redefinition of terms and the adoption of English and Kiswahili ones for talking about the new specialities goes on apace. As yet, however, there is no general term which is the equivalent of the English word 'occupation', much less of the more expressive German *Beruf*. The word used is *mulimu*, which simply means 'agricultural work,' being related to the verb *kulima*, 'to cultivate'. Thus, although the Baganda are today entering modern occupational roles in increasing numbers, they would still have some difficulty in discussing in their own language the *idea* of occupation in the modern sense of a specialized calling.

There is also an increasingly differentiated vocabulary for talking about persons of importance as these persons become more diverse in type, and much of this differentiation reflects changes in the structure of the Buganda Government. We have already referred to the new conception of the *mwami* ('chief') as a civil service administrator. Other changes may be seen in the Great Lukiiko, the Buganda legislature. Originally it was merely the gathering of chiefs to *kukiika*—'to do homage'.[7] Since 1900 there have been added to its membership, first appointed 'notables' (*bamanyifu* or *batutumufu*), representatives of the new high-status professions such as medicine, teaching and the clergy; and, later, 'representatives', *babaka*, members elected by the people. This latter term is the traditional one for an emissary of the Kabaka or a chief and its use to refer to popularly elected representatives thus involves a recognition of new popular loci of power. (As we shall see, however, it has not as yet meant 'democracy' in any substantial sense.) Perhaps the most interesting lacuna in the new vocabulary of power and importance is the absence, thus far, of words for 'politics', 'politician' and 'political party', in spite of the fact that for the past several years all three have been very prominent in Buganda. Luganda newspapers customarily speak of *eby'obufuzi*, literally 'things pertaining to rulership' and then recognize the inadequacy of this rendering by adding, in parentheses, the English word 'politics'. Traditional Luganda was rich in words for 'intrigue' (*lukwe*) and related forms of personal struggle for power, but the particular kind of stylized group competition which makes up modern party politics has yet to find adequate expression, and Baganda editors realize this. The editors, however, have found perfectly good phrases to describe their publications (*lupapula lw'ama-wulire*: 'paper of news' and themselves (*mukuŋŋanya w'ama-wulire*: 'assembler of news').

We emphasized in the previous chapter that traditional Buganda essentially lacked both the idea and the reality of cohesive social strata or status groups. In Chapter 9 we shall consider the question of social mobility in modern Buganda, but we may note here that the *idea* of the status group remains absent. There are 'educated people' (*bayigirize*), 'important people' (*bakulu*), 'leaders' (*bakulembeze*) and 'rulers' (*bafuzi*), but there are still no 'gentlemen' or 'aristocrats' in Luganda.

Baganda are thus in the process of developing a new vocabulary to describe the functionally more differentiated occupational and stratification systems which are evolving. If we turn now to an examination of the actual structure of occupational differentiation in modern Buganda, we shall see that this structure has developed rather more rapidly than has the complex of ideas with which Baganda think about it.

The New Civil Servant

The earliest, and perhaps still the most prominent, field for the development of modern occupational roles in Buganda has been that of government. This has been so partly because the state has always loomed large in Ganda life and partly, also, because Uganda has been primarily a 'political colony' rather than an 'economic' one. That is to say, British influence has made itself felt primarily through political administration rather than through large-scale industrial and commercial enterprise of the sort that has characterized the British impact on Central and Southern Africa, for example, or the Belgian impact on the Congo. Economic development in Uganda has until recently been concentrated mainly in small-scale African cash-crop farming. We may appropriately, therefore, begin our examination of modern social differentiation in the field of political institutions.

Since 1890, when the first treaty between Buganda and Britain was arranged by Captain Lugard, Ganda political institutions have been subject to varying degrees of influence by British officials. By the Uganda Agreement of 1900, Britain recognized '. . . the Kabaka of Uganda as the native ruler of the province of Uganda under Her Majesty's protection and over-rule'.[8] Since the making and implementation of this agreement has been the subject of an excellent study by D. A. Low and R. C. Pratt, we need not trace in any detail the overall history of British administration in Buganda, except to say that British influence was weakest in the initial period before World War I, when the relationship was interpreted rather strictly as one of simple 'protection', and in the most recent period since World War II, when there has been an increasing devolution of authority as a prelude to independence for Uganda as a whole.[9] In the interval between the two wars, in contrast, Britain was inclined to interpret her mission rather more in terms of 'welfare' and 'development' and it was during this period, when British officers felt more free to intervene, that much of the basic modernization of the Buganda Government took place. Modern bureaucratic methods of administration and recruitment of officials were introduced and office was separated from land-holding by the distribution of freehold estates among the élite of the time. The estates were allotted in 1900, mainly to persons who were then chiefs and officials, but by the inter-war period, as Wrigley has pointed out in Chapter 1, many of the allottees of 1900 had died or retired; the land had passed to their heirs and their places in government had been taken by others. The Great Lukiiko, which had been recognized by the 1900 Agreement, slowly changed from an administrative gathering of chiefs into an active and more representative legislature. During this period, also, the Protectorate Government was slowly developing the functions and organs of a modern state, and increasing numbers of Baganda entered its service.

One further word of introduction is perhaps necessary to explain the relationship between the two governments. Until the end of World War II, they developed essentially independently. African participation was largely limited to the tribal governments—developed in the other provinces as well on essentially the Buganda pattern—while the Protectorate Government, aside from tutoring and overseeing the tribal administrations and providing technical services, concerned itself mainly with the affairs of the immigrant communities, European and Asian. Until 1945, for example, there were no

Africans in the Uganda Legislative Council. This pattern of development was regarded as desirable both by British officials and by the Baganda, who always viewed their separate relationship with Britain through the Agreement of 1900 as the charter of their liberties in the face of what they saw as the constant threat of domination by the European settler element in neighbouring Kenya Colony; they resisted participation in such central government institutions as the Legislative Council as weakening their national integrity and independence. Consequently after World War II, when Britain wished to shift the emphasis towards African participation in central government in gradual preparation for national independence, she encountered stiff opposition from the Baganda. The goal of a strong Uganda Government, which post-war British officials felt to be desirable as an aid to economic development, has had to give way, in the face of Ganda opposition, to a more decentralized pattern. By the new Agreement of 1955, the autonomy of the Buganda Government was increased, and the subsequent period has seen still further devolution of functions and staff.

The Buganda Government in 1956 (the date which will, so far as possible, be taken as 'the present' for the purposes of this chapter) was served by 3,887 regular employees and expended £1,240,413 while governing the nearly two million African inhabitants of Buganda.[10] Table 1 provides an outline of its structure, a background against which we may consider how far its employees have come to be 'civil servants' in the modern sense.

In traditional Buganda, the kingpin of the network of diffuse, personal political relations which made up the state was the Kabaka. Chiefs and officials, and in a more general sense the people as a whole, were his personal servants (*baddu*). We may therefore note with interest that the Baganda today distinguish —somewhat hesitantly—between the public and private personalities of the Kabaka. In his former role, he receives from the Buganda Government an annual allowance of £7,500 and funds for the upkeep of the palace, the state cars and other symbolic appurtenances of constitutional kingship. In his private capacity he enjoys a privy purse replenished by the rents from the 350 square miles of estates which were allotted to the throne in 1900. On these estates, the post-1900 kings have reproduced the old organization of king's officials—the *baton-gole*. Each estate is managed by a *mutongole* bearing the title of one of the pre-1900 *batongole*.[11] Administration of the estates is supervised by the *Katikkiro w'Ebyalo bya Kabaka*, the *Katikkiro* of

TABLE I

THE KABAKA'S GOVERNMENT, 1956
(in parentheses, numbers of employees)

A. PRIVATE SPHERE* (number of employees not available).
   1. The Privy Purse (*Nkuluze*.
   2. Royal Estates (*Byalo bya Kabaka*), consisting of 41 estates with a combined population of 29,983.

B. PUBLIC SPHERE (total 3887)†
   1. Central Administration.
      Prime Minister (*Katikkiro*) (61).
      Treasury (*Omuwanika*) (77).
      Justice (*Omulamuzi*) (124).
      Education (10).
      Natural Resources (29).
      Health (25).
      Police (215).
      Prisons (438).
      Land Office (13).
      Works (93).
      Administration of the Capital (*Kibuga*) (45).
   2. Private Secretary and Palace Establishment (159).
   3. The Great Lukiiko (not counted as 'employees').
      Elected Members (60).
      Ministers (6).
      County Chiefs (20).
      Kabaka's Nominees (6).
   4. Territorial Administration (2598).
      20 Counties (*masaza*).
      133 Sub-Counties (*magombolola*).
      923 Parishes (*miruka*).

the King's Villages, and the funds derived from them and from other unofficial sources are handled by the *Omuwanika w'Enkuluze*, the Treasurer of the Privy Purse.

* Information kindly supplied by the *Omuwanika w'Enkuluze* (Treasurer of the Privy Purse).
† Information kindly supplied by the Kabaka's Government.

This financial distinction between the public and private spheres should not, however, lead us to the conclusion that the Kabaka is today a strictly modern constitutional monarch, whose relationship to the official Buganda Government is largely symbolic. The difficulty of determining just how much personal authority he wields is increased by the fact that the Baganda have learned well from their British mentors the lesson that modern monarchy works best behind a screen of allusion and symbolic fiction. As in Britain, the government is the king's and everything is done in his name. In fact, as one would expect, there is in these phrases a good deal more substance than there is at present in Britain. The personal influence of the Kabaka upon appointments, promotions and policy-formation in the modern Buganda Government has usually been substantial, and this has been particularly true in the period since 1955, the year in which Kabaka Mutesa returned from exile clothed in the double mantle of protector of traditional institutions and modern anti-colonial hero. The institutional provisions of the Agreement of 1955, which British officials viewed as contributions towards a constitutional monarchy, included a ministry responsible to the Great Lukiiko, and an appointments board designed to insure disinterested selection of civil servants. In the political atmosphere of recent years, however, it is not surprising that these new institutions have tended to provide new fields for the exercise of the king's personal influence rather than effective checks upon it. The appointments board, chosen by the Kabaka, and the Great Lukiiko and ministry, elected as 'king's men,' have all been extremely responsive to royal influence.

Still, the Buganda Government of today is not simply the traditional despotism in modern dress; its servants are no longer simply personal servants of the king. For one thing, they are engaged, and work, on something like modern civil service terms. There is a printed budget which shows, along with other expenditures, the salary scale of each post and the salary of each individual civil servant. There is a regular pension system. A table of organization in the office of the *Katikkiro* (Prime Minister) defines divisions of functions and regular channels of communication which are, in general, adhered to. If there is personal influence and corruption, there is also commitment in principle to the modern civil service ideal of regularity and dis-interestedness. There is the full modern bureaucratic apparatus of typewritten communication, with carbon copies and voluminous files. An official gazette, *Akiika Embuga*, publishes postings and other official announcements.[12] In an act which was not *merely* symbolic, the government moved in 1957 from its old buildings inside the palace walls to a magnificent new structure which faces the palace across a broad valley at the opposite end of the avenue *Kabaka Anjagala* ('The King Loves Me'). What all this indicates is that the Buganda Government has become a social entity in its own right apart from the king-ship, an entity to which its members have a very substantial loyalty. It possesses an authority which can no longer be adequately expressed in the traditional phrase *Bwakabaka bwa Buganda*, 'The Buganda Kingdom', an extension of personal kingship.

One reason why government can no longer be simply an extension of the king's will is that it has assumed functions the performance of which requires more than personal loyalty and general intelligence. The successor to the *mukungu* and the *mutongole*, and the official who has most in common with the traditional chief, is the county or sub-county chief.[13] Like his nineteenth-century predecessor, he has general responsibility for a territory.[14] Unlike the old *mukungu* or *mutongole*, however, he serves alongside a much more highly differentiated body of specialist officials in relation to whom he acts as co-ordinator and agent rather in the fashion of a modern Western 'execu-tive'.[15] Each of the ministries and departments shown in Table 1 employs specialists who have received technical training, either in schools or 'on the job', frequently both. Although in many cases the level of technical specialization is not high, still the work of government has become complex enough that disregard of technical qualifications would seriously impair it. Indeed, even the basic skills necessary to a modern civil servant in any department or ministry—fluency in writing and reading, book-keeping arithmetic, and some knowledge of English—are still rare enough to have scarcity value. However despotic he might wish, or might be able to be, that is to say, the Kabaka remains dependent upon a limited pool of educated persons able to perform the tasks which his people have come to expect of government—the provision of roads, police protection, education, medical care, agriculture and veterinary services. Many of these services have in the past been provided in large part by the Protectorate Government, but the people have learned to appreciate them and the gradual withdrawal of the Protectorate Government leaves the Buganda Government with popular demands to meet. Then too, the members of the government itself are often motivated by nationalist sentiment and *esprit de corps* to show that they can perform as well as the Protectorate Government. National pride provides a kind of 'super-ego' for the support of modern institutions which otherwise may not be deeply rooted in Ganda society.

These influences—the technical demands of devolved functions and the growth of an *esprit de corps* among its servants—combine to make the modern Buganda Government an important field for the development of the specialized skill and sense of identification with the job which are characteristic of modern occupational roles. At the time of the return of the Kabaka from exile in 1955, there was a widely publicized 'purge' of chiefs and officials who were believed to have been insufficiently devoted to the king's cause. In retrospect, however, it is remarkable, considering the depth to which Baganda were moved by the occasion, how few were the victims. Many who were by no means personal favourites of the monarch and whom he might have taken the occasion to be rid of, remained undisturbed in their posts.

Thus far, we have considered only the Buganda Government. A further group of Baganda, fewer in number but on the average more highly trained, hold modern-type occupational roles in the Uganda Government. The distribution of these persons by department is given in Table 2 (completely unskilled jobs are excluded from both Table 1 and Table 2). In Uganda Government employ are many more university-trained persons —physicians, veterinarians, agricultural officers, a few scientists and engineers. Here they are recruited and serve on regular British civil service terms. One important function of the Protectorate Government has been the provision of on-the-job training for many persons who later came to serve the Buganda Government, either through individual appointment or in the devolution of functions which has occurred in recent years. They

TABLE 2

BAGANDA IN THE PROTECTORATE GOVERNMENT, 1954*

Department	Number of Ganda Employees
Accountant General	
Embossing Operators	3
African Housing	
Engineering Assistants	2
Assistant Estates Manager	1
Agriculture	
Senior Assistant Agricultural Officers	4
Assistant Agricultural Officers	27
Instructors	27
Artisans and Mechanics	4
Laboratory and Field Assistants	22
Assistant Farm Managers	4
Commerce	
Assistant Economic Officer	1
Mechanical Assistant	1
Community Development	
Senior Community Development Officer (Women)	1
Assistant Community Development Officers	4
Assistant Probation Officer	1
Community Development Assistants	18
Probation Assistants	4
Driver-Operators (Cinema Vans)	3
Co-operative Development	
Assistant Co-operative Officers	3
Co-operative Assistants	36
Education	
Education Officers	4
Assistant Education Officers	6
School Music Organizer	1
Instructors†	9
Schoolmasters†	1

* Information taken from the Staff List, 1954, Uganda Government. Baganda were located by possession of Ganda names. Since non-Baganda sometimes adopt Ganda names, this procedure may have led to the inclusion of some non-Baganda.

† Most schools, though grant-aided, are owned by religious groups and consequently their teachers do not appear here.

Department	Number of Ganda Employees
Forestry	
Assistant Foresters	2
Rangers	18
Game and Fisheries	
Game Assistant	1
Geological Survey	
Assistant Chemists	4
Technical Assistants	3
Artisans	3
Drivers	3
Hydrological Survey	
Hydrological Inspector	1
Information	
Information Officer	1
Adviser on Information Services	1
Assistant Information Officer	1
Engineering Assistant	1
Labour	
Labour Inspectors	6
Driver	1
Medical	
Medical Officers	11
Senior Assistant Medical Officers	2
Assistant Medical Officers	15
Medical Assistants	93
Senior Nursing Orderlies	22
Dispensers	32
Assistant Health Inspectors	30
Laboratory Assistants	19
Orthopaedic Assistant	1
Entomological Assistants	2
Vehicle Mechanic	1
Artisans	2
Driver	1
Police	
Assistant Superintendents and Cadets	2
Inspectors	8
Sub-Inspectors	25
Carpenters	2

Department	Number of Ganda Employees
Cobbler	1
Mechanics	6
Schoolmaster	1
Printing	
Intertype Operator	1
Machine Operators and Bookbinders	57
Driver	1
Prisons	
Jailers	6
Instructor	1
Building Instructor	1
Public Works	
Senior Engineering Assistants	4
Engineering Assistants	22
Sub-Overseer	1
Draughtsman	1
Road Inspectors and Headmen	5
Artisans	41
Survey, Land and Mines	
Inspecting Surveyors	7
Surveyors	21
Computers	3
Draughtsmen	36
Driver	1
Assistant Surveyors	4
Assistant Computers	2
Tsetse Control	
Tsetse Surveyor	1
Veterinary	
Senior Assistant Veterinary Officers	2
Assistant Veterinary Officers	10
Veterinary Assistants	30
Laboratory Assistants	5
Clerical Division	
Special Class	1
Executive Class, Grade B	14
General Class, Grade I, II, III	289
TOTAL	1,076

have brought with them, not only specific skills, but also civil service norms of conduct which must have contributed substantially to the institutionalization of these norms within the Buganda Government.

In the most recent period, the transfer of persons to the Buganda Government through devolution has been matched by an accelerated recruitment of Baganda into the national service in accord with the policy of 'Africanization' in preparation for independence. These twin processes, exemplifying the dominance of government in the life of so many rapidly developing non-Western countries, reinforce, at least for the immediate future, the prominence of the civil servant in Buganda's modern occupational structure.

The New Professions: Religion, Education, Medicine and the Law

Outside the civil services of the two governments, four major learned professions are represented among Baganda today: two, religious ministry and teaching, are old, well-established and have numerous members, while the others, medicine and the law, have developed much more recently and as yet have few practitioners.

Christianity arrived in Buganda in 1877 with the first party of Anglican missionaries of the Church Missionary Society, who were followed in 1879 by the first group of Roman Catholic White Fathers of Algiers. Representatives of Islam had come considerably earlier; the first important Muslim visitor was, apparently, Sheikh Ahmed bin Ibrahim, a trader and missionary of Zanzibar, who met Kabaka Suna in 1844 and was active in establishing trade with the coast.[16] The Baganda were eager converts, in spite of severe persecution during the reign of Mwanga, and by the end of the century the traditional religion had essentially been destroyed as an organized force, though elements of it persist in modern Ganda belief and attitude. The three new faiths, however, engaged in two decades of intense rivalry, which not infrequently broke out into violence, and left a legacy of religious intolerance in present-day Buganda. The Protestant faction having prevailed with British aid, there has been since 1900 a kind of unwritten Anglican 'establishment', with certain posts in the government being reserved for Muslims and Roman Catholics. The latest available estimates of the strengths of the three groups give the Roman Catholics 700,000, the Protestants 514,000 and the Muslims 288,000.[17]

All three have put down deep roots in Ganda society. Magical curing and sorcery are still quite common, but these practices exist within the framework of a Christian-Islamic society, much as they must have done in the European and Islamic Middle Ages. The word *ddini* (Arabic-Kiswahili: 'religion') refers to a complex accepted as a necessary part of Ganda life by all except a few back-woods pagans and still fewer modern secularists; it refers only to Christianity and Islam, not to the traditional religion of the ancestors and the *balubaale*. For fifty years there has been no ideological issue between paganism and the new creeds, for the latter have long since become the official repositories of ultimate values. Perhaps the best evidence of this is the fact that for many years there has existed within the Anglican communion, sometimes threatening to secede, a fundamentalist revival movement whose members are known as *balokole* 'the saved'.[18] In this revival there are almost no nativistic elements; it is, on the contrary, an orthodox Wesleyan-type movement bent upon rescuing the Church from decadence and worldliness. Its leaders look to Billy Graham, not to the syncretist Bantu prophets of central and southern Africa.[19] Besides this there have been two small break-away movements; one of these has over the years shrunk to relative insignificance, while the other has returned to doctrinal regularity by affiliating with the Eastern Orthodox communion.[20]

When, therefore, we look at the religious ministry in modern Buganda we must see it against the background of a society in which two world religions are firmly established; and in which the country parson's confirmation class, the bishop saying mass in the cathedral and the returning band of Mecca pilgrims are familiar and entirely legitimate figures.

The Roman Catholics are divided into three dioceses under an archbishop at Rubaga, near Kampala. The clergy are mainly Baganda, though there remain a number of European priests, including the archbishop. Baganda priests number 147, including a bishop and six deans. The Ganda Bishop of Masaka, in the heavily Roman Catholic county of Buddu, is a figure of tremendous prestige in Buganda—perhaps second only to the Kabaka. The Anglican clergy, organized under a province with its centre at the cathedral church of St. Paul at Namirembe, near Kampala, is even more heavily dominated by Baganda; only the archbishop and a handful of others are European, while there are 102 Baganda priests, including bishops and rural deans. Both Anglican and Roman Catholic churches maintain theological colleges in Buganda.

Baganda Muslims are Sunnis of the Shafiite school and are led by Prince Badru Kakungulu, a grandson of Kabaka Suna. Badru's father, Prince Mbogo, had been the political leader of the Muslims during the religious wars of the eighteen-eighties and nineties, and after the establishment of the Protectorate, Mbogo, and later his son, acted as lay leader and patron of the community. For many years the Muslim community was relatively poor, lacking the outside resources which religious philanthropy in Europe made available to the Christians, and as a group were ill-educated, both in Islamic thought and in secular learning. During recent years, however, the Indian Ismaili Khoja followers of the Aga Khan resident in Buganda have provided substantial financial assistance, with the result that Muslim education has been greatly strengthened. The Ismailis, who from an orthodox Sunni point of view are schismatic, have apparently not used their great resources for the purpose of proselytization, but instead have channelled their assistance through the non-sectarian Muslim Welfare Society. The Islamic centre is at Kibuli, near Kampala, where a large mosque and educational establishment is presided over by a Sheikh al-Islam, a Chief Qādī and a Mufti, all of them Baganda. For many years the community has been divided into two sects, known as 'Juma' and 'Juma-Zukuli', over a question of ritual procedure, and they still maintain parallel organizations. In 1956, each group had twenty functionaries with the title of '*sheika*', or '*muwalimu*', in charge of territorial divisions—usually counties—as well as several hundred local *bawalimu* licensed to perform marriages.

Being in relatively close proximity to Mecca and including within its number many prosperous traders and farmers, the Muslim community today contains many who have been able to perform the pilgrimage and others who have been to Cairo and other Islamic centres for training. Such contact with the outside world, together with the recent increases in educational facilities for Muslim children, promises to raise the level of sophistication within the community and thus to remove the sense of backwardness from which its members have often suffered in comparison with their Christian countrymen.

Like the churches and mosques, schools have long been familiar and valued features of the Buganda landscape; indeed, the development of the two kinds of institutions—religious and educational—has been very closely related, for modern education was introduced by the missions and until recently has been essentially controlled by them. Education—*buyigirize*—tended for turn-of-the-century Baganda to be accepted together with religion—*ddini*—as forming a single complex of 'progressive civilization' which almost everyone was avid to acquire. Throughout all the vicissitudes which the relationship between the Baganda and their British protectors has undergone, the legitimacy of Britain's role as bringer of education and religion has seldom been challenged.

The reasons for this eager acceptance of new religious and secular culture are no doubt many and complex, and an adequate analysis of them would take us too far from our subject. The basic outlines of the phenomenon are, however, reasonably clear. As we saw in our brief consideration of traditional religion, the value-system of nineteenth-century Buganda was strongly instrumental in emphasis. Only the nation, its welfare and its expansion, tended to be 'sacred'; other values and beliefs, as well as particular social structural arrangements, tended to be measured by their utility for national aggrandizement. There was, consequently, little commitment to traditional ways of thinking and acting as such. Christianity, Islam and modern secular learning were attractive, therefore, both for their association with the obviously greater power of the invaders, and for their intrinsic merits as more reasonable ways of ordering the natural and moral universe. With the triumph in 1900 of a new generation of chiefs trained by the missionaries, both Christian and Muslim, these new elements of secular and religious culture became part of the culture of the Baganda and progressively lost their association with Europeans as colonial rulers. Thus the late Kabaka Daudi Cwa, who was an active ideologist of the new, twentieth-century Buganda, distinguished in an interesting pamphlet between, on the one hand, education (*buyigirize*) and civilization (*bulabufu*), which are good and necessary to the Baganda, and, on the other hand, 'foreignization' (*kwezaya*), which must be avoided.[21]

It is in the context of this ideological development that the Baganda have been able to make modern education their own. Originally the catechist or *muwalimu* and the schoolteacher were the same person; the thatched mud-and-wattle hut served as both a place of prayer and a classroom, where little groups of children were taught their 'letters' along with the Gospels or the Koran. Increasingly, however, the association between religion and education has weakened. Most schools are still owned by the three main religious groups, but their principal financial support and control of their curricula have passed to the two governments, which have also in recent years begun to build secular schools of their own. Along with its other implications, this increasing divorce of church and school has meant an increasing professionalization of teaching. New teacher-training institutions bring together trainees of all faiths and the Teachers' Association, with its annual meetings, helps to maintain a sense of common vocation.

In 1955 there were in Buganda 539 schools employing 3,354 teachers to teach 74,617 pupils.[22] Of these the vastly greater part in each case were affiliated with the Anglican or Roman Catholic churches; there were only 46 Muslim schools and only 9 Buganda Government secular schools.[23] Supervision of all primary and junior secondary schools, secular or denominational, however, is in the hands of the Buganda Government Ministry of Education, while secondary schools are the concern of the Uganda Department of Education.

'Teachers', of course, are by no means a homogeneous group —indeed they form perhaps the most heterogeneous of all the new occupations which we shall consider. A master at King's College, Budo, the élite Anglican boarding school, is likely to have been educated at Makerere College or overseas—perhaps beyond the undergraduate level—and to have a style of life and social circle which place him in the upper ranks of Ganda society. The teacher in a rural primary school, on the other hand, may be essentially confined, both socially and intellectually, to the village world. In spite of such differences, however, and in spite of a corresponding range of financial rewards, it remains possible to speak of the role of 'the teacher' (*musomesa*, literally: 'one who causes others to read')—a role which, whether its occupant teaches a halting literacy in Luganda to village children or physics to the next generation of university entrants, is honoured by a people who look to education as the means to almost every desirable end, either personal or national.

Teachers and the functionaries of Islam and Christianity have existed long enough and in sufficient numbers to be regarded as occupying established roles in Ganda society. Baganda have definite expectations about how a clergyman or teacher will behave. Medicine and the law, however, are much more recent roles for Baganda and as yet are only superficially integrated into Ganda society, though Baganda were served by European lawyers and mission doctors for fifty years before either profession contained any of their countrymen, and in this limited sense the roles are therefore familiar ones. Lawyers and physicians are less integrated partly because the services which they provide are as yet less universally required. The practitioner of native curing methods (*musawo*; the term is also used for the modern physician) is still active; and in the Buganda Government courts, which have jurisdiction in most of the litigation in which Baganda engage, professional lawyers are barred, each litigant acting as his own advocate. The traditional religious system, however, no longer exists as such and neither does the traditional 'school'—the corps of pages at the court or in the household of a chief. The average Muganda, therefore, needs a physician or lawyer less than he needs a teacher, a priest or a *muwalimu*. A further reason why physicians and lawyers are fewer, is, of course, that their education is more extended and technical and requires a secondary school background which Buganda has only recently been able to provide. Today a Muganda may be trained in medicine at Makerere College. To become a lawyer he still must go outside Uganda. In 1956 there were 12 physicians in private practice, in addition to the 6 employed by the Buganda Government and some 30 in the Protectorate Government service.[24] Five lawyers were in private practice and another held a post as resident magistrate in the Protectorate service.

Nevertheless, in spite of—perhaps because of—their scarcity, lawyers and physicians are important in Buganda life. Both professions are prominent in the leadership of political parties and both loom large in the dreams of ambitious young Baganda.[25] With their European-recognized technical qualifications, they represent to their fellows that achievement of modern knowledge and skill which signifies both great personal success and increasing national independence of European control. But perhaps their greatest significance lies in the fact that they are professions in which the independent practitioner, purveying his own technical skill, represents a common form of organization. They thus represent an important departure in the direction of occupational universalism in a society in which the particularistic patron-client pattern characteristic of the traditional period often carries over into modern institutions. Other modern occupational roles, such as those of the civil servant, teacher or religious functionary, are carried out exclusively in hierarchical organizations which are much more vulnerable to particularism. The norms of universalism and functional specificity are present in the conceptions of church, state and school which have been introduced by Europeans, but hierarchical organization allows particularism and diffuseness to develop *sub rosa*. The schoolboy who aspires to medicine or the law, however, as so many do, works toward success through independent professional competence rather than through the time-honoured way of loyal service to a master.

Farmers and Traders

The average Muganda is still a cultivator who produces his own staple food—the banana—and manufactures and uses many of the traditional craft products. Bark-cloth making, for example, is still a living craft, the product being used for burial wrappings and temporary partitions in houses, though rarely any longer for clothing. Baskets and pots are still made and even the smith survives by making knives of the particular shape favoured by Baganda women for felling and peeling bananas. It is possible that Baganda are still sufficiently rooted in the traditional subsistence economy that most of them could survive quite well if the goods and services which flow from the money economy were by some disaster cut off and they were thrown back into self-sufficiency. The population of Kampala— particularly the non-Baganda, who often have no banana gardens—would no doubt suffer severely, but the village folk could probably provide for themselves the necessities of life.

We conjure up this imaginary disaster in order to stress the fact that the continued existence of a relatively rich subsistence economy (and the absence of a population problem) has formed a kind of cushion against the economic imperatives which else-where in the 'underdeveloped' world, and particularly in Asia, have often made development so urgent. Baganda do, of course, participate in a money economy to a degree which is relatively unusual for East Africans and they greatly value the goods and services which this participation provides. But the incentive for most is the 'carrot' of the essentially luxury goods which the proceeds from their cotton and coffee will buy, not the 'goad' of actual privation or landlessness. And this profitable cash-crop agriculture has in turn provided another 'cushion' at a higher level; on their rich and plentiful land the Baganda have been able to add to subsistence agriculture a pattern of small-scale cash crop cultivation which enables them to buy the new goods and services without going into wage labour. Thus most of the industrial labour force in Buganda consists either of immigrant foreigners or else of Baganda who 'commute' to work from country homesteads where they can keep one foot in agriculture.[26]

It is against this background of environmental beneficence that modern Ganda agricultural practice must be seen. Wrigley deals with the economic side of the matter in Chapter 1; we are interested here in the sociological question: how far has the occupational role of modern, capitalist 'farmer', as contrasted with the semi-subsistence peasant, emerged in present-day Buganda?

There is, of course, no obvious point at which to draw the line between peasant and farmer; these are ideal types and in the real world we find instead a range of variation. On the one hand, there are probably almost no 'pure' subsistence cultiva-tors left. Everyone grows a bit of cotton or coffee and with the proceeds buys tea, sugar, soap, cotton clothing and a bicycle.

The average taxpayer in Buganda in 1956 received Shs. 678 (about £34 or $95) for his cotton and coffee.[27] On the other hand, there are only a few real 'agricultural capitalists', of the sort described in Richards' study, who farm one hundred acres or more with hired labour, after the fashion of the European-owned coffee plantations which exist in small numbers in Uganda and in larger numbers elsewhere in East Africa.[28] Some of these Ganda commercial farmers grow coffee, while others produce bananas in large quantities for sale to those members of the Kampala population who live in areas too densely populated to permit banana culture. And of course there is a continuous range between these two extremes. In one sense all are 'modern farmers', for all are engaged in production for the money economy. The language recognizes this by calling all of them by the new occupational term *balimi* —'cultivators'. Thus agriculture of any kind has become an occupation, as contrasted with the old residual, diffuse low status of *mukopi*, if only to distinguish it from the other occupations which have differentiated out in modern Buganda.

However, the peasant who with his own labour and that of his wife and children, grows subsistence crops plus a plot of cotton for cash with which to purchase the imported extras is but one step removed from the nineteenth-century *mukopi*. The really new phenomenon in the occupational structure is the farmer who treats his holding as an enterprise to be managed in the interests of maximum profitability. The emergence of this type has been made possible by Buganda's unusual '*mailo*' land-tenure system, introduced in 1900 as part of the Protectorate Agreement between Great Britain and representatives of the Kabaka.

Available data do not allow us to determine how many *mailo* holders there are in present-day Buganda nor how these are distributed by size of holding. Neither is there any satisfactory way of determining how many *mailo* holders have devoted their land to plantation development, as against passive land-lordism. Mukwaya, in his study of land tenure, quotes the opinion of the government registrar of titles that there were extant in 1950 approximately 58,000 separate titles.[29] Many persons, of course, hold more than one title. In a study of two sub-counties, Mukwaya found that 78 persons held 98 pieces of land—a ratio of 0·8. Applying this ratio to the registrar's estimate, we might guess that there were in 1950 some 46,000 *mailo* owners or, allowing for a continuation of the trend towards fragmentation noted by Mukwaya, perhaps 50,000 in 1956. The holdings of the owners in Mukwaya's sample were distributed by size as shown in Table 3. Perhaps half own more than the ten acres which, according to the Land Tax of 1939, makes a man more than a simple peasant. Applied to the above estimate of the total number of *mailo* owners, this ratio would indicate that there were in 1956 something like 25,000 persons who might be called 'landlords' and 'farmers' as contrasted with 'peasants'.

TABLE 3

DISTRIBUTION OF MAILO OWNERS BY NUMBER OF
ACRES OWNED IN MUKWAYA'S 1950 SAMPLE

Number of Acres	*Number of Owners*
1–20	415
21–100	181
101–300	45
301–600	32
over 600	14
Total	687

There is another, more direct, but not necessarily more reliable measure: namely, the returns from the land tax, which is levied at Shs. 1·50 for tenants and owners of less than ten acres of *mailo*, Shs. 5 for holders of more than ten acres of *mailo* having fewer than six tenants, and Shs. 15 or Shs. 25 (depending upon the fertility of the area) for holders of more than ten acres of *mailo* with six or more tenants. According to the tax returns for 1956, owners of ten or more acres of *mailo* numbered 15,530.[30] As the Annual Report notes, however, collections have been imperfect and the returns thus yield an underestimate of the number of owners of large holdings.[31] We may guess that the best estimate lies between the figures arrived at in the two different ways. Thus there were perhaps 20,000 substantial *mailo* holders in 1956. Among these, landlords were doubtless more numerous than farmers, for reasons which we have discussed, although the latter have been steadily increasing in number in recent years.

Ganda commercial activity has also been increasing in fields outside agriculture. Unlike the other African peoples of Uganda, the Baganda have been able to buy and sell land quite freely. The Busulu and Envujo Law restricted the *mailo* holder's ability to develop his holding as he might choose, but it in no way inhibited his ability to pledge or sell his rights in it to another African. Thus Baganda have been able, on the one hand, to liquidate their inherited rights in land to acquire capital for investment in other enterprises and, on the other, to invest in land capital acquired by other means. There has even developed a small speculative market in *mailo* titles in which persons in Kampala try to buy cheap and sell dear without ever bothering to visit the holdings concerned. Thus the economy of Buganda, though similar in its main outlines to the economies of neighbouring areas (especially neighbouring parts of southern Uganda) has had a flexibility and a diversity which the latter, with their various customary land tenures, have not enjoyed.[32] An important symptom is the fact that in 1953 more than half the African traders of the Protectorate— 6,683 out of 11,634—were resident in Buganda, though the kingdom contains little more than one-quarter of the total population.[33] Commerce is thus another major entrepreneurial occupation which we must consider in our review of social differentiation in contemporary Buganda.

Perhaps more than any other modern occupational field, commerce appears to ambitious Baganda to have been thoroughly pre-empted by non-Africans. Africanization in church and state is an end actively sought by the missions and the Central Government, and the same is to some extent true of the larger and more bureaucratically organized European business concerns which, by taking in Africans, hope to ease the difficulty of the coming political transition.[34] Most retail distribution and light industry, however, is in the hands of Indians, who for centuries have been established in the Indian Ocean ports and who since the turn of the century have built up an intricate network of trading relations throughout inland East Africa.[35] This complex, which is made up of a large number of small firms, often linked by kinship and possessing a reservoir of contacts and trading skill, appears from the vantage point of ambitious Baganda to be both impenetrable and very difficult to compete with.

In this context it is understandable that the little one-room rural *dduuka* (shop), which is the most common form of Ganda trading enterprise, seldom makes much profit. In 1952, it has been estimated, African traders in Uganda enjoyed a total turnover of some £10,000,000; if some half the traders were Baganda, then perhaps the latter were responsible for £5,000,000 of this.[36] Relatively little of it, however, appears to have represented net profit. It was estimated that only 20 per cent. of the traders averaged as much as £249 in net profit, while 18 per cent. made no profit at all, the shop often being supported by the trader's agricultural holding.[37] The slimness of profits is attributed to the fact that most traders deal mainly in such low-margin staple items as sugar, cigarettes and kerosene, being unable for lack of contacts or experience to merchandise successfully the more profitable lines, such as hardware, clothing and piece goods.[38] These relatively unprofitable little retail enterprises provide other rewards; trading carries prestige for the person who engages in it and the Baganda as a people derive a good deal of satisfaction from seeing Ganda enterprises compete successfully with those of Indians, even if they must be, in effect, subsidized by agriculture. The situation does not, however, make for the growth of a vigorous and distinct commercial 'calling'. Shop-keeping remains largely a side-line.

Some few Baganda have surmounted these limitations to become entrepreneurs in a more substantial sense. In 1955–6, 85 Baganda were registered as directors of 36 limited companies.[39] Some of these enterprises did not involve much African entrepreneurship. Some, for example, were quasi-public undertakings like the Uganda Development Corporation, in which directors have more the character of public servants than entrepreneurs. In other cases, like the *Uganda Argus*, the main English-language newspaper, and Uganda Breweries, a firm producing European-type beer, Baganda were junior partners to European or Indian entrepreneurs. Of the 36 firms with African directors, however, 28 were all-

African affairs, engaged in such varied activities as coffee curing; the distribution of fish, meat or banana beer; publishing in Luganda; and building construction. Few of these concerns are said to be highly profitable and many, no doubt, end up in receivership. Many of them represent the first, tentative efforts of Baganda to enter the more complex kinds of entrepreneurial activity. Although they may fail, they provide the experience essential to later success and their very existence indicates that a more substantial kind of Ganda business enterprise is in the making.

Perhaps most important of all as fields for entrepreneurial activity are the several hundred co-operative societies, particularly those engaged in marketing and processing cotton and coffee. Here again there has been failure due to inexperience and peculation, particularly in societies not registered under the Co-operative Societies Ordinance and hence deprived of assistance from the Department of Co-operative Development. There has also been considerable success, however, and the societies have consequently taken deep root in Ganda economic life. The leaders of the societies, which numbered 379 in 1954, represent a substantial group of Baganda who have made a successful occupational specialty out of co-operative enterprise.[40] Thus, while the occupational tag *mukulembezi w'ekibiina ekye-gassi* ('co-operative society leader') perhaps carries somewhat less prestige today than *musuubuzi* ('merchant'), it represents a greater reality in the occupational structure.

Wage Workers

During recent decades a significant amount of industrialization has taken place in Buganda—almost all of it as a result of Indian and European enterprise. There are cotton ginneries and coffee curing works, cigarette and furniture factories, breweries, construction firms and machine shops. Except for the ginneries and coffee curing works, which are dispersed over the countryside in order to be nearer the sources of their raw materials, most of these undertakings are located near Kampala, though there is another growing industrial complex just across the Nile in Jinja, where the Owen Falls Dam furnishes a supply of electric power. In 1956 commerce and industry, the public services (most prominently the railway and the Public

Works Department) and plantation agriculture, employed some 100,000 Africans in Buganda, a sizeable part of the adult male African population.[41] Demographically and economically, wage labour is becoming important.

That it is as yet relatively unimportant culturally and politically is attributable largely to the peculiar ethnic composition of the labour force, and especially to the place in it occupied by the Baganda. As we have seen, the relative prosperity of agriculture has been a potent factor in keeping Baganda 'down on the farm' and out of wage labour. At the same time, there has existed close at hand a plentiful supply of labour in the form of immigrants from less favoured neighbouring areas such as northern Uganda, Rwanda and Burundi. In consequence, as Elkan has shown in his study of two factories, Baganda tend to appear in the wage labour force mainly in the more highly paid, highly skilled or white-collar positions, while the ranks of unskilled labour in Buganda tend to be filled with foreigners.[42]

Baganda get the better jobs for several reasons, apart from the fact that only the better-paid jobs are sufficiently rewarding to attract them out of agriculture. First, since Buganda has been the centre of educational development for the whole region, they are on the whole more sophisticated. Second, commercial and industrial development has also centred in Kampala and thus Baganda have had better opportunities to learn valuable skills on the job. Finally, the fact that their homeland surrounds Kampala makes it possible for them to combine urban and rural life in a way which is not so readily available to the immigrants. Baganda townsmen often buy small plots on the periphery of the town—the *mailo* land tenure system facilitates this—from which they 'commute' daily to urban employment.[43] In this way they are able to grow much of their food, and even some cash crops, and to lead a more traditionally Ganda style of life while remaining in employment. They are thus more stable employees—and hence receive more rapid advancement —than immigrants who, in order to maintain their social positions at home and their rights in land there, must migrate back and forth, contributing both to the instability, and hence to the inefficiency, of Kampala's labour force, and to their own lack of progress in the job hierarchy.[44] Those who stay in

Buganda, as many Banyaruanda and Barundi do, often take up land in the country and 'become Baganda'.[45] Bantu-speaking people from the neighbouring kingdoms are of course more readily assimilable than are the Nilotes.

The wage labour force in Buganda thus tends to consist, on the one hand, of foreign migrants who are essentially birds of passage and, on the other, of Baganda commuters who, while deeply rooted in the life of the surrounding countryside, and of Buganda as a whole, regard the town as no more than a place of work—one which, moreover, is dominated by Indians and Europeans and hence is fundamentally 'un-Ganda' and 'un-African'. This lack of identification with the town is reinforced by the curious dual administration which prevails in the Kampala urban agglomeration. There is, on the one hand, the area of the Municipality, dominated by Indian business men and British administrators and planners. Africans who live there are housed in special estates and 'labour lines' planned and controlled by the Uganda Government. On the other hand, immediately adjacent to the Municipality lies the *Kibuga*—the capital of Buganda—with its palace, the Buganda Government buildings, and thousands of dwellings constructed according to Ganda notions.[46] It is with the *Kibuga* that Baganda identify, but the *Kibuga* remains essentially a court town; industry and commerce centre in the alien Municipality.

All this may serve to explain why, in spite of the substantial growth of industry and commerce, wage labour has not yet become politically and culturally important—why there is little that one could call an 'urban proletarian sub-culture' and only a rudimentary labour movement. We may hazard a guess that when and if 'class-consciousness' in a Marxian sense does develop it will not be the Baganda who produce it but rather the immigrants, who according to the most recent estimates make up between one-third and one-half the population of the kingdom. Then the Baganda may find themselves in the position of turn-of-the-century Anglo-Saxon Americans: a native middle class set above an immigrant proletariat, a situation filled with interesting (and explosive) political potentialities.[47]

Politicians and Publicists

Political parties, in the sense of associations formed to support or oppose policies, points of view, or factions in government, have existed for many years in Buganda. Before the intrusion of Europeans, competition for office appears to have been conducted mainly among individuals or small groups bound together by kinship or clientship. Also, it tended to be clandestine, for open political competition held no place in traditional Ganda ideology, which regarded the state as a monolith governed unilaterally by a despotic king. The first explicitly political associations were formed by the adherents of the three introduced religions, who contended for possession of the state during the eighteen-eighties and -nineties. The 1900 settlement put a brake on open religious conflict by apportioning offices among Protestants, Roman Catholics and Muslims. Since the Great Lukiiko was at this time made up entirely of officials, this meant that the relative strengths of the three groups in the legislature were also fixed. As the Great Lukiiko has become more representative, however, and as the legislature of Uganda has come to have elective seats, open religious politics has tended to revive. Although officially there are no religious parties, some of the modern parties have in fact been closely associated with one or another religious group.

Another source of party organization appeared shortly after 1900 as a result of the land settlement. We have described how in nineteenth-century Buganda some villages were held as estates by heads of descent groups, some of whom also held chieftainships in the territorial hierarchy. There are indications that at an earlier period such persons—known as *bataka*—held more extensive estates and more important offices, and that their political importance had declined with the growth of royal power. By the eighteen-nineties, though some *bataka* still held hereditary or appointive offices, others held only small estates, limited in some cases, perhaps, to little more than the ancestral burial ground which formed the sacred core of the *butaka*—the clan or lineage land. Now the group of chiefs who in 1900 negotiated the Agreement with the British Commissioner, Sir Harry Johnston, included some office-holding *bataka*, but excluded others, especially, no doubt, those who lacked important territorial offices. No doubt, also, the conflicts of the 'eighties and 'nineties, out of which a cohesive group of Christian and Muslim chiefs emerged victorious, also acted to reduce the importance of hereditary authority. In any case, the 1900 settlement distributed most of the agricultural land of Buganda among the victorious oligarchy in individual freehold (*mailo*). Over the ensuing twenty years, there emerged a political movement claiming to represent *bataka* whose clan and lineage lands had thus been alienated, and ever since that time, '*butaka*' has been a potent symbol of protest around which political associations have from time to time gathered. During the disturbances of 1945 and 1949, and again during the crisis of 1953–5, when the Kabaka was deported, the word *butaka*—often abbreviated to *Bu*'—has been a rallying cry for opposition to chiefs, to the Protectorate Government, to the Kabaka or, sometimes, to all of these together.

The persistence of *butaka* as a symbol of protest is clearly not attributable solely to the loss of land or authority in 1900 by clan and lineage heads. Although many actual *bataka* in this proper sense doubtless did lose by the 1900 Agreement, others were high in the chiefly oligarchy and did very well from it.[48] Some important leaders of the first organized movement to fly the *butaka* flag—the 'Federation of Bataka'—in fact themselves received substantial allotments. An outstanding example is Joswa Kate, who was allotted sixteen square miles. He was also *Mugema*—head of the Grey Monkey clan and chief of the central county of Busiro—one of the three hereditary county chiefs remaining at the end of the nineteenth century. His case suggests how it was that *butaka* sentiment represented something more than protest over immediate loss of land. Powerful clan and lineage heads had traditionally had uneasy relations with the Kabaka, who resented their independent hereditary authority and took every opportunity to reduce it.[49] The *Mugema* in particular, the most powerful of the hereditary chiefs, has tended for at least a century to feud with the king's government; Mutesa I, Daudi Cwa and Mutesa II have all attempted, with varying degrees of success, to reduce his influence.[50] Thus *butaka* sentiment represents, among other things, a traditional conflict between the central power and independent hereditary authority based upon descent groups —a conflict of which the post-1900 Bataka movements were merely the most recent phase.

But *butaka* as a political symbol also means something else, something less 'aristocratic', more popular. To the ordinary *mukopi* it means a complex of sentiments—economic, domestic and religious—centred upon his holding of land, for *butaka* is not something which only a clan or lineage head might possess; in a wider sense it is an effective *rootedness in the land* which a *bakopi* line might acquire through generations of residence and cultivation. The graves of ancestors in the banana garden both hold profound religious meaning and provide the strongest claim to possession (apart from the king's will) known to Ganda customary law. The frequent uprooting of *bakopi*, resulting from the shifting political fortunes of their masters, which seems to have characterized traditional Buganda must, however, have made *butaka* the object of anxiety as well as attachment. And with the coming of European settlement in the neighbouring Kenya highlands (and for a short time in Buganda itself) these traditional insecurities were naturally stimulated.

Thus the *butaka* symbol, which has been prominent in every major political agitation since 1900, expresses a rather wide range of sentiments arising out of the strains and tensions inherent in nineteenth-century Ganda society. To it, and to the religious divisions, have been added in recent times a number of other ideological sources of political party formation, including the frustrations experienced by many Baganda in their attempts to engage in business enterprise and the simple desire for independence and equality which has swept through all of Africa since World War II.

However, in 1956 party politics was not yet an 'occupation' or 'profession' in Buganda. Parties existed, but they were not yet articulated with government in such a way as to provide careers and livelihoods for their leaders. A few party leaders had achieved office in the Buganda or Uganda Governments (service in the chiefly hierarchy has been the orthodox route to ministerial rank in the Buganda Government; achievement in one of the learned professions the commonest basis for appointment to the Protectorate Executive Council), but these had a tendency to become separated from their parties, for in neither the Great Lukiiko nor the Legislative Council was there as yet a 'government' or 'administration' formed by the majority party and capable of rewarding its leaders with office. The Uganda Government was still dominated by European officials, while the Government of the Kabaka was hostile to the parties, as it tends to be to any independent centre of authority, and had thus far prevented them from functioning in the Great Lukiiko in orthodox parliamentary fashion. Membership in neither legislative body was sufficiently rewarding financially to provide a livelihood. Consequently, party life remained divorced from government and party leadership remained a part time, amateur activity, in spite of the enormous prominence of politics, politicians, and even the parties themselves in recent years.

This was the situation in 1956, the year for which the data for this chapter were gathered. By 1962, the parties had acquired a much firmer footing in the political structure and new political alignments had emerged. A Uganda-wide party whose strength lay mainly outside Buganda, the Uganda People's Congress, was preparing to form the first independent Uganda Government in collaboration with a Buganda national party, the *Kabaka Yekka* ('the king alone') Movement. These developments, which will be further discussed in the Epilogue, foreshadow the growth of a more professionalized body of politicians, but for the present it is probably correct to characterize the typical Muganda politician as an amateur.

Politicians are thus on the whole members of the other occupational groups which we have already considered, though of course a man's fame may rest upon his political avocation rather than upon the vocation from which he makes his living, which is why we must discuss politicians in a survey of modern social differentiation. In 1956, there were three main political associations: the Progressive Party, the Democratic Party and the Uganda National Congress. The Bataka still existed under the name 'Bataka Community', but their influence was slight, much of their following and their appeal having been taken over by the newer groups. There were also a number of minor parties of little real consequence. Of the 32 top Ganda leaders (Baganda members of executive or central committees, which also of course included non-Baganda) in the three main parties, we have occupational information for 25. Six were school masters, 6 merchants, 3 landowners or 'gentleman farmers' and 3 physicians. There were also 3 journalists, a lawyer, a building contractor and a printer.[51] Only one, the

President-General of the Uganda National Congress, could be said to be a 'professional politician' in the sense of having had for a substantial period no other occupation. This man had been engaged for twenty years in the organization of parties and politically oriented agricultural co-operative associations; from them and from a degree of private wealth he got his living, but he was exceptional. Most politicians must work at something else in order to support their party activities.

The occupation which best complements the politician's avocation is journalism, for by managing or editing a newspaper he is in a position to reinforce directly his party's efforts. For political journalism Buganda offers a situation which is, by African standards, unusually favourable, for it is one of the few areas in trans-Saharan Africa where the press can reach a really mass audience. In most of Africa, newspapers and other literature are published mainly in the metropolitan languages —French and English—with the result that readership is limited to the educated.[52] In Buganda, however, literacy in Luganda early became very widespread and a substantial literature has been produced which is capable of reaching perhaps a majority of the population. There were in 1956 fifteen weekly or bi-weekly Luganda papers with a combined circulation of 87,100.[53] The papers are often carelessly laid out and their standards of veracity are frequently uncertain (though probably no more so than in many Western countries half a century ago—or even more recently!), with the result that editors and publishers are not infrequently convicted of libel or sedition. But they have, through an enterprising combination of political, human interest ('Abusolomu Musoke Offers Shs. 10 Reward for Information Leading to Recovery of Lost Wife') and marvel ('Cow Gives Birth to Three-legged Calf') stories achieved an avid readership and thus have acquainted an unusually wide audience with the printed word. Of course not all editors and publishers are active politicians or party publicists, but the leading ones are. The publishers of the three most popular papers—*Uganda Eyogera* ('Uganda Speaks'), *Uganda Empya* ('New Uganda') and the *Uganda Post* (printed in Luganda, despite its English title), were in 1956 members of the top leadership of the Progressive Party or the Uganda National Congress. Others often took part in politics at lower levels. Combining as he does the appeal of politics with that of successful business enterprise, it is not surprising that the *mukuŋŋanya wa mawulire* ('assembler of news') is a figure of great prestige in present-day Buganda.

*   *   *   *   *

We have now concluded our survey of social differentiation in modern Buganda, having seen how the relatively simple structure of nineteenth-century society has become much more complex. We next turn to an analysis of how this process of differentiation has affected the fluidity of Ganda society.

Social Mobility, Traditional and Modern

WESTERNERS are apt to think of the modernization of traditional systems of social stratification primarily as a loosening of
hereditary ties—as a reduction, to use somewhat more professional language, of the role in society of ascribed status and an
increase in the role of achievement. We think of it in this way,
perhaps, because our own traditional society—the society of
medieval Europe—was a relatively caste-ridden one. The
ancestors of modern Europeans and Americans thought of their
social world as being divided into fixed layers occupied by
persons of differential worth. Each layer, or 'estate', had its
own distinctive sub-culture and sense of common interest and
destiny. Each tended to be what Max Weber has called a
'status group'.[1] Thus, around the nobility there gathered a
culture of chivalry and a sense of international solidarity so
powerful that it could consider the killing in battle of an enemy
knight by a common soldier, not as a deed of valour, but as a
capital crime.[2] Nobility was, furthermore, thought by medieval
Westerners to be biologically inherited; adultery was abhorred,
not so much as a sin in itself but rather because it was apt to
mix noble blood with that of varlets.[3] Even within the peasant
estate there was strong class-consciousness. An English franklin
despised a villein and might take to the law any man who
addressed him by the latter term.[4] Thus medieval Western
society could be conceived of by its philosophers as an anthropomorphic organism whose parts were the various 'ranks of the

Reprinted by permission from Lloyd A. Fallers, ed., *The King's Men.
Leadership and Status in Buganda on the Eve of Independence* (London:
Oxford University Press, 1964). Dr. Fallers assisted by S. B. K. Musoke.

people', each with its distinct and immutable function.[5] Although mobility was possible, particularly through the towns and the church, men like Robert Grosseteste, the villein Bishop of Lincoln, stood as glaring and barely tolerable exceptions to the established order.[6] In this setting, modernization quite naturally appeared primarily as a solvent of ascribed status. The differentiation of new occupational roles meant, above all, new opportunities to escape through mobility from hereditary inferiority. Popular political movements reinforced these aspirations by demanding equality of opportunity or the elimination of inequality itself.

In Buganda, however, as we have seen, mobility on a very substantial scale is nothing new. Since well before the establishment of British administration, a process of progressive political centralization had increasingly opened positions of power and wealth to men of talent. Rising to a position of influence through loyal and able service to a lord was both culturally approved and empirically possible, and in the course of the nineteenth century was becoming ever easier and more acceptable. We cannot, therefore, view the twentieth-century changes in stratification in Buganda as simply a repetition of the earlier European experience, in which the dominant theme was increasing mobility.

However, we must be more precise. To say that mobility was approved and that it actually occurred in nineteenth-century Buganda is not to say that modernization has not increased it. For modernization has, as we have seen, created many new occupational roles; it has, in fact, almost created occupational specialization as such in Buganda. Even though the principle of status achievement had been accepted, and even glorified, in traditional culture, it is quite possible that this differentiation has increased actual mobility by creating more positions into which persons at the 'bottom of the heap' might move.

This effect is perhaps easier to visualize than to describe. In Fig. 11 the two shapes represent, very crudely, the different opportunities for mobility offered by societies in different stages of economic development and, hence, with different degrees of occupational differentiation. In society A, an undifferentiated peasantry produces all the goods and services necessary for the support of both itself and the small *élite* of rulers and religious specialists. We may take this figure to represent, very roughly, the 'shape' of nineteenth-century Buganda society. The proportions of the population allocated to the various levels are almost —though not quite—sheer guesswork. Although there are, of course, no occupational or income surveys to supply us with

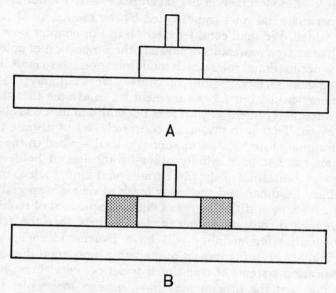

Fig. 11. The effect of occupational differentiation upon mobility.

data, we do have one clue: Sir Apolo Kagwa, in his account of taxation in the nineteenth-century kingdom, remarks that 'Every *mutongole* who had (at least) five men (under him) took his share of the tax', suggesting that the proportion of ordinary *bakopi* to headmen at the lowest level was something in the neighbourhood of five-to-one.[7] In the diagram, we have consequently given the middle level of the pyramid one-fifth the volume of the level beneath it. Without even this much documentary evidence, we have then gone ahead and given the 'top *élite*'—the persons above the level of the lowest headmen —one-fifth the volume of the latter. An important point to notice is that, even if mobility were perfect—that is to say, if every person had an equal chance to reach one of the higher positions, the chances of his doing this in such a society would still be relatively small. In a peasant society, where the *élite* is relatively small and the occupationally undifferentiated mass of ordinary folk relatively numerous, mobility is difficult, whatever the cultural attitude towards it may be.

The other figure, B, we may take to represent society A after a degree of modernization has taken place—after a number of new occupational roles (represented by the shaded area) have been added. We shall consider later on in this chapter how far the shaded area represents accurately the proportion of holders of new occupational roles which modernization has so far added to Buganda society. Again, of course, we shall have to be extremely crude, but for the moment let us assume that these new roles do represent at least *some* net addition at levels above the lowest. That is to say, more concretely, let us assume that the addition of the new occupational roles described in the last chapter has not been wholly offset by the loss of holders of lower-level *élite* roles of the more traditional kind, such as those of village headmen and the lower levels of religious specialists. If this is so, even if the degree of cultural approval of mobility has remained constant during the two periods, then the actual opportunities for mobility will have increased. Such, very roughly, has been the impact of modernization upon the social stratification systems of traditional societies everywhere, however different the process may have seemed to peoples with different values and beliefs concerning mobility.[8]

Of course we have, in thinking about these imaginary constructions, made a number of *ceteris paribus* assumptions which are in varying degrees unjustified. When we examine some of these, the problem of assessing the changes in stratification brought about in Buganda by the process of modernization becomes more complicated. In the first place, we have assumed that competition for higher positions is perfectly free, and that it has operated with equal freedom through the nineteenth and twentieth centuries. But competition for mobility, it is safe to say, is never wholly free in any society and the principal reason is very clear: men of power and wealth tend to be able to confer competitive advantages upon their children, whatever the values of the society may say. Even where high positions are in fact open to talent, and where ideology strongly supports mobility, children of the *élite* have advantages, for they are in a better position to acquire that part of talent which is the result of training. Thus, as we shall see, the nineteenth-century Ganda chief of high rank could more easily place his son in the traditional 'school for chiefs'—the corps of palace pages—than could an ordinary *mukopi* villager. Furthermore, the impediment to perfect mobility does not end with the bestowal upon the sons of the great of differential advantages in the race to the top. If mobility upward is to be free, so also must downward mobility be, for the talented poor cannot compete successfully unless there are vacant positions to compete for. But, just as the *élite* are able to give an added push to their abler progeny, so also they are often in a position to cushion the descent [of the less gifted of their heirs by easing them into sinecures. In consequence, the intelligent and energetic peasant's son may find the road upward clogged by a sluggish downward traffic. Particularly is this so in a society like that of nineteenth-century Buganda, in which fertility was highly correlated with rank. Polygyny made chiefs enormously more prolific than peasants and better diet gave their children better chances of survival; this added to the burden of downward mobility which the system had to bear.

Factors like these operate also in present-day Buganda, but of course we cannot simply assume that they operate to the same degree, for many things have changed. Perhaps most important, modern school education has, to a great extent, replaced personal service as the training—and recruiting—ground for *élite* status. The decline in polygyny and, perhaps, a higher general level of nutrition, have reduced effective status-differential fertility. We shall have to consider how far these changes have altered the ability of the *élite* to pass on their status to their children, and in which direction. Again, our answers cannot be very precise, but we may be able to make a few well-informed guesses.

The final unrealistic element in our imaginary comparison of mobility in old and new Buganda is our assumption that the cultural side of stratification has not changed—that mobility during the two periods has received the same support from the Ganda value system. Here there are, broadly speaking, two developments of which we must take account. First, open or 'universalistic' recruitment to the *élite* has clearly received some reinforcement on the ideological plane from Western contact.

Schools, churches and the civil service all emphasize it constantly and it would be a mistake to assume that these ideas are simply rejected by Baganda as foreign. Their impact has been very substantial, in part because of their congruence with the traditional emphasis upon achievement, and in part as a consequence of the development of a new national ideology in which the acceptance of Western ideas could be regarded as a means of maintaining the traditional autonomy and integrity of Buganda. Thus churches, schools and civil service came to be regarded as Ganda churches, schools and civil service and their characteristic values as Ganda values, or at any rate as consistent with the latter.

At the same time, however, the period of British administration has also seen other cultural developments which have operated in an opposite direction. In nineteenth-century Buganda, there was relatively little cultural differentiation between *bakopi* and *élite*. There were courtly manners and there was the sophistication of the capital, but these were qualities that a clever peasant could acquire; differences were insignificant compared with the cultural gulf which separated, for example, the medieval Anglo-Norman knight from the villein. It was in part this relative lack of cultural differentiation which underlay the essential 'classlessness' (in the sense of the absence of cohesive and clearly delineated strata; *not*, of course, in the sense of egalitarianism) in nineteenth-century Buganda. However, the triumph during the 'eighties and 'nineties of a new group of chiefs—what Wrigley has called the 'Christian revolution'[9]—brought into being something that had not existed before: a relatively cohesive *élite* with a distinctive ideology involving commitment to Christianity and technical progress in association with the British administration. The 1900 Agreement underwrote the dominance and exclusiveness of this group by reinforcing their position as a political oligarchy and by giving them an economic base—the *mailo* estates. The churches honoured them as patrons of religion. We must, therefore, consider how far this incipient gentry became one in the full sense—how far, that is to say, they have been able to perpetuate their dominance by maintaining control of wealth, power and educational opportunity and, equally important, how far they have remained a cohesive, culturally differentiated group.

These are the questions which we shall pursue in this chapter. First we shall examine somewhat more closely the pattern of mobility in nineteenth-century Buganda. Then we shall consider the impact of the changes of the turn-of-the-century period and their consequences for stratification and mobility in contemporary Buganda.

Stratification and Mobility in Nineteenth-century Society

In nineteenth-century Buganda, as we have seen, some élite positions were 'achieved', while others were 'ascribed'. These terms of Linton's are very useful for purposes of preliminary description, and indeed they correspond roughly with a distinction which Baganda themselves draw when they say that some positions are *bw'ensikirano* ('hereditary'), while others are not. The simple dichotomy, however, obscures complexities and inter-cultural differences of some magnitude and we must try to take account of these.

We may, first of all, examine those positions which Baganda describe as *bw'ensikirano* and which English speakers would call 'hereditary', making use of the nearest available translation. These are the *bataka*, heads of clans or lineages and holders of those state offices which in the past were joined with clan or lineage headships. In what sense are (or were) these offices 'hereditary'? The limiting case of ascribed or hereditary status would of course be one in which each person's adult status could be determined from birth by fixed rules pertaining to descent and birth-order. Father-to-son inheritance, with primogeniture, would be one way of securing a high degree of predictability, while another would be collateral, or brother-to-brother, inheritance by order of birth. In nineteenth-century Buganda, however, things were never so predictable. The positions described as *bw'ensikirano* were 'hereditary' or 'ascribed' only in the sense that they were held within rather large patrilineal descent groups. Within a group, it was not at all clear who would inherit a particular position, for there was no birth-order rule. And, although positions often passed from father to son, this was by no means invariably the practice, even when sons were available. Hence a position might be filled from a wide range of eligible candidates.

An example will perhaps make clearer the broad sense in

which *bw'ensikirano* or *butaka* (they come to the same thing; *bw'ensikirano* refers to the mode of recruitment, *butaka* to the piece of land which always seems to have been an incident of such recruitment) positions were 'hereditary'. An illuminating case is provided by the office of the *Kayonga*, the head of one of the constituent minor lineages of the major lineage of the *Nankere* of the Lungfish clan. The *Nankere* lineage and its estates in northern Busiro have been described in Chapter 7 and illustrated in Fig. 9. Here we shall be concerned with the internal affairs of the minor lineage of the *Kayonga*. Like many other clans and lineages in present-day Buganda, the *Nankere* people have in recent times kept written records of their affairs, including a chronicle of important legendary and historical events and genealogies of their members. A few of these written records, including that of the *Nankere* lineage, have been published. The genealogy in Fig. 12, showing the descent of the headship of the *Kayonga* minor lineage in recent generations, and the tales which we shall present to elucidate it, are taken from the published volume.[10]

The chronicle of *Kayonga* begins in the time of Jjunju, the twenty-sixth Kabaka, with the story of how the headship passed from Kigongo to his brother Bembe. Elsewhere it is said that there were '. . . many holders of the office (before Kigongo) whose names cannot be recorded here because the book in which they were written was lost. . . .'[11] We begin therefore with Kigongo:

In the time of Kabaka Jjunju, when Kigongo was *Kayonga*, some hunters went pig hunting. They hunted at Kikandwa and killed three pigs. Kunyiga, father of Kigongo, said: 'Here, let me have the back meat of one to eat; tell Kigongo that Kunyiga has eaten one.' But when they told Kigongo about it, he cried: 'What! He has taken the back meat? Go, bring it to me!' When they arrived at the house of Kunyiga, they found the meat already cut up and in the cooking pot. Kunyiga emptied it out and they took it away.

After a time, Semakookiro became Kabaka and he sent for the *Kinyolo* of the Grey Monkey clan and told him: 'I want to pass through the maturation ritual.'[12] But, since it was the turn of the *Kayonga* to carry out the ritual, Kunyiga spoke up and said: 'You needn't take the trouble to find someone else. I shall carry out the ritual myself.' So the *Kinyolo* went to see Kunyiga at Namagoba and

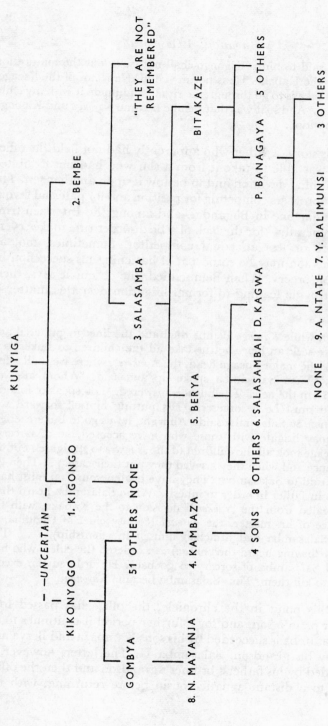

Fig. 12. Inheritance of the headship of the minor lineage of the *Kayonga*.

Kunyiga said to him: 'Kigongo shall not carry out the maturation ritual for the Kabaka. He is not my child. He is not of the lineage. If the Kabaka is to go through the ritual, let him do it with my child Bembe. . . .' And so it was that Bembe became *Kayonga* and Kigongo lost his position.

In this story, a father who apparently had not held the office himself was able to take it from a son who had not exhibited sufficient filial devotion and to bestow it upon another son. The theme of brothers competing for position and for paternal favour is a familiar one in Buganda—and among the Interlacustrine Bantu generally—for the lack of a birth-order rule makes every son more or less an equal competitor. Sometimes, too, an ambitious son may be suspected of hastening his succession by means of sorcery. When Bembe died, the chronicle says, there was a struggle leading to formal litigation over this matter of sorcery:

After a while *Kayonga* Bembe died and the lineage gathered and said: 'We seek an heir. Let us take all the children to Bukerekere (home of the major lineage head, the *Nankere*), where we shall select an heir.' Then Salasamba spoke up and said: 'Whom are you taking? I am the heir.' The lineage answered: 'You speak of inheriting. You must be a sorcerer.' (His putting himself forward was suspicious.) So Salasamba said: 'All right, let us go to Bukerekere so that I may litigate with those who have accused me of sorcery.' The lineage took all the children to the *Nankere* to straighten out the inheritance and when they arrived they put their case. . . . Then the *Nankere* said to Salasamba: 'They have beaten you. You must have killed your father in order to inherit.' When Salasamba heard that, he appealed from the *Nankere's* decision to the Kabaka, with the assistance of his master, the *Kitunzi* (county chief of Ggomba, to whom Salasamba had attached himself in clientship). . . . The Kabaka (having heard the charge) . . . ordered the elders who had accused Salasamba of sorcery to go back. He ordered the executioners to kill them. Thus Salasamba became *Kayonga*.

To this point in the chronicle, the office has passed to a brother or to a son, and for a further period it continues to do so. Salasamba is succeeded by his sons Kambaza and Berya and then by his grandson, Salasamba II. The latter, however, is succeeded by his father's brother's grandson and then the office passes to a distant agnatic cousin before returning, with the present incumbent, to the line of Berya. In each of these latter cases nearer agnates were available. Baganda say, however, that such distant collateral inheritance is a good thing because it 'holds the lineage together'. So long as such cases occur, the group forms a single undivided lineage unit. If it fails to occur for too long, the lines most distant from those in which the inheritance of the headship has begun to concentrate will become disaffected—will begin to complain: 'They are destroying the relationship'—and will tend to split off and form a separate lineage. The chronicle of *Kayonga* provides an interesting example of this. It is related that Salasamba and Kikonyogo were companions (the exact kin relationship between them is not clear, but they appear to have been close agnates):

There was a time when Salasamba and Kikonyogo were together in clientship, when Salasamba was a man of *mutongole* Semwanga of the Otter clan and Kikonyogo was a man of Nakato. At that time Semakookiro (later Kabaka) was still a prince living in Kyaggwe. These two men, Salasamba and Kikonyogo, being clients of those two *batongole*, were thus both men of Prince Semakookiro.

When Semakookiro became Kabaka, he took Nakato, master of Kinkonyogo, and made him *Mukwenda* (county chief of Ssingo) and he took Semwanga, master of Salasamba, and made him *Kitunzi* (county chief of Ggomba.) After a time Nakato died at Mityana . . . and the Kabaka took his clients and gave them other offices. The Kabaka asked: 'Where is Nakato's boy, of whom they speak?' And then the Kabaka said: 'This Kikonyogo will not go to a regular office, but instead will go to Namutamba to serve Prince Koko.' When Kikonyogo arrived there, he thought to himself: 'It is possible that when I die Prince Koko will seize all my property. I shall go to Buyonga to my friend Salasamba, who is *Kayonga*, so that he may give me a holding where I may keep my things.' When he arrived at Buyonga, Salasamba gave him a holding at Lumuli, near those of his brothers Kiddu and Nkambira, and Kikonyogo put in their charge all his cattle and other belongings. The things stayed at Lumuli and he returned to the prince. Presently the time came for him to die. When he was dying, Salasamba had already died and his son Kambaza was in the office of *Kayonga*. Kambaza sent Gombya and Kiddu and Nkambira to the funeral gathering at Namutamba and when they arrived they supported Gombya and put him on the stool to succeed Kikonyogo.

By the early years of this century the lines had diverged, and when Nasanaeri Mayanja succeeded Yairo Balimunsi, the descendants of Salasamba considered him illegitimate. He is described as having 'usurped' (*kubulya n'ensowoole*) the office and after him, as we have seen, it returned to a descendant of Salasamba.[13] The line of Kikonyogo is now described as a minimal lineage (*lunyiriri*) distinct from the main stem (*kasolya*) of the minor lineage (*mutuba*).[14] Since the chronicle was prepared by the descendants of Salasamba, who objected to Nasanaeri Mayanja's succession, one suspects that the account in the above story of Gombya being 'put on the stool of Kikonyogo' is meant to indicate that, even at that time, Kikonyogo's line was becoming distinct and hence his descendants could have no valid claim on the minor lineage headship.

The story of Kikonyogo also illustrates another important feature of the Ganda unilineal descent system: the influence upon lineage affairs of the administrative organization of the state. Kikonyogo achieved success in the administrative system; married many wives and fathered many children; and no doubt this is another reason why his descendants have come to form a distinct minimal lineage. In the case of the many headships of clans or lineages which were combined with state offices, the influence of state politics was even more direct and the meaning of *nsikirano* ('inheritance') was further broadened. Kagwa gives an excellent account of the vicissitudes of the office of the *Kibaale*, who was both head of the Antelope clan and major-domo of the palace. In some cases the position was filled by consultation among members of the clan, but on other occasions the Kabaka intervened and in effect simply appointed a clan member of his own choice.[15]

All these events Baganda speak of in the idiom of 'inheritance', and it is thus evident that they mean by it something broader than English-speaking people do. For Baganda, *nsikirano* applies simply to any position which is filled from among, and on behalf of, the members of a descent-group—a kind of 'inheritance' in which there is clearly room for a good deal of achievement. But if traditional ascribed positions were not hereditary in any strict sense, neither, of course, were those positions described by Baganda as 'not hereditary' (*obutali bw'ensikirano* or *butongole*) completely open to talent. There was, as we have seen, no developed notion of class—no notion that only a chief's sons should become chiefs—and only a minor development of status culture. But there were means by which chiefs and *bataka* might confer upon their children differential advantage in the competition for appointive office and we must now examine these.

The traditional conception of appointive office is quite clear; one may hear it today from any articulate Muganda. The required qualities were cleverness and loyalty; the path to advancement was through personal service or clientship. This process, however, involved two distinguishable elements or stages. Advancement came with able and loyal service, but for this purpose innate ability was not enough. First a person had to be trained and this required that he grow up in a great household, where he might learn by serving and observing the powerful. To this end, a father placed his pre-adolescent son in the palace or in the household of a chief. Nsimbi describes the most famous and important of these in-service training schools, the *kigalagala*, or corps of palace pages:

... until the time when children began to learn in school, the palace and the courts of chiefs had in them many boys and girls who were placed there to serve and to be trained. Boys placed in the palace to serve the Kabaka were called pages (*bagalagala*). ... The *Ssaaba-kaaki* ruled all the pages in the palace who served the Kabaka and he appointed officers among them. The corps of pages had in it a *mumyuka*, a *ssaabaddu* and the other titled ranks of office. The office of *Ssaabakaaki* was not hereditary, but could be bestowed upon any-one the Kabaka chose.[16]

The biographers of a number of prominent twentieth-century Baganda who grew up under the old order have made it possible for us to view these institutions through individual experience. Thus the biographer of Jemusi Kibuka Miti writes:

Some time after his son Mudiru had been placed to serve in the palace, Lukaayi Kacocco took another of his children, Kibuka Miti, and gave him to Kaddu, the *Musalosalo* (a *mutongole* chief), who introduced him to the Kabaka. ... Long ago, before there were schools, the palace was the chief school. Almost every chief of the Kabaka who had children chose some for service in the palace, that they might learn good behaviour. And often it happened that when there were chieftainships to be distributed, the Kabaka thought first of his pages, and not of others, because, as I have explained, the palace was like a school. You could distinguish at once the behaviour of a person brought up in the palace from that of others. Miti was aged twelve or thirteen when he entered the palace.[17]

The Rev. B. M. Zimbe, writing of his own experiences in the corps of pages, is even more succinct concerning its training functions:

. . . there was a custom that the Kabaka of Buganda only wanted to be given young boys aged ten to fourteen years because they said that a big boy does not learn and does not know how to serve. They had a saying: 'If a tree grows crooked, it cannot be straightened later without breaking.'[18]

Thus the pattern of achievement through training in personal service is plain. We must next ask: how far could, and did, chiefs and *bataka* control access to such in-service training to the advantage of their children? How far, that is to say, was there in nineteenth-century Buganda a kind of incipient gentry—a body of powerful descent-groups capable of perpetuating themselves in high positions through control of recruitment, in spite of the ideological emphasis upon achievement? Although we cannot give a quantitative answer, there is a good deal of qualitative evidence of which we may take note.

It is often said that the pages were the sons of chiefs. Thus Nsimbi tells us: 'The pages in the palace were placed there by leading *bataka* and chiefs. They were called "children of the *bataka*".'[19] Certainly we get the impression from published clan chronicles and genealogies that nineteenth-century Baganda were not lacking in the dynastic spirit. Members who achieved high office are enumerated, and their deeds recounted, with evident pride. In part, one might argue, *just because of* the ideological commitment to the notion that servants of the Kabaka were freely chosen for their ability, there was great honour for the descent-group which produced many of them. Baganda descent-groups strove to place their sons in the corps of pages and their daughters in the royal harem, just as modern Westerners—members of societies in many ways even more deeply committed to 'equality of opportunity' than nineteenth-century Baganda—help their children to be 'more equal than others' by buying for them 'good education' and encouraging 'good marriages'.[20] There is, in short, not a contradiction, but rather a perfectly understandable relationship between the emphasis upon achievement and the dynastic impulse.

One of the most successful chiefly 'dynasties' of which we have record is that descended from Senteza *Kajubi*, a major lineage head in the Grasshopper clan, who lived in the reign of Jjunju, the twenty-sixth Kabaka. Our informant is Sir Apolo Kagwa, great-great-grandson of Senteza, who set the fashion in clan chronicles, as he did in so many spheres of twentieth-century Ganda life, with his *Book of the Grasshopper Clan*.[21] One of Senteza's sons, whose name was Bunya, attached himself to Prince (later Kabaka) Semakookiro, and when the latter 'ate the kingship', Bunya was made *mumyuka* (second in command) to the county chief of Busujju. Later he was promoted to *Kangawo*—county chief of Bulemeezi. Although his descendants prospered, Bunya himself suffered a fate characteristic of traditional Buganda politics. A woman of his line was taken to wife by the Kabaka and bore the latter a prince, Kamanya, who, when he reached manhood, became overtly impatient to succeed his father. Bunya, as Kamanya's classificatory mother's brother, who stood to profit from such an eventuality since the king's mother's people were always richly rewarded with offices, was suspected of conspiring with Kamanya and the Kabaka sought an excuse to be rid of him. The story is a long and intricate one, involving Bunya's stealing the wife of another chief and the latter's planting in Bunya's household a stool and leopard skin (royal regalia), obvious 'evidence' of his treasonable dealings with the ambitious Kamanya. On the pretext of discovering these incriminating items, the Kabaka seized Bunya and some twenty of his agnates and had them drowned in a swamp. His surviving sons fled and went into hiding with kinsmen.

With the accession of Kamanya, however, the fortunes of the line naturally revived (Bunya was clearly guilty of plotting with Kamanya, even though the evidence against him had to be fabricated and for a completely different reason—a good example of the complexity of Ganda politics). Sir Apolo writes triumphantly:

And this was what reawakened the Grasshopper clan: When Kamanya, their child, became Kabaka, he sought out his mother's

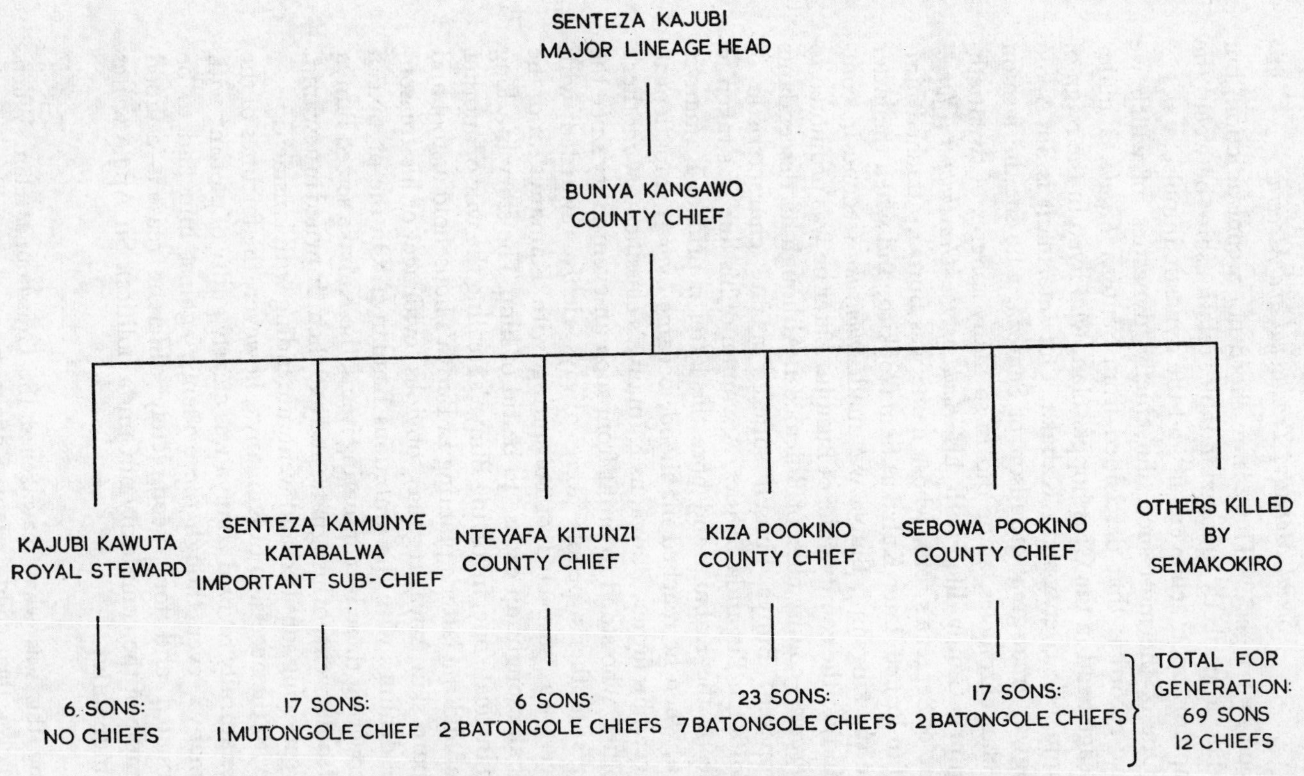

Fig. 13. Offices held by sons and grandsons of Bunya *Kangawo*.

people where they had been hiding—some with *Sekiboobo* Zizinga of the Rat clan, some with *Kago* Nkali of the Colobus Monkey clan, some with Kasuku *Makamba* of the Civet Cat clan—and when they were collected he gave them chieftainships. We shall read in this book about each one they were given.[22]

The political careers of five of Bunya's surviving sons and of his sixty-nine recorded agnatic grandsons are summarized in Fig. 13. Three of the sons became county chiefs, while one became the steward of the king's kitchen (*Kawuta*) and another became *Katabalwa*, chief of the largest subdivision of the great western county of Buddu. None of the grandsons reached such high rank, but twelve became *batongole* of varying degrees of importance. In the account of succeeding generations (not shown in Fig. 13, for lack of space), where Sir Apolo writes of events of which he has personal knowledge, one can see more clearly just how the process of dynasty-building worked. Members of the lineage who had already established themselves in office helped younger agnates gain entrance to the corps of pages. Thus Sir Apolo, when still a boy, went to live with his father's brother's son, Ibulaimu Sempa Basudde, who at that time was a *mutongole* chief, the *Musuna*. The latter secured for him a position in the palace mosque (Kabaka Mutesa was at that time pursuing an interest in Islam), which he shortly succeeded in leaving for a better post in the treasury. Later, when Sir Apolo had become firmly entrenched, he in turn was able to place in the corps of pages many younger agnatic cousins and nephews.

In considering the case of the descendants of Bunya *Kangawo*, one may tend to be impressed by how many became chiefs, but we may suggest that what is really remarkable here, in view of the strength of patrilineal descent and patrilineal descent-group solidarity in Ganda society, is how *few* were successful. Five-sixths of the grandsons descended into obscurity. The figures, of course, ought not to be taken too seriously, but if anything they surely exaggerate the number of chiefs among Bunya's descendants, since undistinguished men are more likely to have been forgotten. In part, of course, this is a necessary consequence of the fact that, where the *élite* are greatly outnumbered by their children—a nearly universal phenomenon, here exaggerated by the practice of polygyny—there *must* be a large volume of downward mobility simply because there are not enough *élite* positions to go round. But this case also suggests something else, namely, that while kinship ties might gain for a lad a position in the palace—a toehold on the bottom rung of the ladder—it could not so easily secure for him promotion to the higher levels. Except for the king's own mother's people, whom he tended to appoint simply because he considered them unusually disposed to be loyal, promotion depended upon the royal evaluation of a man's performance.

There are two further considerations of which we must take account in assessing traditional mobility. First, we must remember that our clan chronicles and memoirs give us a view of only the upper levels of the system of recruitment to appointive office through household service. In Sir Apolo's Grasshopper chronicle, only service in the palace page corps is regularly mentioned and the positions described as having been given by the Kabaka to clan members are limited to relatively high ones. The lowliest positions mentioned are those of first-level subordinates to royal *batongole* such, for example, as the office of *mumyuka* (second in command) to the *Mukuta*, to which a son of Kiza *Pookino* was appointed. We know, however, that *batongole* and *bakungu* chiefs appointed by the Kabaka, and probably some of the *bataka* as well, in turn appointed their own officers, also called *batongole*, whom they put in charge of their estates. Such must have been the 'chiefs of the villages' (*baami b'ebyalo*) who, from the standpoint of the *bakopi*, formed that part of the authority hierarchy with which they were in direct contact. Such must have been the '*batongole* in charge of five or more men' of whom Sir Apolo writes in his account of taxation.[23] We also know that each chief's household tended to contain a miniature corps of pages and that service therein could be the beginning of a career. Kagwa, for example, tells of a man named Kiyanzi who was '. . . brought up in the home of the *Sengoba*. . . . When he grew up he acquired fame by carrying Kabaka Kyabagu on his shoulders when he returned from Jinja. Because of this he was appointed to the office of *Sekayiba*.'[24] We must assume, then, that the processes which we have traced at the level of the palace and the royal appointees went on also at lower social levels—that, though the bright son of a *mukopi* had only a microscopic chance of becoming a royal page and receiving a royal chiefly appointment, he stood a very real chance of joining the household of a *mutongole* chief and becoming a low-level *mutongole* himself.

This is not to say that the peasant lad had no chance at all of entering the palace as a page, for there was another interesting feature of the traditional recruitment system which increased the likelihood of his rising spectacularly, but which at the same time obscured the event when it did occur. Nsimbi describes it thus:

All those who were placed to serve in the palace were sent by the clans. However, because they feared the fierceness of the Kabaka, some of the chiefs and *bataka* feared to give him their own children. Some therefore sent their servants, whom they represented as their children. Some served the Kabaka well and he gave them chieftain-ships. He thought of them as the actual children of those who sent them. . . . Those who received chieftainships were known as the children of the clans of their sponsors.[25]

By this sort of fiction, mobility from the peasant level might be reconciled with the continued political prominence of par-ticular lineages: a process analogous to the 'fictional agnation' which has been reported for many 'segmentary' societies.[26] There is, of course, no way of knowing how often this sort of thing occurred, but there is evidence that it was not uncommon. One of the favourite ways of undercutting one's political rival was to put about the story that he was not really the son of his 'father' but rather a slave boy captured in a raid on Bunyoro, or the child of a peasant. It was a charge which was so often true that it was readily believed.[27]

Thus, to summarize: in nineteenth-century Buganda those *élite* positions which were called 'hereditary' were in fact filled by selection from among quite wide ranges of eligible persons. At the same time, appointive offices, which were increasing in numbers and importance, were to some unmeasurable extent monopolized by a kind of incipient gentry, which held a measure of control over recruitment. At the lower levels, however, and even to some extent higher up, there was opportunity for entrance into the *élite* by children of ordinary peasants.

We must now consider how far the events of the turn-of-the-century period affected this pattern.

The Growth and Decline of the Gentry

During the two decades which preceded the signing of the Agreement with Britain in 1900, and in the provisions of that document itself, the gentry tendency in Ganda society was greatly strengthened. Throughout the nineteenth century there had existed, as we have seen, an *élite* class of persons with great power and wealth—an *élite* 'class' in Marx's and Weber's sense of a category of persons occupying an 'objectively' advantageous political and economic position.[28] However, the chiefs and *bataka* who made up this *élite* were not, in anything like the full sense, a gentry or upper 'status group', for they lacked both a developed sub-culture and a sense of common identity and interests. The *bataka* were divided among themselves by the very nature of their offices, which identified them with exclusive corporate descent groups cutting across differences in wealth and power; the *bakungu* and *batongole* chiefs were divided by their vertical personal ties of subordination and superordination and were prevented by the king's power of appointment from solidifying into a cohesive body. The development of an *élite* sub-culture was inhibited both by these structural features and by the absence of a written literary tradition which might have provided the medium for an elaboration of a gentry culture.[29] By the end of the nineteenth century, however, all these impediments had been greatly weakened and a real gentry with common interests, a common sub-culture and a sense of common destiny and identity was in the making. We must examine the factors which produced this new tendency and also the forces which have in the end prevented it from coming to fruition.

We may perhaps say that an *élite* sub-culture began to take shape when, in 1854, the Arab trader Ahmed bin Ibrahim acquired sufficient influence over Kabaka Suna to persuade the latter to submit to Koranic instruction.[30] During his reign and that of his successor, Mutesa, Islam spread among the chiefs and retainers at the capital and at the headquarters of the county chiefs. Numbers of mosques were built. With Islam went literacy in Kiswahili, the coastal *lingua franca* (written in Arabic script), and a much greater awareness of the outside world. Mutesa himself kept the fast of Ramadan for a number of years. Just why Islam, and later Christianity, were so readily accepted by the most powerful members of society is a question to which there is no simple answer. We may suppose, however, that an explanation would involve reference to the highly instrumental character of nineteenth-century Ganda culture, which disposed persons to accept any ideology associated, as Islam and Christianity were, with an obviously more efficient technology.[31] For the pages and young chiefs who were at the critical points in their careers, the new creeds were doubtless especially attractive as marks of sophistication. For the Kabaka, there was obvious political wisdom in learning enough about the visitors to enable him to judge their importance for purposes of alliance and defence. In addition, however, it is clear that there was among the *élite* of the time a sense of moral and intellectual ferment, as if the traditional religious culture had ceased to explain the world satisfactorily, and consequently for some the meaning of Islam or Christianity became very profound indeed, ultimately leading them to the extremity of martyrdom.[32] But whatever deeper cultural forces were involved, it is clear that by the later decades of the century the monotheistic religions and their associated languages and secular culture had become a new *élite* idiom which the ambitious were avid to acquire. Almost every great household seems to have contained Muslim or Christian 'readers'.[33]

The eighteen-eighties and -nineties involved members of this rising group of men in events of a sort which subsequently provided excellent materials for a myth of *élite* identity and leadership. After a period of cautious, and somewhat playful, interest in Islam and Christianity, first Mutesa and then his son Mwanga (Mutesa died in 1884) began to sense the power of the political forces which lay behind these new creeds and became increasingly hostile to them. For a time there was intermittent petty persecution—harassment of mission adherents and seizures of property—stimulated, perhaps, by attempts on the part of Anglicans, Roman Catholics, and Arabs to gain royal favour at each others' expense. In the late eighteen-eighties, Mwanga evidently decided to act more forcefully against what he had come to regard as a serious threat to his authority. In 1885 and 1886, a number of Baganda Christians and Muslims were mutilated and burned and the Anglican bishop-designate was murdered in Busoga, on Mwanga's orders, on his way up from the coast. Finally, in 1888, the king attempted to rid himself of all Christians and Muslims by marooning them on an island in Lake Victoria. The plot failed and he was driven from his throne—not the first king in the history of Buganda to be deposed, but certainly the first to be overthrown in the name of ideology.

The years following were occupied in continual struggles among the adherents of the three new religions. First the Muslims achieved ascendancy under the new Kabaka, Mwanga's brother, Kiwewa. The European missionaries fled to the southern shore of Lake Victoria and the Christian Baganda escaped into Ankole to the west. Kiwewa soon fell out with his Muslim supporters and was killed, being succeeded by another brother, Kalema, a circumcised Muslim. Mwanga, who had escaped by canoe, made peace with the Christian exiles and the missionaries and with their support fought his way back to power. Meanwhile, European governments had been interesting themselves in the East African interior. In 1890, acting under the terms of an Anglo-German agreement defining spheres of interest, Captain F. D. (later Lord) Lugard arrived at Mwanga's capital and obtained his signature to a treaty granting responsibility for the maintenance of law and order to the Imperial British East Africa Company. In 1894, a British Protectorate was declared and the Company handed over its authority and duties to the Government. The 'maintenance of law and order' could not, however, be assured by paper agreements and declarations and it was some time before the British administration possessed sufficient armed force to accomplish it. There were further clashes between Christians and Muslims and between Anglicans and Roman Catholics. The century ended with a final, futile attempt by Mwanga to regain his independence. Allying himself with dissident Muslims and with the *Mukama* (king) of Bunyoro, Kabarega, he waged a two-year losing battle against the British administration, which was allied with a majority of the Baganda led by Christian and Muslim chiefs. Mwanga was exiled and his infant son, Daudi Cwa, was proclaimed Kabaka under a chiefly regency. All important chieftainships were divided among the victors.

Thus the Agreement of 1900 was negotiated, on behalf of the Baganda, by a group of men who had been converted as young pages and chiefs, had survived the persecutions of the eighteen-eighties, had fought intermittently for nearly a decade, and had emerged the undisputed leaders of their society. As a group they were tough, stern and deeply pious in an old-fashioned, 'church militant' way which reminded one British officer of the Scottish Covenanters.[34] They had, of course, enjoyed the support of European missionaries and soldiers, without which they might well not have prevailed, and under whose control they ultimately found themselves, but they were no mere 'mission boys' or puppets. The churches had built up strong lay organizations, led by the men who were chiefs in 1900, which had maintained faith and discipline for extended periods during the persecutions and wars without European support, either moral or military.[35] Their exploits on behalf of 'God and progress' were soon elaborated into a national legend which took its place alongside the stories of the ancient kings and which remains to this day one of the most vivid elements in the Ganda historical consciousness.

The chiefs of 1900 thus enjoyed a double legitimacy. They had in many cases begun their careers, and risen successfully, in the service of independent Baganda kings, and therefore could fairly claim to embody the continuity of the traditional state; but they had also, with remarkable success, guided the kingdom through the dangers of a period which saw the culmination of European empire-building in East Africa. True, Buganda emerged into the twentieth century a dependent nation, a province of the Uganda Protectorate ruled, ultimately, by British colonial officials. But the kingdom remained intact, with a substantial measure of home rule—symbolized by Britain's official designation of the Kabaka as 'His Highness', a title reserved for substantial Muslim sultans and Indian princes—while at the same time acquiring what were recognized to be the benefits of association with the West. The Agreement which accomplished all this, while not in legal fact a treaty binding the British Government, has been persistently, even tenaciously, regarded as such by the Baganda and also— possibly to some extent in response to the moral pressure of this Ganda view of the matter—by the British as well.[36] Baganda have thus been able to believe that the British were voluntarily *invited* by Baganda traditional authorities to 'protect and teach' them. Thus, although it has been possible in later times of crisis for some to charge that the chiefs of 1900 '. . . betrayed their master, Mwanga, and sold the birthright of the Baganda for a mess of pudding [*sic*] . . .', still most Baganda, most of the time, have concluded that, everything considered, they drove a remarkably good bargain—a verdict with which the external observer, with a somewhat fuller appreciation of the international political forces at work at the time, can only agree.[37]

It is perhaps worth pausing briefly to document this basic ideological acceptance, within a traditional political framework, of Western religion and techniques and of the legitimacy of the chiefs who entered into the association with Britain, for it is a phenomenon somewhat uncommon in colonial polities. Throughout the many disputes which have subsequently arisen between the Protectorate government and Ganda leaders, the latter have nearly always taken their stand upon what they regarded as the *correct interpretation* of Britain's responsibility to 'educate and protect' Buganda rather than upon a rejection of these responsibilities as such. We have already called attention in Chapter 3 to Kabaka Daudi Cwa's pamphlet on 'education, civilization and foreignization', in which he argues for an acceptance of the useful elements in Western culture and a rejection of the corrupting ones. He writes in one passage:

. . . I have considered it my duty to warn very strongly all members of this younger generation of Baganda that while they should strive to acquire education and civilization, they should also take very great care that acquisition of Western education and civilization do not destroy their best native traditions and customs, which in my opinion are quite as good as those found among Western civilized countries, but only require developing and remodelling where necessary. . . .[38]

Daudi Cwa was, of course, committed by his office to association with Europeans and hence not entirely a free agent, but even the most anti-government pamphleteers have tended to plead within the same ideological framework. For example, the author of *Buganda Nyaffe*, a pamphlet banned as seditious shortly after World War II and regarded by the Government as perhaps the most bitterly anti-European piece of writing ever published in Uganda, charges the British with attempting to 'enslave' the Baganda and 'steal' their land. He nevertheless opens his argument with praise for the arrangements made in 1900:

The considerations which brought about the introduction of the *mailo* system among the Baganda were these: (1) When Europeans came here, Kabaka Mutesa I ruled Buganda and the surrounding countries, all of which bowed to him. (2) In all the wars which the Baganda fought against Kabaka Mwanga II, they were concerned to protect the great friendship which Mutesa I had established with the Queen of England and to maintain peace with the Europeans in the country. (3) Over a long period, much Ganda blood was spilled in wars against (those) . . . who tried to expel the Europeans.

For these reasons, the British government was pleased with the Baganda and in order to confirm their friendship secured their possession of their ancestral land through the *mailo* system. In these affairs, we were greatly helped by the missionaries, who had been invited by Kabaka Mutesa to preach the Gospel of the light of Truth.[39]

The chiefs of 1900 were, then, accepted as the legitimate bearers of a new cultural synthesis—a modernized and Christianized Ganda culture. During the early years of the twentieth century, their leadership was rewarded by new sources of wealth and new ways of spending it. In 1900–2, when *mailo* estates to the extent of 9,003 square miles were allotted among 3,945 chiefs of all ranks, there was of course little immediate change. Although there was a good deal of shifting about, most of those who received allotments held offices which in any case would have been supported by estates under the old regime, and of course the acquisition of paper titles did not affect the holder's ability to exploit his land at all. He could command *corvée* labour and exact tribute in foodstuffs and handicraft products, as chiefs had always done, but in the absence of changes in the basic economy he could do no more. The *mailo* allotment did, however, lay the foundation for a later development which greatly strengthened the tendency for the chiefs to become a cohesive, hereditary gentry. Since the estates were heritable private property, they formed an economic basis for status which was independent of office—a basis which became increasingly valuable as a cash economy developed, making possible the assessment of money rents. Nineteenth-century chiefs could consume few goods and services not available to the *bakopi*, though of course they consumed, and, more importantly, controlled, larger quantities. The men of 1900, however, as the spread of cotton cultivation increased their cash incomes, had available to them all the products of the industrial West. They could, furthermore, pass on the new sources of income to their children, no matter how their political careers fared.

Leadership in the formation of the new *élite* style of life came from the senior chiefs, who had been associated with Europeans during the troubles of the 'eighties and 'nineties. Sir Apolo Kagwa, who was *Katikkiro* from 1890 through the first quarter of the twentieth century, and whose earlier career we have already traced, has left a charming account of how at first he 'alone adopted new customs and work habits . . . they laughed at me at first . . . but later others followed . . .', beginning, on 31 January 1890, with his purchase of a watch.⁴⁰ He then went on to reform the slipshod procedure of the Great Lukiiko, purchased a horse (September 1892); built a two-storey brick house (July 1894); bought a kerosene lamp (January 1896); and a bicycle (1898) and began writing his first book. Perhaps most important of all because it concerned a more intimate and personal side of life, in January 1894, he adopted the custom of eating while seated at a table instead of upon mats spread on the floor, and of drinking tea instead of banana beer.

In the introduction of Western patterns of household behaviour, it is clear that the missionaries played a crucial role by entertaining Ganda chiefs in their homes. Some had of course lived with the Baganda in close intimacy during the religious wars. By 1908 Hattersley, Educational Secretary of the Anglican mission, could write: 'The Baganda are an extremely nice people to deal with, and the upper class of chiefs, when they come in for a meal, either dinner or for tea, are as courteous and gentlemanly as it is possible to be.'⁴¹ Calling upon the young Kabaka Daudi Cwa before going on furlough to England, the Hattersleys '. . . were served with afternoon tea in quite the approved fashion. . . '.⁴² Thus a late Victorian style of home furnishing and entertaining became part of the new *élite* sub-culture and spread among the chiefs as income from their *mailo* estates provided them with the financial means.

The missionaries also played a critical role in another respect. 'Knowing that in the ordinary course of events such boys (the sons of chiefs) were destined to become future leaders of the country, we cast about for some means of getting hold of them'.[43] The answer was found in an *elité* educational system, patterned after the English boarding schools:

After much thought and prayer, and in consultation with the chiefs, it was decided, with the approval of the Bishop and the Church Council, that the best way out of the difficulty was to build a set of boarding-houses, each with its own house-master. The chiefs were delighted with the idea and readily promised to build the boarding-houses and to pay for the support of their children.[44]

Day schools, which seem to have charged no fees, had existed since 1896, but in the new Mengo High School, opened in 1905, parents of pupils paid £6 13s. 4d. towards dormitory costs and £2 10s. 8d. in fees—substantial sums at a time when the cash economy had only began to develop. The school was not closed to the sons of *bakopi*, but it is clear from Hattersley's discussion that admission depended upon some kinsman paying the fees, for there were no funds for scholarships. At about the same time the Roman Catholic Mill Hill Fathers opened a boarding school at Namilyango.[45] More recently, St. Mary's College, Kisubi (Roman Catholic) and King's College, Budo (Anglican) have become the leading institutions.

There can be no doubt about the great influence of these schools in fixing the form of the new style of life, for they enjoyed full control over a large number of *élite* children during the formative years, and the masters gave as much attention to character training and manners as to academic subjects.[46] In addition, however, we must form some impression concerning the degree to which the limited access to education increased the tendency of the *élite* to become hereditary. For this purpose, we must try to compare the ability of descent-groups to monopolize access to the new education with their ability to control recruitment through the nineteenth-century institution which the schools replaced—the system of placing children as servants in the palace and in the households of great chiefs. As always we can only estimate, but three factors would seem to have made the post-1900 *élite* somewhat more compact and self-perpetuating than its predecessors had been.

First, at any rate during the early decades of the century, the recruitment 'funnel' would appear to have been somewhat narrower than it had been earlier. Places in boarding schools were few, as compared with the great numbers of the serving-boys in traditional great households, and sending a child to one of these schools required the expenditure of scarce resources, while it cost nothing material to get a boy accepted as a palace page. Thus a smaller group of upper *élite* was probably able to monopolize access to the channels of recruitment to posts of distinction. Second, a chief could send his own son to boarding school with greater confidence for, unlike the nineteenth-century kings and chiefs, the schoolmasters were unlikely to feed him to their pet crocodiles if he misbehaved. A traditional source of mobility—the sending of slaves or underlings' children in place of sons—was thus eliminated. Finally, the conversion of most of the *élite* to Christianity probably narrowed somewhat the span of the descent-group that typically acted as a unit in promoting the mobility of its members. Although all the chiefs did not at once (or later) become in actual practice monogamous, the pressure of church membership did act to single out a man's sons by his *mukyala ow'empeta* ('ring wife'—the one married in church) for educational support and testamentary preference. Furthermore, the practice of collateral succession essentially ceased in favour of a father-to-son pattern, with a strong tendency towards primogeniture.[47] Consequently, less 'achievement' was hidden within the interstices of 'ascription'; *nsikirano* came to mean something rather closer to 'hereditary', in the English sense of the word, than it had in the nineteenth century.

Thus the new *élite* was culturally more differentiated and more self-perpetuating. It was also more powerful politically, for it took shape during a period when the kingship—the political pivot of the traditional state—was at the lowest point of its recent history. Throughout the eighteen-nineties, the throne was occupied by Mwanga, a Kabaka who, after his restoration, could never be more than a creature of the senior Christian chiefs and the British officials and missionaries. There then followed the seventeen-year minority of Daudi Cwa, during which the chiefly oligarchy, under the leadership of the three ministers and regents—Stanislas Mugwanya, the Roman Catholic Chief Justice; and Apolo Kagwa and Zakaliya Kisingiri, the Anglican Prime Minister and Treasurer—continued to rule. Thus the new *élite* had more than a quarter-

century in which to consolidate their position without the intervention of the Kabaka in Buganda Government affairs. Most
important, the royal power was not during this period exercised
in appointments to office.[48]

The cohesiveness and influence of what had now become
something very like a gentry reached its peak around 1920–5
and thereafter probably began to recede. One immediate
reason for this was that Kabaka Daudi Cwa had meanwhile
come of age and had begun to assert his traditional authority.
This authority was, of course, circumscribed by the supervisory
powers of the British administration, but henceforth such
autonomy as remained to the Buganda Government was
divided between the Kabaka and the chiefs, and was further
diminished by the administration's ability to exploit the
division. More broadly, British officials began during this
period to intervene more and more in Buganda government
affairs in the interest of what they considered good government.[49] Apolo Kagwa and Stanislas Mugwanya, the pillars of
the chiefly oligarchy, who had led their fellows through thirty
years of war and transition, were both retired during the
'twenties following disputes with Protectorate officers.[50] Their
successors never exercised anything like their authority. Some
of the interventions of the administration, furthermore, served
to undermine the foundations of the whole *élite* class, for by this
time British colonial administrators had come to be more
interested in promoting the welfare of ordinary folk than in
maintaining the power and dignity of their rulers. The Busulu
and Envujo Law of 1928, for example, which was extracted
from an extremely reluctant Great Lukiiko (at that time made
up almost entirely of landowning chiefs), limited the rents and
dues payable by tenants and guaranteed their security of
tenure, thereby limiting both the incomes of *mailo* owners from
their estates and the uses to which the estates might be put.
Generally speaking, Uganda Government policy has moved
in a similar 'democratizing' direction ever since—broadening
educational opportunity through the construction of more
schools and the establishment of scholarship funds, stimulating
economic growth at the peasant level, making the Great
Lukiiko more representative, and extending, wherever possible,
civil service modes of recruitment and administration.

All this helped also to diffuse much more widely key elements of the gentry culture. Monotheistic religion, literacy and a somewhat Westernized style of household life—features which in 1900 made up the sub-culture of an *élite*—have today become part of the common culture of at least a majority of Baganda. The gentry, in short, came into existence in the wrong century. Before it could consolidate its position, it encountered the opposition of 'welfare state' conceptions of public policy of a sort which were threatening the dominance of gentry classes everywhere in the modern world.

Stratification and Mobility Today

In a sense everything we have done thus far has been preliminary to a consideration of social stratification and social mobility in contemporary Buganda. In order to make possible a better understanding of present-day patterns, we have sketched the evolution of social differentiation—the social division of labour—over the past century and we have attempted to see how stratification and mobility worked within the nineteenth-century institutional framework. Drawing upon our knowledge of this institutional legacy and of the forces which have influenced it since the establishment of British administration, let us now try to see how present-day Ganda society is stratified and how individual Baganda find their places in it.

It may be useful to begin with some rough diagrammatic summaries of the 'shape' of modern Ganda society, some attempts to represent graphically the quantitative relationships between the various 'levels' of society. The 'shape' of a society in this sense is important because it sets limits upon the amount of social mobility which is possible, quite apart from cultural factors. Fig. 14 is a very crude attempt to represent present-day occupational stratification among the some 360,000 adult males who paid taxes to the Buganda Government in 1956.[51] At the top place we have a small *élite* of 10,000, consisting of the 1,076 Protectorate government civil servants; the 211 Buganda government civil servants who made Shs. 500 or more per month; the 3,354 teachers, 289 Christian priests and Muslim sheikhs and 54 doctors and lawyers; the 85 company directors, some 1,200 traders who made more than £250 per year net profit, and the 2,500 (more or less) owners of more than ten acres of *mailo* land with five or more tenants.[52] Of course, by changing our criteria slightly we might easily have halved or doubled the number of this 'top *élite*', without, however, changing very much the overall shape of the pyramid. One might argue, for example, that many of the teachers and clergy-men—a large proportion of whom do not make the £250 per year which was the criterion for the inclusion of traders—should not have been listed in this top group. Teachers and clergymen, however, are not paid in precisely the same coin as traders and civil servants—either in Buganda or elsewhere in the world—and their location in the stratification hierarchy at a level above their spending power, while doubtless uncomfortable for them, probably represents roughly the social reality of their positions. The middle group of 50,000 includes some 20,000 'substantial' farmers and landowners mentioned in

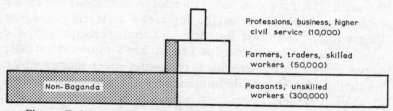

Fig. 14. Estimate of the occupational structure of present-day Buganda.

Chapter 8, as well as the 5,000-odd traders who made less than £250 per year.[53] It also includes some 25,000 skilled workers—an exceedingly crude estimate arrived at simply by taking one-fourth of the wage-labour force recorded for Buganda in the labour census.[54] The broad base consists simply of the 300,000 remaining adult males who paid taxes in 1956. Many of these are not Baganda; in this diagram and in those which follow we have, therefore, shown a non-Baganda population of 40 per cent., guessing—for there are no published data—at their distribution throughout the hierarchy.[55]

Fig. 14 is thus no more than an hypothesis erected upon a series of guesses, but perhaps it helps one to visualize what the past half-century has done to the social hierarchy in Buganda. Although the pyramid is still very broad, it is probably less broad than in the nineteenth century, for many new positions have been added—particularly in the middle ranges—which formerly did not exist, while relatively few, one would guess, have been lost. As a matter of fact, Fig. 14 undoubtedly underestimates the number of traditional middle-range positions which have carried over into modern times. The lower *batongole* chiefs, who must have made up the bulk of this level under the old regime, have counterparts today in their namesakes who serve as assistants to the parish chiefs (Southwold, 1964) The modern *batongole*, however, are hidden in Fig. 14 among the peasants and unskilled workers—or at any rate those who are not substantial traders or farmers, as a few are, are so hidden— for they are not paid by the Buganda Government and hence do not appear in our sources of data. It would not be quite accurate to say that with modern social differentiation they have in fact sunk to the simple peasant level, for locally, as Southwold demonstrates (1964) they may be figures of some moment. We may conclude, therefore, that today there are somewhat more places in the hierarchy at levels above the lowest than there were formerly and that, consequently, the able and ambitious peasant lad today has a somewhat greater opportunity to rise—provided, of course, other factors which we shall discuss shortly do not block his progress—than had his great-grandfather.

Figs. 15 and 16 represent other ways of illustrating the present-day social hierarchy based, respectively, upon the distribution of land, as measured by Land Tax returns, and distribution of income, as measured by Graduated Tax returns.[56] The point to which we want to draw attention is simply that, crude as these diagrams certainly are, they are remarkably similar in shape. Allowing for differences in the number of categories distinguished, they all show a broad, un-differentiated base making up some six-sevenths of the population; a middle group of approximately one-seventh, con-sisting of the relatively few men engaged in the more specialized forms of production and exchange; and a tiny *élite* of the wealthy, educated and powerful. Although the base of the pyramid may have narrowed in relation to the upper levels during the past fifty or sixty years, Buganda clearly still has a relatively broad-based social hierarchy of the sort which is typical of peasant societies everywhere.

Thus far we have assumed, as one must when one tries to represent society as a pyramid or a hierarchy, that the various categories of persons we have considered are all commensurable in terms of a single scale of prestige. In particular, we have assumed that 'neo-traditional' categories of persons (as we may

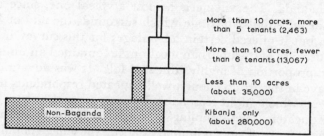

More than 10 acres, more than 5 tenants (2,463)

More than 10 acres, fewer than 6 tenants (13,067)

Less than 10 acres (about 35,000)

Non-Baganda

Kibanja only (about 280,000)

Fig. 15. Distribution of land ownership, 1956, estimated from Land Tax returns.

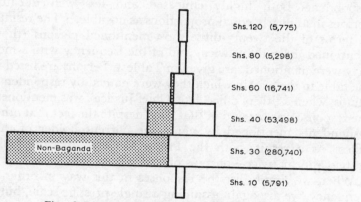

Shs. 120 (5,775)

Shs. 80 (5,298)

Shs. 60 (16,741)

Shs. 40 (53,498)

Non-Baganda

Shs. 30 (280,740)

Shs. 10 (5,791)

Fig. 16. Distribution of Graduated Tax payments, 1956.

call those traditional roles which have carried over, in somewhat modernized form, into contemporary society), such as county chiefs and the king's ministers, may for purposes of this sort of representation be equated with quite new kinds of persons, such as doctors, politicians and clergymen. What we suggest when we do this is that county chiefs and clergymen are judged by themselves and by others to 'belong together' in some sense, though we have thus far introduced no data to support this notion. At this point, therefore, we may examine some data which, though again very crude, may enable us to form some

judgment as to how far this assumption of a single, homogeneous prestige scale is justified.

In December 1954, and January 1955, fifty men in the village
of Mutundwe, Kyaddondo, were each asked whom they considered to be the six 'most important people' (*abasinga obukulu*)
in Buganda. The village is a most atypical one, since it lies
within the suburban fringe which surrounds the city of Kampala, but it offered certain advantages for this survey in that,
just because of its suburban location, it contained an unusually
large proportion of highly educated folk. It was advantageous
to have in the group enough well-educated respondents to give
answers which might reasonably be compared with those of the
less-educated. The 'sampling' was extremely rough-and-ready.
In the absence of any preliminary data on the village population,
the interviewers were simply asked to include among the
respondents both highly educated and less well-educated
persons in as nearly equal proportions as possible.[57] The results,
in terms of the twenty-three most-mentioned persons (those
mentioned more than twice) and of the frequency with which
they were mentioned, are given in Table 4. Persons are listed in
the table in the way in which they were named by respondents;
that is, when a title of office, like 'Chief Justice', was mentioned,
the response was entered in that way, despite the fact that other
respondents mentioned by name the current holder of that
office. As a result, both the Prime Minister and the Chief
Justice appear twice—once as offices and once as persons.

When we simply list the responses in this way in order of
frequency, we are again assuming a single prestige scale, but it
is interesting—and a partial confirmation of the validity of our
assumption—that, apart from the clustering of the Kabaka and
his ministers at the top, neo-traditional offices and the more
modern kinds of *élite* persons are interspersed. The men of
Mutundwe do not appear to place the newer *élite* roles either
higher or lower *en bloc* than the neo-traditional offices. To the
extent that this is so, there is some basis for saying that (for
example) a county chief and a party leader or editor are more
or less 'on the same level'. And this is consistent with much else
that we have said about modern Buganda. To a remarkable
degree, for reasons which we have discussed, the traditional and
the modern have merged to form a society which is unusually

single-minded about its values, considering that it is in the midst of rapid social change.[58] County chiefs and party leaders do indeed consider themselves, and are considered by others, to form in some sense a single *élite*.

The same phenomenon seems to exist on the level of the local

TABLE 4

PERSONS SELECTED BY MEN IN MUTUNDWE AS AMONG THE SIX 'MOST IMPORTANT BAGANDA'

Persons	*Times mentioned*
H.H. the Kabaka	27
Prime Minister	26
Chief Justice	25
Treasury Minister	22
I. Musazi (party leader)	12
Bishop Kiwanuka (Roman Catholic)	11
E. Kalibbala (U.N. employee)	7
S. Kulubya (Legislative Council and retired minister)	7
County Chief of Kyaddondo	5
E. M. K. Mulira (party leader and editor)	5
H. Mukasa (retired county chief)	5
M. Mugwanya (Chief Justice)	5
Queen	4
County Chief of Kyaggwe	4
Bishop Lutaya (Anglican)	4
M. Kawalya-Kagwa (Legislative Council and retired) Prime Minister)	4
P. Kavuma (Prime Minister)	4
J. Sengendo (Headmaster)	4
Queen Mother	3
Chief of the Capital	3
Y. Kyazze (retired Treasury Minister)	3
L. Basudde (wealthy farmer and Legislative Council)	3
A. Kironde (lawyer, party leader, Legislative Council)	3

community prestige scale. The same fifty men of Mutundwe were at the same time asked to name the six most important men of the parish. Their ten most frequent responses—those which occurred more than five times—are given in Table 5 in order of frequency.

Here the local representatives of the neo-traditional hierarchy, the parish chief and his deputy, fall midway down the list among doctors, politicians, and business men. On the level of the national *élite* the parish chief would not, of course, rank in such distinguished company, but in the local community he is a person of importance, just as, in the prestige hierarchy of

TABLE 5

PERSONS SELECTED BY MEN IN MUTUNDWE AS AMONG THE SIX 'MOST IMPORTANT IN THE PARISH'

Persons	Times mentioned
J. Sengendo (headmaster)	30
M. Walusimbi (wealthy business man)	28
M. Nsimbi (author and civil servant)	28
E. Muwazi (doctor and politician)	23
R. Muwanga (civil servant)	15
Y. Lwanga (deputy parish chief)	15
Y. Semakula (parish chief)	14
S. Ndugwa (doctor)	9
E. Kigozi (building contractor)	7
S. Zake (Anglican clergyman)	6

Gettysburg, Pennsylvania, the Mayor of the town would rank with Dwight D. Eisenhower as 'among the six most important citizens'.

What these data indicate thus far is that both the neo-traditional hierarchy and the more modern occupations contribute to the present-day *élite*. Respondents, when asked to name the 'most important people in the country', will name both kinds of persons. That is not to say, however, that all Baganda agree as to who are the most important of all. They do not. In particular, as we might expect, the more educated a person is, the more importance he is likely to give to members of the newer *élite* occupations and the less likely he is to rate highly the more traditional offices of state. This tendency is shown in Tables 6 and 7, the data for which come from the same sample of Mutundwe men. Although of course the figures cannot be taken too seriously, they are internally consistent and thus have, perhaps, a little more significance than the size and nature of the sample would suggest. The less education these men have had, the more likely they are to rate highly the neo-traditional offices, on either the national or local level. Their better-educated neighbours exhibit an opposite tendency to rate more highly the newer *élite* occupations. Thus we must qualify our earlier assertion that modern and neo-traditional

TABLE 6

RELATIONSHIP BETWEEN THE EDUCATIONAL LEVEL OF MUTUNDWE MEN AND THEIR TENDENCY TO RATE TRADITIONAL OFFICES HIGHLY IN NATIONAL IMPORTANCE

	Educational level			
	Primary 1–6	Secondary 1–3	Secondary 4–6	Higher
Times traditional offices were mentioned	85	27	26	6
Times others were mentioned	21	25	49	24
Total	106	52	75	30
Traditional offices as per cent of total	80	52	35	20

occupations have been assimilated to a single prestige scale. They have, indeed, to an important (and, for Africa, unusual) degree, but there would also appear to be an incipient tendency for Baganda to divide in terms of relative education on the question of who, among the *élite*, are at the very top.

Having achieved some understanding of the shape of present-day Ganda society and of the ways in which Baganda today allocate prestige, we come, finally, to the problem of social mobility—to the question of how *élite* positions are filled. We know that much mobility existed in the past and that, at least for a time, the changes brought about by British administration probably reduced it somewhat. It remains for us to try to determine how far the 'democratizing' tendencies of the past thirty or forty years—some of which have been the results of explicit public policy and some the less clearly intended con-

sequences of economic development and differentiation—h
made mobility easier.

In order to gain some indication of the characteristics and
social origins of the *élite*, a study was made during 1957–58 of
298 of its members.[59] Again the sampling was haphazard,

TABLE 7

RELATIONSHIP BETWEEN THE EDUCATIONAL LEVEL OF
MUTUNDWE MEN AND THEIR TENDENCY TO RATE THE
PARISH CHIEF AND HIS DEPUTY HIGHLY IN LOCAL
IMPORTANCE

	Educational level			
	Primary 1–6	Secondary 1–3	Secondary 4–6	Higher
Times chief and deputy were mentioned	15	6	5	3
Times others were mentioned	35	35	48	28
Total	50	41	53	31
Chief and deputy as per cent of total	30	15	9	10

though an attempt was made to include at least some members
of each major *élite* occupation or category. However, because
the sample is not properly 'stratified', that is to say, because it
does not include numbers of persons in each category in proportion to their numbers in the total population of the *élite*,
what it can tell us about the profile of the *élite* as a whole is
statistically less significant that what it says about some of the
more important constituent sub-groups.[60] Tables 8, 9, 10 and
11 give the data on education, fathers' occupations and
whether or not individuals' fathers or grandfathers received
estates in the 1900 *mailo* allotment. This last is perhaps our best
measure of social mobility, for in 1900 *élite* membership must
have correlated very highly indeed with *mailo* ownership.
Although there certainly were those in 1900 who felt themselves

to have been unjustly dealt with in the allotment, this seems most often to have involved persons' receiving less land than they considered their due rather than the total exclusion of persons who ought to have been included. Low's account of these events suggests that the ruling oligarchy among the chiefs went to some trouble to allocate an estate of some kind to

TABLE 8

EDUCATIONAL LEVELS REACHED BY MEMBERS OF THE *ÉLITE* SAMPLE

	Primary	Secondary	Makerere College	Overseas	Total
Party leaders	—	5	2	3	10
Editors	—	3	—	1	4
Elected Lukiiko members	23	30	3	3	59
Nominated Lukiiko members	2	5	—	—	7
Legislative Council members	—	2	1	5	8
County Chiefs	2	14	2	1	19
Buganda government civil servants	—	40	8	8	56
Uganda civil servants	—	2	4	9	15
Ministers	—	4	—	2	6
Anglican clergy	1	19	1	1	22
Roman Catholic clergy	—	22	—	7	29
Muslim sheikhs	14	—	—	1	15
Doctors	—	—	2	—	2
Lawyers	—	—	—	8	8
Large landowners	1	4	—	1	6
Traders	4	5	—	1	10
Miscellaneous (mostly retired civil servants)	6	9	4	3	22
Totals	53	164	27	54	298

every person of importance.[61] Most of the data given in Tables 8, 9, 10 and 11 were gathered by interviewing the persons concerned. In the matter of *mailo* allotments to individuals' fathers or grandfathers, however, it was in most cases possible to check interview results against the 1900 allotment lists.[62]

TABLE 9

SCHOOLS ATTENDED BY MEMBERS OF THE *ÉLITE* SAMPLE

	King's College, Budo	St. Mary's, Kisubi	Other	Total
Party leaders	3	6	1	10
Editors	1	1	2	4
Elected Lukiiko members	6	4	49	59
Nominated Lukiiko members	3	1	3	7
Legislative Council members	6	1	1	8
County Chiefs	10	5	4	19
Buganda government civil servants	22	15	19	56
Uganda civil servants	4	8	3	15
Ministers	5	—	1	6
Anglican clergy	8	—	14	22
Roman Catholic clergy	—	1	28	29
Muslim sheikhs	—	—	15	15
Doctors	1	1	—	2
Lawyers	5	1	2	8
Large landowners	4	—	2	6
Traders	2	1	7	10
Miscellaneous (mostly retired civil servants)	6	7	9	22
Totals	86	52	160	298

First, looking at the probably not very significant overall figures, given in the totals at the bottom of each table, we may note that between one-third and one-half of the group, depending upon the criterion selected, appear to be direct descendants of *élite* members. Roughly one-third (102) are descendants of *mailo* allottees of 1900 and somewhat more than one-half (166) are sons of chiefs, teachers or clergymen. Nearly one-half attended either King's College, Budo, or St. Mary's, Kisubi, the two boarding schools which, particu-

TABLE 10

OCCUPATIONS OF FATHERS OF MEMBERS OF THE *ÉLITE* SAMPLE

	Chief	Clergy	Teacher	Mukopi	Other	Total
Party leaders	4	—	1	5	—	10
Editors	1	—	3	—	—	4
Elected Lukiiko members	32	—	7	20	—	59
Nominated Lukiiko members	5	—	—	2	—	7
Legislative Council members	5	—	—	2	1	8
County Chiefs	15	—	2	1	1	19
Buganda government civil servants	36	2	2	16	—	56
Uganda civil servants	5	—	1	6	3	15
Ministers	3	1	—	2	—	6
Anglican clergy	1	1	2	18	—	22
Roman Catholic clergy	3	—	1	24	1	29
Muslim sheikhs	1	—	3	10	1	15
Doctors	1	—	—	1	—	2
Lawyers	3	1	1	1	2	8
Large landowners	6	—	—	—	—	6
Traders	2	—	—	8	—	10
Miscellaneous (mostly retired civil servants)	15	—	—	6	1	22
Totals	138	5	23	122	10	298

larly during the early decades of this century, specialized in educating the sons of the *élite*. Thus there is a very significant hereditary element in the present-day *élite*. But this we would expect to find, in almost any society; what is more surprising here is rather the large number of men who apparently have risen from relatively humble origins. Well over one-third (122)

TABLE II

LAND ALLOTTED IN 1900 TO FATHERS OR GRAND-FATHERS OF MEMBERS OF THE *ÉLITE* SAMPLE

	No land allotted	*Land allotted*	*Total*
Party leaders	3	7	10
Editors	3	1	4
Elected Lukiiko members	46	13	59
Nominated Lukiiko members	4	3	7
Legislative Council members	3	5	8
County Chiefs	7	12	19
Buganda government civil servants	34	22	56
Uganda civil servants	10	5	15
Ministers	3	3	6
Anglican clergy	21	1	22
Roman Catholic clergy	28	1	29
Muslim sheikhs	14	1	15
Doctors	2	—	2
Lawyers	4	4	8
Large landowners	—	6	6
Traders	8	2	10
Miscellaneous (mostly retired civil servants)	6	16	22
Totals	196	102	298

claim to be the sons of ordinary *bakopi* and two-thirds are the sons of men who were left out of the 1900 *mailo* allotment. Contemporary Buganda would appear to be a relatively 'open' society.

Undoubtedly associated with this tendency to openness is the fact that present-day *élite* Baganda are on the whole quite highly educated. Almost five-sixths of the entire group have been to secondary school—a rare distinction in a society in which education is still a very scarce commodity. Just how scarce it is, is indicated by Fig. 17, which shows the number of places available at the various levels of the educational system.[63] Although probably most children acquire some schooling—

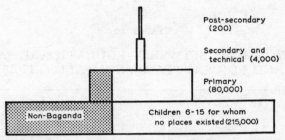

Fig. 17. Estimate of places in the school system available to residents of Buganda, 1956.

enough to make them literate, there were in 1956 only about one-third as many places in schools as there were children between the ages of six and sixteen. Above the primary level the 'funnel' narrowed even more sharply. Educational facilities are constantly expanding, but even universal full primary education is clearly still a long way off.

Now an educational system—particularly where schooling is both scarce and closely tied to *élite* status—is potentially either a door open to talent or a door barred to the humble and powerless. It may facilitate mobility by giving the bright poor boy a relatively objective opportunity to show what he can do, or it may exclude him because the *élite* are able to control entrance to the advantage of their own offspring. Although at the turn of the century, apparently, education tended to be essentially an *élite* monopoly, today this is clearly not so, as Table 12 indicates. The table shows the relationship, among members of our sample, between educational attainment and descent from *mailo* allottees of 1900. It is clear that, while *élite* descent confers an advantage in the competition for education, sons and grandsons of the chiefs of 1900 by no means enjoy a monopoly of it. Some four-fifths of those educated at the primary level were not descended from 1900 *mailo* allottees.

Even among those educated at Makerere College or overseas only slightly more than one-third are sons or grandsons of the turn-of-the-century *élite*.

How are we to account for this relatively free access to education in a society which not many decades earlier had seemed to exhibit marked oligarchic tendencies? Two factors are probably responsible. First, efforts on the part of the educational author-

TABLE 12

RELATIONSHIP BETWEEN EDUCATIONAL ATTAIN-MENT AND DESCENT FROM *MAILO* ALLOTTEES OF 1900

	Educational level		
	Primary	Secondary	Makerere College or overseas
Father of grandfather received *mailo* in 1900	10	55	31
Neither father nor grandfather received *mailo*	42	108	52
Totals	52	163	83
Descendants of *mailo* allottees as per cent of total	19	34	37

ities—both mission and government—to broaden educational opportunity by providing scholarship aid for the able poor have certainly had an effect. This factor will increase in importance as financial outlays for education by both central and local governments increase. But there is also a second factor of which the importance is often neglected or misunderstood. Unquestionably, many members of our sample who appear in the tables as sons of *bakopi*, or as descendants of men who were not important enough to receive land in 1900, were nevertheless aided in gaining an education by *élite* kinsmen other than their parents —by a mother's brother, for example, the traditional friend of a Muganda in time of need, or by a father's brother or even an affine. Such aid may range from provision of food and a place to sleep while attending a nearby day school, to payment of fees at an expensive boarding school. We do not know how often this sort of thing occurred among our *élite* sample, but we know it to be common on the basis of our general knowledge of Buganda life. In one sense, of course, it is 'nepotism'—the opposite of free competition for educational opportunity. But just as, in traditional Buganda, the relatively wide span of the effective descent-group and the lack of a birth-order rule left room for a good deal of 'universalistic' selection of heirs, so in modern Buganda the tendency to help poor young kinsmen to acquire schooling produces something like the same result. Wealthy Baganda do not—indeed cannot—help all their young kinsmen who might appeal for support; and today they tend, as we have said, to help their own sons, particularly those by the 'ring' wife, first. It is, however, in their interest to help the most able of their other young kinsmen, likely to achieve high positions in later life and thus likely to confer glory— and perhaps more concrete advantages—upon their kinsmen, including their benefactor. It is thus a mistake to believe with reference to either nineteenth-century or modern Buganda that any sort of mobilization of kinship ties militates against social mobility. Where educational resources are scarce and methods of selection at best haphazard, the rich uncle is probably best regarded as fulfilling some of the functions of a scholarship board.

So much for the general characteristics of our *élite* sample. It is a generally well-educated group and one relatively open to talent. But it is by no means homogeneous in these respects, for there are marked differences among sub-groups. For example, the chiefs, civil servants, ministers, landowners and leading politicians are much more closely related to the 1900 *élite* than are the other groups. The tendency of these categories of persons to form a relatively cohesive and hereditary 'inner *élite*' is illustrated in Fig. 18, which shows the genealogical links among a group of them.[64] These people are the descendants of the gentry of 1900, and to the extent to which a gentry may be said to exist in present-day Buganda they are among its leading members. However, some of the groups in our sample are much less gentry-like. The clergy, for example, as has often

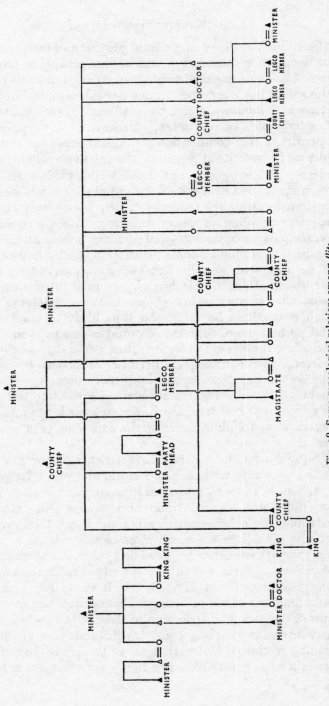

Fig. 18. Some genealogical relations among *élite*.

been the case in other times and places, are almost universally recruited from humble backgrounds. So also, though less universally, are the elected members of the Great Lukiiko.[65] Though exercising a good deal of authority, the Great Lukiiko has not, on the whole, attracted the wealthy and well born. Together these two groups make up the greater number of those persons in our sample whose fathers were *bakopi*, whose ancestors received no land in 1900 and who attended schools other than the two *élite* boarding schools. But these divisions are not absolute. There are chiefs, leading politicians and higher civil servants who also rose from peasant origins and there are clergy and Great Lukiiko members who are sons of the *élite*. In one degree or another, the major sub-groups share the characteristics of the *élite* as a whole: a belief in education, an appreciation of talent combined with a recognition of responsibility to kin and, above all, a faith in the ability of neo-traditional Ganda institutions to deal successfully with the exigencies of life in the modern world.

Problems for the Future

A social stratification system—what we usually call in everyday life a 'class system'—is a society's way of applying its values to the behaviour of its members so as to call forth their efforts on behalf of agreed ends. A social stratification system says: 'These are the activities to which it is worth devoting your life and these are the rewards which are held out to you in return for performing them well.' In these three chapters, we have tried to show how stratification in this sense has operated in Buganda over the past one hundred years of changing circumstances.

In its social stratification system, as in so much else, Buganda has been unusual among African societies. It was unusual in the past in the degree to which it was able to mobilize the energies of its members for national aggrandizement and in the general fluidity of its social structure. These two features were related, for individual achievement was geared to national expansion. The Kabaka claimed the right to subordinate to this all other values and in return he rewarded his faithful servants—and the nation as a whole—with wealth, power, and self-esteem. Buganda's experience with colonial administration has also been unusual, partly because of the nature of the traditional society and partly because of the circumstances of the establishment of the relationship with Great Britain. Because nineteenth-century Buganda was flexible, yet highly disciplined and bursting with energy, she attracted the British on terms which allowed her people to believe that they had contracted for a tutor, not a ruler. Although this was not an entirely accurate image of what had occurred, the force of the myth has been sufficient to make it in practice nearly true. Furthermore, because the traditional society was a relatively open one, a new set of men, committed to an at least partly new ideology, could take power at the turn of the century without violence to the integrity of the society. New men, new religion, the endless new ideas and techniques embodied in Western education—all these could be absorbed and yet the Baganda could believe that they were living in the same society, under leaders of a familiar kind. Indeed, the traditional kingdom gained added legitimacy from the sense that it had triumphed over new problems, had successfully put the new men and new techniques to work in the service of traditional goals.

From one point of view, all this has been a striking success, for few African societies have come through the encounter with the West with both a commitment to progress and a clear sense of continuity with the past. It is this peculiar 'progressive conservatism' which gives the Baganda their self-confidence—their lack of that fundamental self-doubt which makes so many East Africans alternate between self-abasement and aggressive self-assertion. This same tendency has allowed the Baganda to accommodate in a single stratification system both the servants of the neo-traditional state and the representatives of new *élite* occupations. Where so many African societies have been split by conflicting loyalties to new and old *élites*, relatively few Baganda have ever faced a choice between them.

This very success has, however, left a legacy of problems, of which the most important is the question of the terms upon which the Baganda will in the future live with their neighbours. Perhaps they will not be required to live with them in close political intimacy. Perhaps the future self-governing Uganda will be a federation loose enough to permit Buganda to remain an essentially self-contained polity. Or perhaps—though this

seems very unlikely—the other peoples of Uganda will ultimately accede to Buganda's demands—repeated from time to
time over the years—for complete independence. In all likelihood, however, the Baganda will be required to establish some
modus vivendi with the other peoples of Uganda, and even those
of neighbouring territories, for the attractions of wider unity—
once Africans have achieved political domination in the neighbouring territories—will be very great. In that case, Buganda's
neo-traditional social structure, with all its advantages in other
respects, will pose severe problems.

For modern Ganda society and its characteristic *élite* are in a
fundamental sense possessions of the Baganda alone. Even
though Buganda lies at the heart of a wider Uganda, and even
though she has supplied this wider unit with essential services,
institutions and personnel, the adjustments which have maintained her peculiar sense of continuity in the course of extensive
change have taken place in terms of Ganda culture and Ganda
national identity. What the modern county chief and the
London-trained lawyer have in common is their Ganda-ness.
This is what makes them members of a common *élite*. Without
this there would be no basis for common identity, for there is
no all-Uganda national culture.

There are many symptoms of this isolation of the Baganda
from their neighbours: the continued, and even growing,
vitality of Luganda as a literary language; the demands for
political autonomy; the lack of social contact between members
of the Baganda *élite* and their non-Baganda peers living in
Kampala. In the course of the past century the Baganda have
made many remarkable adjustments; the most difficult task of
all—the achievement of a common social structure and common cultural idiom in terms of which they can co-operate with
neighbouring peoples—still lies ahead of them.

Notes

Preface

[1] Galbraith, 1958; Harrington, 1962.

[2] "The Negro American, 1, 2" (transcript of the American Academy Conference on the Negro American, *Daedalus*, Fall 1965, Winter 1966. The benchmark for these and other recent discussions is of course Gunnar Myrdal's *The American Dilemma*, 1944.

[3] Mills, 1957; Rose, 1967.

[4] Jencks et al., 1972; Bell, 1972.

[5] Rawls, 1971.

Introduction

[1] Louis Dumont prefers "hierarchy," but that term seems to me to suffer from the same defects as "stratification." It implies a particular pattern of inequality: that of an organizational chain of command. See Dumont's *Homo Hierarchicus,* 1970, especially pp. 19–20 and Appendix A.

[2] Shils, 1961.

[3] This is essentially the view I have come to hold of Marion J. Levy, Jr.'s, brave and rigorous attempt to determine the "structural and functional requisites of any society." See his *Structure of Society,* 1952. If I cannot accept its upshot, I nevertheless admire Levy's effort to follow out to the end a view which many others simply accept without examination: namely the view that the world is divided among discrete and comparable societies.

[4] Weber's editor refers here to Morris Cohen's discussion in his *Reason and Nature.*

[5] "Intersubjective" seems to convey better what Weber means here. See Schutz, 1962, pp. 2–47.

[6] Weber, 1968, 1:15.

[7] Lewis, 1961, pp. 395–436, 473–80.

[8] Dumont, 1970.

[9] Gierke, 1900, pp. 131–32.

[10] Gierke, 1900, pp. 22–23

[11] Dumont, 1970, chapter 11.

[12] I am not, of course, questioning the value of this notion in linguistics; but the fact that cultural complexes of their constituent concepts are mediated by language does not mean that the operations used by linguists are necessarily appropriate to their analysis.

13 Dumont, 1970, pp. 72–78; 167–83. André Béteille says of a Tanjore village: "conflicting claims to higher social rank are often expressed by non-Brahmins in the idiom of the *varna* scheme." Béteille, 1965, p. 97.

14 Palmer, 1959–64. I ignore the prior English revolution, both for the sake of brevity and because it did not become, as the French and American revolutions did, part of an international movement.

15 Palmer, 1959–64, 1:27–52; Marriott, 1960.

16 Palmer, 1959–64, 1:29.

17 See Gallie's notion of the "essentially contested concept" (Gallie, 1964, pp. 157–91).

18 Crick, 1964, chapter 3.

19 Bendix, 1960, chapters 1 and 2; Marx, 1956, pp. 203–12.

20 If both Marx and Weber somewhat overstated the impersonality of the modern employer-employee relationship, the great attention given to "industrial relations" in contemporary societies, both capitalist and socialist, testifies to the *essential* correctness of their insights.

21 The reduction of Weber's intricate and subtle argument in *The Protestant Ethic and the Spirit of Capitalism* to the notion that "the protestant ethic *caused* capitalism" is perhaps the outstanding example of this tendency.

22 Geertz, 1962,

23 Weber was very skeptical of the assertions of those of his contemporaries who believed that race played a significant role in sociocultural differentiation. See *Economy and Society*, pp. 7–8.

24 Weber, 1958a, p. 182.

25 Weber, 1946.

26 Weber, 1946; Crick, 1964. This view of political culture as the professional subculture of politicians may be compared with that of Pye and Verba, 1965, who stress the political aspect of the general culture. While of course the two are related, preserving the distinction draws attention to the creative (or uncreative) role of political professionals vis-à-vis both their own workaday world and the political life of the general public, and to the interaction between these spheres.

27 Tocqueville, 1841, introduction and chapter 3.

28 Billington, 1968.

29 Turner, 1921, pp. 2–3.

30 Palmer here quotes from L. W. Larabee's *Conservatism in Early American History*, 1948, p. 48.

31 Palmer, 1959–64, 1:235.

32 Hartz, 1964, p. 1.

33 Hartz, 1964, pp. 25–26.

34 On the bourgeoisification of trade union leadership, see Mills, 1948.

35 Warner and Lunt, 1941, 1942; Warner and Srole, 1945; Warner and Low, 1947; Warner, 1959.

[36] Warner and Lunt, 1941, p. 81.

[37] Warner and Lunt, 1941, p. 35

[38] Warner and Lunt, 1941, p. 35.

[39] Warner, Meeker, and Eells, 1949.

[40] The principal critiques are: Lipset and Bendix, 1951, and Kornhauser, 1953. Kornhauser reviews most of the pertinent criticism of the 1940s and early 1950s. More recently, a professional historian has worked in Yankee City and has criticized both Warner and his critics. See Thernstrom, 1964.

[41] For Warner's later work on national elites see Warner and Abegglen, 1955, and Warner, 1963.

[42] Davis, Gardner, and Gardner, 1941; Dollard, 1937, Warner, 1936.

[43] The Socialist Party of America, formed in 1901 under the leadership of Eugene V. Debs, who had also led the great American Railway Union strike of 1894, received its largest popular vote—915,302—in 1920 and its largest percentage of the vote—6 percent—in 1912. Congressmen were elected from Wisconsin and New York in 1910, and in 1911 33 towns and cities had socialist mayors. "Foreign language federations" accounted for 32,894 out of 80,126 paid members in 1917 and included Finns, Letts, South Slavs, Italians, Scandinavians, Hungarians, Bohemians, Germans, Poles, Jews, Slovaks, Ukrainians, Lithuanians, and Russians, many of whom published their own newspapers. The party, like the smaller Socialist Labor Party of Daniel de Leon, made free use of class-conflict terminology. See Shannon, 1955.

[44] Baltzell, 1958.

[45] Hofstadter, 1955.

[46] In most societies, of course, the cultural "center" has been religious. In the United States, religious pluralism has made this progressively more difficult. At the same time, the legal institution, culminating in the Supreme Court as interpreter of the constitution, has become increasingly more potent as an arbiter of values.

[47] Dumont, 1970, Introduction and Appendix A.

Chapter 2

[1] Barber and Lobel, 1953.

[2] It is not suggested that women are *solely* in charge of status-symbolic expenditure, merely that they play perhaps the major role in this respect. See also Parsons, 1949, p. 225.

[3] Our thinking concerning the status-symbolic role of consumption patterns owes a great debt, of course, to Veblen's notion of "conspicuous consumption" and more recently to the work of W. L. Warner and his colleagues.

[4] Merton, 1949.

[5] Merton, 1949.

6 Schumpeter, 1947, pp. 73-74.

7 By "irrationality" is meant here irrationality *within the framework of a given value system.* Values themselves, of course, are neither "rational" nor "irrational" but "nonrational." The value of individual achievement is nonrational. Action directed toward achievement may be termed rational to the degree that, in terms of the information available to the actor, it is likely to result in achievement; it is irrational to the degree that this is not so.

8 Merton, 1949.

9 Balfour, 1953.

Chapter 3

1 Barnes, 1948; Gluckman, Mitchell, and Barnes, 1949; Mitchell, 1949.

2 Busia, 1951.

3 Hailey, 1950, 1953.

4 Evans-Pritchard, 1940, 1951, 1953.

5 Fortes, 1945, 1949.

6 Parsons, 1951.

7 Weber, 1947, p. 340.

8 See, for example, Delavignette, 1950.

Chapter 4

1 The general approach to stratification adopted here owes a great deal to Parsons, 1954, pp. 69-88.

2 Marshall, 1957, 1959, 1960.

3 Jones, 1961, p. 5.

4 Geertz, 1956a, passim.

5 Griaule, 1954; Colson, 1954.

6 Skinner, 1964.

7 Bascom, 1959.

8 Forde, 1951, pp. 10-16.

9 Nadel, 1942, pp. 257-97.

10 Bohannan, 1957, passim.

11 Sluiter, 1960; Middleton, J., 1953, pp. 52-56; Kenyatta, 1953, pp. 20-40.

12 Fallers, 1959.

13 Berreman, 1960; Marriott, 1960, pp. 14 ff.

14 Albert, 1960.

15 Redfield, 1956.

16 Fallers, 1961a (reprinted as chapter 5 of this volume).

17 Levy, 1952, pp. 95-98, 390-467.

18 The distinction is related to that made by Herskovits, 1955, pp. 155-56, following Dubois, between "prestige" and "subsistence" economies, although facilities are of course not limited to subsistence goods.

[19] Herskovits, 1926, passim.

[20] Maquet, 1961, pp. 18–19, 129–42.

[21] M. Gluckman, 1960, says that the crucial factor in the creation of the Zulu "empire" of Shaka was land shortage, but he does not explain how this effect was produced, and one does not find his argument convincing. On the contrary, the Zulu polity, as he himself so well describes it, seems an excellent example of a state built upon military and political intelligence and charisma. Land shortage, if such existed, did not prevent the empire from disintegrating when Shaka's leadership ceased to be effective.

[22] Zimbe, B M., 1938, pp. 19–20.

[23] Arnold, 1957.

[24] Forde, 1956.

[25] Elkan and Fallers, 1960, passim.

[26] Smythe and Smythe, 1960.

Chapter 5

[1] Kroeber, 1948, p. 284.

[2] Redfield, 1947; Foster, 1953.

[3] Firth, 1951, p. 87.

[4] Redfield, 1956, p. 78.

[5] Vinogradoff, 1892, pp. 1–39.

[6] Wolf, 1955.

[7] Weber, 1947, pp. 346–58.

[8] Fortes, 1953; Smith, 1956.

[9] Fallers, 1960.

[10] Busia, 1951; Schapera, 1955.

[11] Herskovits, 1938; Fallers, 1960.

[12] Redfield, 1956; Foster, 1953; and Marriott, 1955.

[13] Homans, 1941, pp. 368–70.

[14] Herskovits, 1938; Bascom, 1951; Lloyd, 1955.

Chapter 6

[1] Parsons, 1940, 1953; Weber, 1946. A concern with stratification runs as a minor theme through all of Weber's sociological writing.

[2] Marriott, 1960, pp. 16–17.

[3] Berreman, 1960; Homans, 1941.

[4] Kroeber, 1948, p. 284.

[5] Durkheim, 1947, p. 175.

[6] Fortes, 1953.

[7] Easton, 1959, p. 237. Sir Henry Maine expressed a similar idea: "Ancient jurisprudence . . . may be likened to international law filling . . . the interstices between the great groups which are the atoms of society." (Maine, 1931, p. 138).

8 Redfield, 1956, pp. 60–66.

9 The evolution from personal servant to public official is traced in great detail in Tout, 1920–33.

10 Machiavelli, 1941, p. 104.

11 Gierke, 1958, pp. 22–30.

12 Homans, 1941, p. 237.

13 Painter, 1957.

14 Grunebaum, 1946, pp. 211–12.

15 Gibb and Bowen, 1950, 1:39, 199.

16 Gibb and Bowen, 1950. In the attempted reforms of the last century of Ottoman rule, there was a reassertion of universalistic centralism. By this time, however, the regime was too fundamentally undermined by western influence to succeed in this attempt. See Lewis 1969, pp. 40–205.

17 Marriott, 1960, p. 1.

18 Brown, 1953.

19 See especially Bailey, 1957, 1960; and Weber, 1958*b*.

20 Weber, 1958*b*, p. 337.

21 Marriott, 1960.

22 Greenberg, 1949.

23 Fallers, 1961*a* (reprinted as chapter 5 of this volume).

24 Berle and Means, 1930.

25 Parsons, 1960, pp. 98–131.

26 Parsons, 1938.

27 Davis and Golden, 1954, table 2.

28 Morris, 1960.

29 Morris, 1960.

30 Elkan and Fallers, 1960.

31 Geertz, 1956*b*.

32 Ashby, 1958.

33 Parsons, 1960, pp. 98–131; Galbraith, 1958, pp. 334–56.

34 Bendix, 1951.

35 Becker, 1932, p. 62.

36 See for example, Kant's "Idea for a Universal History with Cosmopolitan Intent," in Kant, 1949.

37 Singer, 1956; Singer, 1961.

38 Singer, 1956, p. 86.

39 Singer, 1956, pp. 86–88.

40 Gibb, 1945, pp. 47–48. See also Ahmed, 1960.

41 Lewis, 1961.

42 Fallers, 1961*b*.

43 Smythe and Smythe, 1960.

44 Warner and Lunt, 1941; Hoggart, 1957; Mitford, 1956.

45 Hoggart, 1957, especially chapter 6.

46 Warner and Lunt, 1941, pp. 92–109.

[47] McIlwain, 1940.

[48] Lindsay, 1957.

[49] Thomas, 1959; Shils, 1956, pp. 47–57.

[50] Tocqueville, 1955.

[51] Burke, 1955.

[52] Talmon, 1960.

[53] Tocqueville 1955.

[54] Gibb and Bowen, 1950, 1:39–199, 2:70–164.

[55] Landes, 1958, pp. 69–101.

[56] Lewis, 1961, pp. 317–55.

[57] Lewis, 1961, pp. 184–87; Berger, 1957.

[58] Harrison, 1960, pp. 96–136.

[59] Rudolph and Rudolph, 1960.

[60] Harrison, 1960.

[61] Lincoln, 1958, p. 402.

[62] An interesting discussion of this notion may be found in Legum, 1960.

Chapter 7

[1] Fortes, 1953, pp. 27–28.

[2] Rattray, 1929, pp. 404–5.

[3] Gluckman, 1960, pp. 166–8.

[4] Warner and Lunt, 1941; Warner, Meeker and Eels, 1949.

[5] Glass, 1954; Lipset and Bendix, 1959; National Opinion Research Center, 1947.

[6] In its general approach the view of stratification presented here owes most to Parsons, 1953, though no attempt is made to follow precisely his theoretical elaboration of it.

[7] Weber, 1946, pp. 186–8.

[8] The despotic role of the Kabaka and its relation to other institutions is discussed in Fallers, 1959.

[9] Princes not chosen to succeed had to formally renounce their rights at the coronation. (See: Richards, 1961. It is clear, however, that this did not always prevent them from plotting against their brother.)

[10] The data for Fig. 2 are taken from Cox, 1950. The boundaries shown are of course very approximate.

[11] Kagwa, 1952, p. 151.

[12] Kasirye, 1955, pp. 43, 59–61.

[13] Kagwa, 1952, p. 163.

[14] Stanley, 1878, Vol. I, pp. 305–6.

[15] Ibid., p. 314.

[16] Tout, 1920–33, makes constant reference to the itinerant

nature of the court, especially in Vols. I and II.

[17] Kagwa, 1953, and Zimbe, 1939, describe many instances. The account of the war against the Bavuma in Stanley, 1878, Vol. I, pp. 301–43, gives the best description of a temporary camp.

[18] Kasirye, 1955, pp. 59–61.

[19] This sketch may be found at the back of Roscoe, 1911.

[20] Speke, 1864, p. 276.

[21] Stanley, 1878, p. 393.

[22] Ibid., p. 394.

[23] Kakoma, Ntate and Serukwaya, 1959.

[24] Mukwaya, 1953, p. 14.

[25] Mair, 1934, p. 217.

[26] Gorju, 1920.

[27] Nsimbi, 1956, p. 222; Kagwa, 1953, p. 6.

[28] Nsimbi, 1956, p. 194; Kagwa, 1953, p. 12.

[29] Cox, 1950, pp. 153–9; Southwold, 1961.

[30] Nsimbi, 1956, p. 215; Musoke and Kikuba (n.d.).

[31] Kakoma, *et al.*, 1959.

[32] Ibid.

[33] M. Southwold, in a private communication, points out that '*mukungu*' is used in three somewhat different senses to mean: 1. all appointed chiefs, including *batongole* (see below), as distinguished from hereditary *bataka*: 2. territorial administrators, as contrasted with *batongale*; 3. junior territorial administrators, as distinguished from *ssaza* chiefs. This is a further instance of the tendency to define by opposition which we noted earlier in this chapter in our discussion of the meaning of '*mukopi*'. We shall, however, continue to use '*mukungu*' in what seems to be its commonest meaning, i.e. territorial administrators as distinguished from both *batongole* and *bataka*.

[34] Cox, 1950; Southwold, 1961.

[35] Nsimbi, 1956, p. 68.

[36] This was true in Busiro (see below).

[37] During the investigation described in Appendix B, our informants frequently had difficulty distinguishing between the two types. Everyone agreed that there was a difference, but there was frequently disagreement about what, precisely, the difference was and about which persons fell into which category.

[38] Nsimbi, 1956, pp. 68–9.

[39] Kagwa, 1953, p. 66.

[40] Nsimbi, 1956, pp. 69–70.

[41] Kagwa (1952, p. 147) says that Kabaka Mutesa I arrested his *Mugema*, Nakabale, and dismissed him from office, but later thought better of it and restored him. The events of Mutesa's reign suggest that other chiefs or *bataka* would hardly have been treated with such caution.

42 Southall, 1954, pp. 241–63.

43 Busia, 1951.

44 Max Gluckman, 1940, pp. 25–55; 1960, pp. 157–67. Perhaps the best analysis of a Southern Bantu segmentary state is that of Barnes, 1954.

45 Herskovits, 1938.

46 Southall, 1954, op. cit.; Fortes, 1953.

47 Weber, 1947, pp. 341–58.

48 Extended accounts of Ganda religion are given by Roscoe, 1911, pp. 271–345; Mair 1934, pp. 223–65; Kagwa, 1952, pp. 209–37; and Taylor, 1958, pp. 190–217.

49 Ibid., pp. 209–11.

50 Ibid., pp. 211–15.

51 Kagwa, 1952, p. 222; Ashe, 1894, pp. 96–7.

52 Mair, 1934, pp. 230–1.

5° Mackay gives an account of the visit to Mutesa's court in 1879 of the priests and medium of Mukasa, the god of Lake Victoria. They had been summoned to be consulted about Mutesa's illness. (Mackay, 1896, pp. 145–77.)

54 Kagwa, 1952, pp. 210–31.

55 Speke, 1864, pp. 425–6.

56 Stanley, 1878, Vol. I, p. 401, estimates 850,000 souls for Buganda, including Buddu; 2,775,000 for 'Mutesa's empire', but he exaggerates the latter by including 500,000 Banyoro, who can hardly be considered a tributary people. See also Kuczynski, 1949, for a discussion of population estimates.

57 A. I. Richards, in a forthcoming book, examines the general problem of political communication in non-literate states.

58 Kagwa's drawing shows only the town-houses of the chiefs. Quite possibly there was an added penumbra of huts of retainers, servants and other lesser folk.

59 Roscoe, 1911, p. 200.

60 Kagwa's plan of the palace in Roscoe (ibid.), shows, for example, the compounds of the *Sseruti* (king's brewer) and *Kauta* (palace cook) just outside the enclosure.

61 Kagwa, 1952, pp. 100–3, outlines this organization.

62 Kagwa, 1952, p. 238.

63 Ibid., pp. 238–46; Roscoe, 1911, pp. 258–67.

64 Kagwa, 1953, pp. 115–18, and Stanley, 1878, Vol. I, pp. 388–93, discuss such cases.

65 Kagwa in Roscoe, 1911.

66 Kagwa, 1952, pp. 163–7.

67 Kagwa does not actually say, but the likeliest hypothesis is that the levies he describes were annual. In traditional Buganda there were two 'years' for every one in the Western calendar, a method of reckoning facilitated by the fact that there are normally two wet and

two dry seasons each year. If the levies took place each Ganda year, the tax burden would therefore be twice as heavy. Kagwa frequently specifies whether he is speaking of Ganda or European 'years', but in this case he fails to do so.

[68] Ibid., p. 167.

[69] Ibid., pp. 152–62.

[70] Stanley, 1878, Vol. I, pp. 304–42.

[71] Kagwa, 1952, p. 153.

[72] In the Buvuma campaign witnessed by Stanley, chiefs personally led their men into battle. In the wars which Kabaka Suna waged against the Basoga and the Banyankole in the eighteen-fifties, according to both Kagwa and Stanley, many chiefs were killed or wounded in personal combat. See: Stanley, 1878, Vol. I, pp. 304–42; Kagwa, 1953, pp. 99–100.

[73] In present-day Uganda the male population over sixteen years of age constitutes 28 per cent. of the total. Applying this ratio to Stanley's estimate of 850,000 as the total population of the Buganda of his day, we arrive at some 240,000 adult males. He estimated the number of Baganda warriors in the Buvuma campaign at 125,000 (Stanley, 1878, Vol. I, p. 306).

[74] Stanley speaks of a small royal bodyguard of musketeers, but does not mention the *Mujasi* (Stanley, ibid., p. 307). Kagwa, 1952, p. 155, says that Kabaka Mutesa created the *Mujasi* as commander of the '*baserikale*' (professional soldiers, from Kiswahili—Arabic *askari*). In speaking of other members of the army he used the native Luganda term *batabazi*, 'warriors'.

[75] Kagwa, 1952, p. 159.

[76] Ibid., p. 162.

Chapter 8

[1] Everett Hughes has developed this theme. See Hughes, 1958, especially Chapter 3.

[2] Warner and Lunt, 1941; Glass, 1954; Lipset and Bendix, 1959. These are, of course, only a few of the most prominent studies.

[3] Parsons, 1954.

[4] Abegglen, 1958.

[5] Hughes, 1958, p. 42.

[6] Apparently some of the Islamic societies of the Near East, which of course exhibited much greater occupational differentiation, were, however, like Buganda in being non-modern societies with relatively high rates of social mobility and despotic polities. G. Von Gruenebaum, writing of the empire of the Abbâsid Caliphs, says: 'The will of the prince could transfer a subject from one class to another with the greatest ease and speed. Thus society remained flexible and

fluid. . . .' (Gruenebaum, 1953, p. 212). Another interesting example is provided by the slave-administered polity of the Ottomans, described by Gibb and Bowen, 1950, Vol. I, Part I, especially Chapter III.

[7] Kagwa, 1952, Chapter 12.

[8] Laws of Uganda Protectorate, 1935, Vol. VI, p. 1374.

[9] Low and Pratt, 1960.

[10] Figures for staff and expenditure are taken from the Estimates 1956–57. Access to unpublished population returns for 1956 was kindly provided by the Kabaka's Government.

[11] As we noted earlier, the term *mutongole* is also used today for the local headmen who act as subordinates to parish chiefs. (See also Southwold, 1964.)

[12] The words are the beginning of the proverb *akiika embuga amanya ensonga*: 'he who comes to the capital knows what's going on'.

[13] Richards has described these chiefs, their duties, and their mode of recruitment. See: Richards, 1959.

[14] The traditional society is not the only source of the diffuseness of the modern chief's role; the latter is in some ways patterned after that of the British administrative officer, who has a somewhat similarly diffuse responsibility for his district. (See: Fallers, 1956, Chapter 8.)

[15] The reference here is to the type of role, found in many spheres of modern life, described by Bernard, 1938.

[16] Accounts of the growth of Islam in Buganda are given in Gee, 1958, and Anderson, 1954, pp. 148–61; of Protestantism in Taylor, 1958; and of Roman Catholicism in Thoonen, 1942, and Zikusooka, 1955. Figures for Baganda Anglican clergy were kindly provided by the office of the Bishop of Uganda; those for Roman Catholic clergy by the Archdiocese of Rubaga and those for Muslim leaders by *Sheika* Ahamada Nsambu, *Hajji* Musa Kasule, *Omw.* Alamanzane Gava and *Sheika* Abudala Hainani Mivule.

[17] Gee, 1958, p. 148.

[18] Warren, 1954.

[19] The classical study of syncretistic and separatist churches in Africa is of course that of Sundkler, 1948.

[20] See Welbourn, 1961, pp. 77–110.

[21] Kaizi, 1948, pp. 242–6.

[22] Annual Report for the Kingdom of Buganda for the year ended 31st December, 1955, pp. 199–200.

[23] There were also 105 private schools with 8,343 pupils which were unaided by the governments because they refused government inspection or were not considered up to standard. Many of the pupils of these schools are non-Baganda.

[24] Data for the Protectorate Government are those given in Table

2 for 1954, although the numbers will not have changed greatly in two years. In Table 2 physicians are listed as 'Medical Officers' and 'Assistant Medical Officers'.

[25] In a study of the ambitions of secondary pupils in a school in neighbouring Busoga, carried out by the writer in 1951, medicine was the clear favourite. Busia reports a similar result from Jahoda's work in Ghana. (See: Busia, 1956.)

[26] See: Elkan and Fallers, 1960.

[27] Report for the year 1956.

[28] Richards, 1954, especially Chapters V and VII.

[29] Mukwaya, 1953, p. 30.

[30] Figures kindly supplied by the Kabaka's Government.

[31] Annual Report for the Kingdom of Buganda for the year ended 31st December, 1955, p. 195.

[32] See: Fallers, 1955.

[33] Advancement of Africans in Trade, 1955, p. 15.

[34] Some firms have, for example, made use of the facilities of the government's Local Government Training School at Nsamizi to train young African executives.

[35] See: Morris, 1956.

[36] Uganda. Advancement of Africans in Trade, 1955, p. 15.

[37] Ibid.

[38] Ibid., p. 16.

[39] *Saben's Commercial Directory and Handbook of Uganda*, 1955–6.

[40] Uganda. Annual Report of the Department of Co-operative Development for the year ended 31st December, 1954, p. 3.

[41] Uganda. Enumeration of Employees, June, 1956, pp. 11–12.

[42] Elkan, 1956, 1961; Fortt, 1954.

[43] Southall and Gutkind, 1956.

[44] Elkan and Fallers, 1960.

[45] Richards, 1954, Chapter VII.

[46] Southall and Gutkind, 1956.

[47] See: Hofstadter, 1955, especially Chapters V and VI.

[48] On 13 March 1922, for example, Kabaka Daudi Cwa was addressed by a group of clan and lineage heads *defending* the 1900 allotment on the ground that they and other *bataka* had received proper allotments (memorandum in the files of the Resident's Office, Kampala). Included were the *Ggabunga*, head of the large Lungfish clan and traditional admiral, who received eleven square miles; and the *Namwaama*, head of the Yam clan, whose allotment was the same.

[49] See: Chapter 7.

[50] Mutesa I had *Mugema* Nakabale arrested and imprisoned in stocks, but later felt it necessary to release and reinstate him (Kagwa,

1952, p. 148). *Mugema* Joswa Kate, as we have seen, was a leader of the *bataka* protest in Daudi Cwa's time. Mutesa II has had greater success, at any rate thus far; in 1955, upon his return from exile, he was able to secure the dismissal of *Mugema* Joswa Kamulegeya, whom he regarded as disloyal.

⁵¹ We are indebted for information on the leadership of the Uganda National Congress to Mr. Neil Ascherson, who carried out a study of the Congress for the East African Institute of Social Research.

⁵² See: Hailey, 1957, pp. 1235–41.

⁵³ Uganda, 1956, p. 126–7. An account of Luganda literature is given in M. C. Fallers, 1960.

Chapter 9

¹ Weber, 1946, 1947.

² Painter, 1957, p. 59.

³ Ibid., pp. 98–99.

⁴ Homans, 1942, p. 237.

⁵ Gierke, 1958, pp. 22–30; Tawney, 1947, pp. 20–39.

⁶ Homans, 1942, pp. 251–2.

⁷ Kagwa, 1952, p. 165. M. Southwold, in a private communication, argues that this greatly underestimates the number of men under each *mutongole* in the nineteenth century and gives as his own estimate about twenty men for each *mutongole*. In each case, of course, to get the total number of persons one should add in women and children, but if these are given the status of their husbands and fathers the proportions of persons at the different levels are unaffected. Southwold's estimate may be correct, but I would argue that there were other persons at the village level besides *batongole* who should be counted as being above the *mukopi* level—stewards (*basigire*) of the *batongole*, for example, and magico-religious practitioners. In any case, the point of the exercise is not to arrive at a numerically accurate representation of the status levels—we know this to be impossible—but rather to represent hypothetically the effect of modern social differentiation upon the status pyramid.

⁸ Lipset and Bendix, 1959, Chapter II; Barber, 1957, Chapter 4.

⁹ Wrigley, 1959B, pp. 33–48.

¹⁰ Kakoma, *et al.*, 1959, pp. 48–77.

¹¹ Ibid., p. 49.

¹² A ceremony in which a young man of the Lungfish clan is sacrificed to celebrate the king's coming of age and to prolong his life. See: Roscoe, 1911, pp. 210–12.

¹³ Kakoma *et al.*, 1959, p. 48.

¹⁴ Ibid., p. 73.

[15] Kagwa, 1949, pp. 73–78.

[16] Nsimbi, 1956, p. 64.

[17] Lwanga, 1954, p. 3.

[18] Zimbe, 1939, p. 3.

[19] Nsimbi, 1956, p. 28.

[20] This perhaps explains the paradox that in contemporary United States the idealization of the 'self-made man' is often accompanied by an absorbing interest in genealogy.

[21] Kagwa (n.d.).

[22] Ibid., p. 9.

[23] Kagwa, 1952, p. 165.

[24] Kagwa, 1953, p. 114.

[25] Nsimbi, 1956, p. 173.

[26] See: Fortes, 1953, pp. 27–28.

[27] Kagwa 1953, pp. 115–17, tells how such rumours were spread concerning *Katikkiro* Kaira in the reign of Kabaka Mutesa. Today one often hears such stories about Sir Apolo Kagwa himself from his detractors.

[28] Weber, 1947, pp. 180–6; Bottomore and Rubel, 1956, pp. 178–202.

[29] It will be obvious that our thinking about the differentiation of a gentry sub-culture owes a very great deal to Robert Redfield's discussion. See: Redfield, 1956.

[30] Taylor, 1958, pp. 25–26.

[31] See above pp. 100–4; 135–6.

[32] Taylor (1958, Chapter 2) has a sensitive discussion of this difficult problem.

[33] Ibid., Chapter 1. Also: Kagwa, 1953, Chapters XVI–XVII; Zimbe, 1939, Chapters 10–19; Lwanga, 1954, pp. 4–23.

[34] J. R. L. Macdonald, quoted by Taylor, 1958, p. 58.

[35] Ibid., Chapter 2.

[36] The legal status of the Agreement and its practical, political and mythological functions are discussed in Low and Pratt, 1960, Chapter 6 and Appendix I.

[37] The international political environment is described in Thomas and Scott, 1935, pp. 2–43. The phrase about betrayal is from a document circulated at the time of the deportation of Kabaka Mutesa II.

[38] Kaizi, 1948, p. 246.

[39] Mukubira (n.d.), p. 1. Surely one of the most important reasons why the arrangements of 1900 have found general acceptance is that many of the Europeans involved—particularly among the missionaries—treated the Baganda with genuine respect and humanity, thereby establishing in the minds of Baganda the notion

that, whatever political difficulties might arise, they had real European friends and allies to whom they might appeal for support. For example, C. W. Hattersley's book *The Baganda at Home* (Hattersley, 1908) is pervaded by the attitude that, given the opportunity to progress, Baganda are fully the equals of Europeans. He writes (p. 157):

'Surely the feeling has taken root in the hearts of most European races that an African is a child of Ham, born to be a slave of those of other nations. Many have been moved to pity him, but pity in most cases breeds contempt. We need more real Christianity to make us realize that the African is of one flesh and of one blood with us all, and has every right to be taught and trained as we have been, and so allowed to take his position in the world. It is only because of the feeling engendered in his heart by the treatment he receives at the hand of the white man—from the conviction that he will never be allowed a fair chance, that he is always one of the despised of mankind—that Ethiopianism has attained such a measure of success. . . .'

Bishop Tucker's *Eighteen Years in Uganda and East Africa* (Tucker, 1911) conveys the same outlook. These were strong doctrines in an age in which Social Darwinist racism was an intellectually and morally respectable point of view and it is hardly surprising that their proponents established for themselves a permanent place in the affection of the Baganda.

[40] Kagwa (n.d.), p. 15. Although certainly a great innovator, Sir Apolo probably overemphasizes his uniqueness in his role. An excellent, though unfortunately unpublished, life of his Roman Catholic counterpart, Chevalier Stanislas Mugwanya, by Mr. Joseph Kasirye, makes it clear that Mugwanya was a man of similar cast. There were others also.

[41] Hattersley, 1908, p. 91.

[42] Ibid., p. 7.

[43] Ibid., p. 160

[44] Ibid., p. 161.

[45] Gale, 1959, pp. 244–7.

[46] Hattersley, 1908, pp. 171–6.

[47] See: Southwold, 1956, pp. 88–96. Where there are sufficient funds it is common, at least nowadays, to assist collateral kin as well. Any well-to-do household located near a day school will likely contain one or more young kinsmen who work for their board and lodging in order to be near enough to attend the school.

[48] Low and Pratt, 1960, pp. 195–6.

[49] Ibid., Chapter 9.

[50] See: Kabaka Daudi Cwa, 1928, 1932: Also: Kasirye, 1953;

Mulira, 1949; Low and Pratt , 1960, pp. 212–19.

[51] Tax returns for 1956 were kindly made available by Dr. W. Elkan, who was given access to them by the Kabaka's Government.

[52] Land Tax returns for 1956. See note 51.

[53] Uganda. Advancement of Africans in Trade, p. 15.

[54] Uganda. Enumeration of Employees, June, 1956, pp. 11–12.

[55] Non-Baganda made up slightly more than one-third of the kingdom's population at the 1949 census. According to the 1959 census, the male population is more than half foreign.

[56] See note 51.

[57] These interviews were carried out by three Makerere College students: Miss E. S. Lubega, Mr. S. E. W. Kadu and Mr. D. R. Munderi.

[58] This is in striking contrast to the situation in Northern Rhodesia, as revealed by the study reported in Mitchell and Epstein, 1959. Mitchell and Epstein did not even include neo-traditional offices in their questionnaire, suggesting that there is in Northern Rhodesia a complete hiatus between modern and traditional sectors of society.

[59] These interviews were carried out by Mr. S. B. K. Musoke.

[60] For example, all members of the Great Lukiiko and all county chiefs and ministers were interviewed, while only two of the forty-eight physicians were included.

[61] Low and Pratt, 1960, Chapter 5.

[62] The Registrar of Titles, Kampala, kindly allowed us access to these records.

[63] These data were collected, with the generous co-operation of many headmasters and Education Department officials, by Mrs. S. Elkan.

[64] Many other members of the *élite* could, no doubt, be linked with this cluster of persons if more extensive genealogical inquiries were carried out.

[65] For data on an earlier group of members of the Great Lukiiko, see: Richards, 1959, p. 68.

Bibliography

Abegglen, J. G. 1958. *The Japanese factory: Aspects of its social organization*. Glencoe, Ill.: Free Press.

Ahmed, J. M. 1960. *The intellectual origins of Egyptian nationalism*. London: Oxford University Press.

Albert, Ethel. 1960. Une étude de valeurs en Urundi. *Cahiers d'études africaines* 21:147–60.

Anderson. J. N. D. 1954. *Islamic law in Africa*. London: Her Majesty's Stationery office.

Arnold, Rosemary. 1957. A port of trade: Whydah on the Guinea Coast. In *Trade and market in the early empires,* ed. Karl Polanyi, C. M. Arensberg, and Harry Pearson, pp. 154–76. New York: Free Press.

Ashby, Eric. 1958. Education for an age of technology. In *A history of technology,* ed. C. Singer, H. J. Holmyard, A. R. Hall, and T. I. Williams, 5:776–97. New York: Oxford University Press.

Ashe, R. P. 1894. *Chronicles of Uganda*. London: Hodder and Stoughton.

Bailey, F. G. 1957. *Caste and the economic frontier*. Manchester: University Press.

———. 1960. *Tribe, caste and nation*. Manchester: University Press.

Balfour, W. C. 1958. Productivity and the worker. *British Journal of Sociology* 4:257–65.

Baltzell, E. Digby. 1958. *Philadelphia gentlemen: The making of an upper class*. Glencoe, Ill.: Free Press.

Barber, Bernard. 1957. *Social Stratification*. New York: Harcourt Brace.

Barber, Bernard, and Lobel, Lyle S. 1953. "Fashion" in women's clothes and the American social system. *Social Forces* 31:124–31. Reprinted in *Class, status and power: A reader in social stratification,* ed. Reinhard Bendix and S. M. Lipset, pp. 323–32. Glencoe, Ill.: Free Press.

Barnes, J. 1954. *Politics in a changing society*. London: Oxford University Press for Rhodes-Livingstone Institute.

Barnes, J. A. 1948. Some aspects of political development among the Fort Jameson Ngoni. *African Studies* 7:99–109.

Bascom, W. R. 1951. Social status, wealth and individual differences among the Yoruba. *American Anthropologist* 53:491–505.

————. 1959. Urbanism as a traditional African pattern. *Sociological Review*, n.s. 7:29–43.

Becker, Carl. 1932. *The heavenly city of the eighteenth-century philosophers.* New Haven: Yale University Press.

Bell, Daniel. 1972. Meritocracy and equality. *Public Interest,* no. 29 (fall), pp. 26–68.

Bendix, Reinhard. 1951. *Social science and the distrust of reason.* University of California Publications in Sociology and Social Institutions, vol. 1, no. 1. Berkeley: University of California Press.

————. 1960. *Max Weber: An intellectual portrait.* New York: Doubleday.

Berger, Morroe. 1957. *Bureaucracy and society in modern Egypt.* Princeton: Princeton University Press.

Berle, A. A., Jr., and Means, Gardiner C. 1930. Corporation. *Encyclopedia of the Social Sciences* 4:414–23.

Bernard, C. I. 1938. *Functions of the executive.* Cambridge: Harvard University Press.

Berreman, G. D. 1960. Caste in India and the United States. *American Journal of Sociology* 66:120–27.

Béteille, André. 1965. *Caste, class and power: Changing patterns of stratification in a Tanjore village.* Berkeley and Los Angeles: University of California Press.

Billington, Roy A. 1968. Frederick Jackson Turner. *International Encyclopedia of the Social Sciences* 16:169.

Bohannan, Paul J. 1957. *Justice and judgement among the Tiv.* London: Oxford University Press.

Bottomore, T. D., and Rubel, M., eds. 1956. *Karl Marx: Selected writings in sociology and social philosophy.* London: Watts.

Brown, D. Mackenzie. 1953. *The white umbrella: Indian political thought from Manu to Gandhi.* Berkeley: University of California Press.

Burke, Edmund. 1955. *Reflections on the revolution in France.* New York: Gateway Editions.

Busia, K. A. 1951. *The position of the chief in the modern political system of Ashanti.* London: Oxford University Press for International African Institute.

————. 1956. The present situation and aspirations of *élites* in the Gold Coast. *International Social Science Bulletin* 8:424–30.

Colson, Elizabeth. 1954. Ancestral spirits and social structure among the plateau Tonga. *International Archives of Ethnography* 47:21–68.

Cox, A. H. 1950. The growth and expansion of Buganda. *Uganda Journal* 14:153–59.

Crick, Bernard. 1964. *In defense of politics.* Rev. ed. Baltimore: Penguin Books.

Daudi Cwa, Kabaka. 1928. *Lwaki Sir Apolo Kagwa yawumula* (Why Sir Apolo Kagwa resigned). Kampala: Gambuze Press.

————. 1932. *Okuwumula kwa Stanislas Mugwanya* (The retirement of Stanislas Mugwanya). Kampala: Gambuze Press.

Davis, Allison; Gardner, Burleigh; and Gardner, Mary. 1941. *Deep South: A social anthropological study of caste and class.* Chicago: University of Chicago Press.

Davis, Kingsley, and Golden, Hilda Hertz. 1954. Urbanization and the development of pre-industrial areas. *Economic Development and Culture Change* 3:6–26.

Delavignette, R. 1950. *Freedom and authority in French West Africa.* London: Oxford University Press.

Dollard, John. 1937. *Caste and class in a southern town.* New Haven: Yale University Press.

Dumont, Louis. 1970. *Homo hierarchicus.* Chicago: University of Chicago Press.

Durkheim, Emile. 1947. *The division of labor in society.* New York: Free Press.

Easton, David. 1959. Political anthropology. In *Biennial Review of Anthropology,* ed. Bernard J. Siegel. Stanford: Stanford University Press.

Elkan, Walter. 1956. *An African labour force.* East African Studies, no. 7.

————. 1961. *Migrants and proletarians.* London: Oxford University Press for East African Institute of Social Research.

Elkan, Walter, and Fallers, Lloyd A. 1960. Labor mobility and competing status systems. In *Labor commitment and social change in developing areas,* ed. W. E. Moore and A. S. Feldman, pp. 238–57. New York: Social Science Research Council.

Evans-Pritchard, E. E. 1940. *The Nuer.* London: Oxford University Press.

————. 1951. *Kinship and marriage among the Nuer.* London: Oxford University Press.

————. 1953. The Nuer conception of the spirit in its relation to the social order. *American Anthropologist* 55:201–14.

Fallers, Lloyd A. 1955. The politics of land holding in Busoga. *Economic Development and Culture Change* 3:260–70.

————. 1956. *Bantu bureaucracy.* Cambridge. W. Heffer and Son for East African Institute of Social Research.

————. 1959. Despotism, status culture and social mobility in an African kingdom. *Comparative Studies in Society and History* 2:11–32.

————. 1961*a*. Are African cultivators to be called "peasants"? *Current Anthropology* 2:108–10.

————. 1961*b*. Ideology and culture in Uganda nationalism. *American Anthropologist* 63:677–86.

Fallers, Margaret C. 1960. *The eastern lacustrine Bantu.* London: International African Institute, Ethnographic Survey of Africa, East Central Africa, part 11.

Firth, R. 1951. *Elements of social organization.* London: Watts.

Forde, Daryll, 1951. *The Yoruba-speaking peoples of south-western Nigeria.* London: International African Institute, Ethnographic Survey of Africa, Western Africa, part 4.

————. ed. 1956. *Efik traders of old Calabar.* London: Oxford University Press.

Fortes, M. 1945. *The dynamics of clanship among the Tallensi.* London: Oxford University Press.

————. 1949. *The web of kinship among the Tallensi.* London: Oxford University Press.

————. 1953. The structure of unilineal descent groups. *American Anthropologist* 55:17–41.

Fortt, J. 1954. The distribution of immigrant and Ganda populations within Buganda. In *Economic development and tribal change,* ed. A. I. Richards, chap. 4. Cambridge: Heffer.

Foster, G. M. 1953. What is folk culture? *American Anthropologist* 55:159–73.

Galbraith, J. K. 1958. *The affluent society.* Boston: Houghton Mifflin Co.

Gale, H. P. 1959. *Uganda and the Mill Hill Fathers.* London: Macmillan.

Gallie, W. 1964. *Philosophy and the historical understanding.* London: Chatto and Windus.

Gee, T. W. 1958. A century of Muhammadan influence in Buganda, 1852–1951. *Uganda Journal* 22:139–50.

Geertz, Clifford. 1956*a*. Religious belief and economic behavior in a Central Javanese town: Some preliminary considerations. *Economic Development and Cultural Change* 4:138–58.

————. 1956*b*. The development of a Javanese economy: A socio-culture approach. Document c/56–1, Center for International Studies, Massachusetts Institute of Technology, Cambridge.

————. 1962. The growth of culture and the evolution of mind.

In *Theories of mind,* ed. Jordan Scher. Glencoe, Ill.: Free Press.

Gibb, H. A. R. 1945. *Modern trends in Islam.* Chicago: University of Chicago Press.

Gibb, H., and Bowen, Harold. 1950. *Islamic society and the West.* New York: Oxford University Press.

Gierke, Otto. 1958. *Political theories of the Middle Ages.* Trans. F. W. Maitland. Boston: Beacon Press.

Glass, D. V., ed. 1954. *Social mobility in Britain.* London: Routledge and Kegan Paul.

Gluckman, Max. 1940. The kingdom of the Zulu in South Africa. In *African political systems,* ed. M. Fortes and E. E. Evans-Pritchard. London: Oxford University Press for International African Institute.

————. 1960. The rise of a Zulu empire. *Scientific American* 202:157–67.

Gluckman, M.; Mitchell, J. C.; and Barnes, J. A. 1949. The village headman in British Central Africa. *Africa* 19:89–106.

Gorju, Pére J. 1920. *Entre la Victoria, l'Albert et l'Edward.* Rennes: Oberthür.

Greenberg, Joseph H. 1949. Studies in African linguistic classification III: The position of Bantu. *Southwestern Journal of Anthropology* 5:309–17.

Griaule, Marcel. 1954. The Dogon of the French Sudan. In *African Worlds,* ed. Daryll Forde, pp. 83–110. London: Oxford University Press.

Gruenbaum, Gustave von. 1953. *Medieval Islam.* 2d ed. Chicago: University of Chicago Press.

Hailey, Lord. 1950, 1953. *Native administration in the British African territories.* London: Her Majesty's Stationery Office.

————. 1957. *An African survey.* London: Oxford University Press.

Harrington, Michael. 1962. *The other America.* New York: Macmillan.

Harrison, Selig. 1960. *India: The most dangerous decades.* Princeton University Press.

Hartz, Louis. 1964. *The founding of new societies.* New York: Harcourt, Brace, and World.

Hattersley, C. W. 1908. *The Baganda at home.* London: Religious Tract Society.

Herskovits, Melville J. 1926. The cattle complex in East Africa. *American Anthropologist* 28:230–72, 361–80, 494–528, 633–64.

————. 1938. *Dahomey: An ancient West African kingdom.* New York: J. J. Augustin.

————. 1955. *Cultural anthropology.* New York: Knopf.

Hofstadter, Richard. 1955. *The age of reform, from Bryan to F.D.R.* New York: Knopf.

Hoggart, Richard. 1957. *The uses of literacy.* Fair Lawn, N.J.: Essential Books.

Homans, George C. 1941. *English villagers of the thirteenth century.* Cambridge: Harvard University Press.

Hughes, E. 1958. *Men and their work.* Glencoe, Ill,: Free Press.

Jencks, Christopher, et al. 1972. *Inequality.* New York: Basic Books.

Jones, W. O. 1961. Food and agricultural economies of tropical Africa. *Food Research Institute Studies* 2:3–20.

Kagwa, Sir A. 1949. *Ekitabo kye bika bya Baganda* (Book of the clans of the Baganda). Kampala: Uganda Bookshop and Uganda Society. (1st ed. 1908.)

————. 1952. *Ekitabo kye mpisa za Baganda* (Book of the customs of the Baganda). London: Macmillan. (1st ed. 1905.)

————. 1953. *Basekakaka be Buganda* (The kings of Buganda). Kampala: Uganda Bookshop; London: Macmillan. (1st ed. 1901.)

————. n.d. *Ekitabo kye Kika kya Nsenene* (Book of the Grashopper Clan). Publisher unknown.

Kaizi, M. 1948. *Kabaka Daudi Cwa: Obulamu, omulembe n'ebirowoozo bye* (Kabaka Daudi Cwa: His life, times and thought). Kampala: Baganda C.S. Press.

Kakoma, S. K.; Ntate, A. M.; and Serukwaya, M. 1959. *Ekitabo eky'abakyanjove ab'e Mamba mu Siiga lya Nankere e Bukerekere* (Book of the Lungfish Clan of Kyanjove, Bukerekere, the lineage of Nankere). Kampala: East African Institute of Social Research.

Kant, Immanuel. 1949. Idea for a universal history with cosmopolitan intent. In *The philosophy of Kant,* ed. Carl Friedrich, pp. 116–31. New York: Modern Library.

Kasirye, J. S. 1953. *Stanislas Mugwanya.* Kampala: Eagle Press.

————. 1955. *Abateregga ku nnamulondo y'e Buganda* (Princes of the throne of Buganda). London: Macmillan.

Kenyatta, Jomo. 1938. *Facing Mount Kenya: The tribal life of the Gikuyu.* London. Secker and Warburg.

Kornhauser, Ruth Rosner. 1953. The Warner approach to social stratification. In *Class, status and power,* 1st ed., ed. Reinhard Bendix and S. M. Lipset, pp. 224–55. Glencoe, Ill.: Free Press.

Kroeber, A. L. 1948. *Anthropology.* New York: Harcourt, Brace.

Kuczynski, R. R. 1949. *Demographic survey of the British colonial empire.* Vol. 2. London: Oxford University Press.

Landes, David S. 1958. *Bankers and pashas*. London: Heinemann.

Larabee, L. W. 1948. *Conservatism in early American history*. New York: New York University Press.

Legum, Colin. 1960. *Congo disaster*. London: Penquin Books.

Levy, Marion J., Jr. 1952. *The structure of society*. Princeton: Princeton University Press.

Lewis, Bernard. 1961. *The emergence of modern Turkey*. London: Oxford University Press.

Lincoln, Abraham. 1958. Message to Congress, July 4, 1861. In *Great Issues in American History*, vol. 1, *1765–1865,* ed. Richard Hofstadter. New York: Vintage Books.

Lindsay, J. O. 1957. The social classes and the foundations of the states. In *New Cambridge Modern History,* 7:50–65. Cambridge: Cambridge University Press.

Lipset, Seymour M., and Bendix, Reinhard. 1959. *Social mobility in industrial society*. Berkeley: University of California Press.

——————. 1951. Social status and social structure. *British Journal of Sociology* 2:150–66; 2:230–58.

Lloyd, P. C. 1955. The Yoruba lineage. *Africa* 25:235–51.

Low, D. A., and Pratt, R. C. 1960. *Buganda and British overrule*. London: Oxford University Press for East African Institute of Social Research.

Lwanga, P. M. K. 1954. *Obulamu bw'omutaka J. K. Miti Kabazzi* (Life of the clan head, J. K. Miti Kabazzi). Kampala: Friends Press.

Machiavelli, Niccolò. 1941. *The Prince and other works*. Trans. A. H. Gilbert. Chicago: Packard and Co.

McIlwain, C. H. 1940. *Constitutionalism, ancient and modern*. Ithaca, N. Y.: Cornell University Press.

Mackay, A. 1896. *Mackay of Uganda by his sister*. New York: Armstrong.

Maine, Henry. 1931. *Ancient law*. London: Oxford World's Classics.

Mair, L. P. 1934. *An African people in the twentieth century*. London: Routledge.

Maquet, Jacques. 1961. *The premise of inequality in Ruanda*. London: Oxford University Press.

Marriott, McKim. 1955. Little communities in an indigenous civilization. In *Village India,* ed. McKim Marriott, pp. 171–222. American Anthropological Association Memoir 83.

——————. 1960. *Caste ranking and community structure in five regions of India and Pakistan*. Poona: Deccan College Postgraduate and Research Institute.

Marshall, Lorna. 1957. The kin terminology of the !Kung Bushman. *Africa* 27:1–27.

————. 1959. Marriage among the !Kung Bushmen. *Africa* 29:335–65.

————. 1960. !Kung Bushmen bands. *Africa* 30:325–55.

Marx, Karl. 1956. *Selected writings in sociology and social philosophy*. Ed. T. B. Bottomore and M. Rubel. London: Watts.

Merton, R. K. 1949. Social structure and anomie. In *Social theory and social structure*, chap. 4. Glencoe, Ill.: Free Press.

Middleton, J. F. M. 1953. *The Kikuyu and Kamba of Kenya*. London: International African Institute, Ethnographic Survey of Africa, part 5.

Mills, C. Wright. 1948. *New men of power*. New York: Harcourt, Brace.

————. 1957. *The power elite*. New York: Oxford.

Mitchell, J. C. 1949. The political organization of the Yao of Southern Nyasaland. *African Studies* 7:141–59.

Mitchell, J. C., and Epstein, A. L. 1959. Occupational prestige and social status among urban Africans in northern Nigeria. *Africa* 29:22–39.

Mitford, Nancy, ed. 1956. *Noblesse oblige*. New York: Harper.

Morris, H. S. 1956. Indians in East Africa: A study in a plural society. *British Journal of Sociology* 7:194–211.

Morris, Morris D. 1960. The labor market in India. In *Labor commitment and social change in developing areas*, ed. W. E. Moore and A. S. Feldman, pp. 173–200. New York: Social Science Research Council.

Mukubira, D. n.d. *Buganda nyaffe* (Buganda our mother). Kampala: Baganda C.S. Press.

Mukwaya, A. B. 1953. *Land tenure in Buganda*. East African Studies, no. 1.

Mulira, E. M. K. 1949. *Sir Apolo Kagwa*. Kampala: Uganda Bookshop.

Musoke. E. M., and Kibuka, A. n.d. Ebyafayo bye Kika kye Ngo ne Sekabaka Kintu (The story of the Leopard Clan and Kabaka Kintu). Manuscript in the library of the East African Institute of Social Research.

Myrdal, Gunnar. 1944. *The American dilemma*. New York: Harper.

Nadel, S. F. 1942. *A black Byzantium: The kingdom of Nupe in Nigeria*. London: Oxford University Press.

National Opinion Research Centre. 1947. Jobs and occupations: A popular evaluation. *Public Opinion News* 9:3–13.

Nsimbi, M. B. 1956. *Amannya Amaganda n'ennono zaago* (Ganda names and their origins). Kampala: Uganda Society.

Painter, Sidney. 1957. *French chivalry*. Ithaca, N.Y.: Cornell University Press.

Palmer, R. R. 1959–64. *The age of the democratic revolution*. Princeton: Princeton University Press.

Parsons, Talcott. 1938. The professions and social structure. *Social Forces* 17:457–67.

———. 1940. An analytical approach to the theory of social stratification. *American Journal of Sociology* 45:841–62.

———. 1949. *Essays in sociological theory*. Glencoe, Ill.: Free Press.

———. 1951. *The social system*. Glencoe, Ill.: Free Press.

———. 1953. A revised analytical approach to the theory of social stratification. In *Class, status and power: A reader in social stratification*, ed. Reinhard Bendix and S. M. Lipset, pp. 92–129. Glencoe, Ill.: Free Press.

———. 1954. *Essays in sociological theory*. Glencoe, Ill.: Free Press.

———. 1960. *Structure and process in modern societies*. New York: Free Press.

Pye, Lucian W., and Verba, Sidney, eds. 1965. *Political culture and political development*. Princeton: Princeton University Press.

Rawls, John. 1971. *A theory of justice*. Cambridge: Harvard University Press.

Redfield, Robert. 1947. The folk society. *American Journal of Sociology* 52:293–308.

———. 1956. *Peasant society and culture*. Chicago: University of Chicago Press.

Richards, A. I. 1961. African kings and their royal relatives. *Journal of the Royal Anthropological Institute* 91:135–50.

———, ed. 1954. *Economic development and tribal change*. Cambridge: W. Heffer and Son for East African Institute of Social Research.

———, ed. 1959. *East African chiefs*. London: Faber and Faber.

Richards, A. I., and Reining, P. 1954. Report on fertility surveys in Buganda and Buhaya. In *Culture and human fertility*, ed. Frank Lorimer. Paris: UNESCO.

Roscoe, J. 1911. *The Baganda*. London: Macmillan.

Rose, Arnold M. 1947. *The power structure: Political process in American society*. New York: Oxford.

Rudolph, Lloyd I., and Rudolph, Susanne. 1960. The political role of India's caste associations. *Pacific Affairs* 33:5–22.

Saben's commercial directory and handbook of Uganda, 1955–56. Kampala: Saben's Commercial Directories.

Schapera, I. 1956. *Government and politics in tribal societies.* London: Watts.

Schumpeter, J. A. 1947. *Capitalism, socialism and democracy.* New York: Harper.

Schutz, Alfred. 1962. *The problem of social reality.* The Hague: M. Nijhoff.

Shannon, David A. 1955. *The Socialist Party of America: A history.* New York: Macmillan.

Shils, Edward A. 1956. *The torment of secrecy.* New York: Free Press.

————. 1961. Center and periphery. In *The logic of personal knowledge: Essays presented to Michael Polanyi on his seventieth birthday.* London: Routledge and Kegan Paul.

Singer, Milton. 1956. Cultural values in India's economic development. *Annals of the American Academy of Political and Social Sciences* 305:81–91.

————. 1961. Review of Max Weber's *Religion of India. American Anthropologist* 63:143–51.

Skinner, Elliott P. 1964. West African economic systems. In *Economic transition in Africa,* ed. Melville J. Herskovits and Mitchell Harwitz, pp. 77–97. Evanston, Ill.: Northwestern University Press.

Sluiter, Greet. 1960. Kikuyu concepts of land and land kin. M.A. thesis, University of Chicago.

Smith, M. G. 1956. Segmentary lineage systems. *Journal of the Royal Anthropological Institute* 88:39–80.

Smythe, Hugh, and Smythe, Mabel. 1960. *The new Nigerian elite.* Stanford: Stanford University Press.

Southall, A. W. 1954. *Alur society.* Cambridge: W. Heffer and Son for East African Institute of Social Research.

Southall, A. W., and Gutkind, P. C. W. 1956. *Townsmen in the making.* East African Studies, no. 9.

Southwold, M. 1956. The inheritance of land in Buganda. *Uganda Journal* 20:88–96.

————. 1961. *Bureaucracy and chiefship in Buganda.* East African Studies, no. 14.

————. 1964. Leadership, authority and the village community. In *The king's men,* ed. Lloyd a Fallers, pp. 211–55. London: Oxford University Press for the East African Institute of Social Research.

Speke, J. H. 1864. *Journal of the discovery of the source of the Nile.* New York: Harper.

Stanley, H. M. 1878. *Through the dark continent.* 2 vols. New York: Harper.

Sundkler, B. G. M. 1948. *Bantu prophets in South Africa*. London: Lutterworth Press.

Talmon, J. L. 1960. *The origins of totalitarian democracy*. New York: Frederick A. Praeger.

Tawney, R. H. 1947. *Religion and the rise of capitalism*. New York: Pelican Books.

Taylor, J. V. 1958. *The growth of the Church in Buganda*. London: S.C.M. Press.

Thernstrom, Stephen. 1964. *Poverty and progress: Social mobility in a nineteenth-century city*. Cambridge: Harvard University Press.

Thomas, E. M. 1959. *The harmless people*. New York: Knopf.

Thomas, Hugh, ed. 1959. *The establishment*. New York: Clarkson N. Potter.

Thomas, H. R., and Scott, R. 1935. *Uganda*. London: Oxford University Press.

Thoonen, J. P. 1942. *Black martyrs*. London: Sheed and Ward.

Tocqueville, Alexis de. 1955. *The Old Régime and the French Revolution*. New York: Doubleday Anchor Books.

————. 1841. *Democracy in America*. Trans. Henry Reeve. 4th ed. New York: J. and H. Langley.

Tout, T. F. 1920–33. *Chapters in the administrative history of medieval England*. Manchester: University Press.

Tucker, A. R. 1911. *Eighteen years in Uganda and East Africa*. London: Longmans Green.

Turner, Frederick Jackson. 1921. *The frontier in American history*. New York: Henry Holt.

Uganda. 1956. London: Her Majesty's Stationery Office.

Uganda. 1955. *Advancement of Africans in trade*. Entebbe: Government Printer.

————. 1955. *Annual Report of the Department of Co-operative Development for the year ended 31st December, 1954*. Entebbe: Government Printer.

————. 1956. *Enumeration of employees, June 1956*. Entebbe: East African Statistical Department, Uganda Unit.

Vinogradoff, P. 1892. *The villainage in England*. London: Oxford University Press.

Warner, W. Lloyd. 1926. American caste and class. *American Journal of Sociology* 42:234–37.

————. 1959. *The living and the dead: The symbolic life of Americans*. New Haven: Yale University Press.

————. 1963. *The American federal executive*. New Haven: Yale University Press.

Warner, W. Lloyd, and Abegglen, James. 1955. *Big business leaders in America.* New York: Harper.

Warner, W. Lloyd, and Low, J. O. 1957. *The social system of the modern factory: The strike.* New Haven: Yale University Press.

Warner, W. Lloyd, and Lunt, P. S. 1941. *The social life of a modern community.* New Haven: Yale University Press.

————. 1942. *The status system of a modern community.* New Haven: Yale University Press.

Warner, W. Lloyd; Meeker, Marchia; and Eels, Kenneth. 1949. *Social class in America: Manual of procedure for the measurement of social stratification.* Chicago: Science Research Associates.

Warner, W. Lloyd, and Srole, Leo. 1945. *The social system of American ethnic groups.* New Haven: Yale University Press.

Warren, M. 1954. *Revival: An inquiry.* London. S.C.M. Press.

Weber, Max. 1946. Politics as a vocation. In *From Max Weber: Essays in sociology,* ed. Hans Gerth and C. Wright Mills, pp. 77–128. New York: Oxford University Press.

————. 1947. *The theory of social and economic organization.* Ed. and trans. A. M. Henderson and Talcott Parsons. New York: Oxford University Press.

————. 1958a. *The Protestant ethic and the spirit of capitalism.* Trans. Talcott Parsons. New York: Scribner's Sons.

————. 1958b. *The religion of India.* New York: Free Press.

————. 1968. *Economy and society.* Ed Guenter Roth and Clause Wittich. New York: Bedminster Press.

Welbourn, F. B. 1961. *East African rebels.* London: S.C.M. Press.

Wolf, Eric. 1955. Types of Latin American peasantry: A preliminary discussion. *American Anthropologist* 57:452–71.

Wrigley, C. C. 1959. The Christian revolution in Buganda. *Comparative Studies in Society and History* 2:33–48.

————. 1944. The changing economic structure of Buganda. In *The king's men,* ed. Lloyd A. Fallers, pp. 16–63. London: Oxford University Press for East African Institute of Social Research.

Zikusooka, B. 1955. *Abatuleetera eddini Katolika* (They who brought us the Catholic religion). Kisubi: White Fathers.

Zimbe, B. M. 1938. *Buganda ne Kabaka* (Buganda and the Kabaka). Kampala: Gambuze Press.

Index